Competency Based Education and Training

Competency Based Education and Training

Edited by

John Burke

 The Falmer Press

(A member of the Taylor & Francis Group)
London • New York • Philadelphia

UK   The Falmer Press, Falmer House, Barcombe, Lewes, East Sussex, BN8 5DL

USA   The Falmer Press, Taylor & Francis Inc., 1900 Frost Road, Suite 101, Bristol, PA 19007

First published in 1989
Reprinted 1990

British Library Cataloguing in Publication Data
Competency based education and training.
  1. Competency-based education
  I. Burke, John
  371.3

ISBN 1-85000-626-1
ISBN 1-85000-627-X Pbk

Jacket design by Caroline Archer

Typeset in 11/13 Bembo by
Chapterhouse, The Cloisters, Formby L37 3PX

Printed in Great Britain by BPCC Wheatons Ltd, Exeter

Contents

List of Abbreviations

ABCTG	Administrative, Business and Commercial Training Group (ILB q.v.)
APL	Accreditation of Prior Learning
ATB	Agriculture Training Board
BTEC	Business and Technical Education Council
CAST	Curriculum Advice and Support Team
CATE	Committee for the Accreditation of Teacher Education
CBE	Competency Based Education
CBET	Competency Based Education and Training
CBL	Competency Based Learning
CD	Curriculum Development
CGLI	City and Guilds of London Institute
CPD	Continuing and Professional Development
CPRS	Central Policy Review Staff
CPVE	Certificate of Pre-Vocational Education
DACUM	Developing *a* Curriculum
DES	Department of Education and Science
EARAC	East Anglian Regional Advisory Council
EAV	Examining and Validating (*also referred to as EV*)
ED	Employment Department (*previously known as Department of Employment which led to confusion with DOE, Department of Environment*)
FE	Further Education
FEH	Further and Higher Education
FESC	Further Education Staff College
FEU	Further Education Unit
FTE	Full Time Equivalent
GCSE	General Certificate of Secondary Education

HCTB   Hotel and Catering Training Board
HE   Higher Education
HMI   Her Majesty's Inspectorate
HOD   Head of Department
HTB   Hairdressing Training Board
ILB   Industry Lead Body
IMS   Institute of Manpower Studies
IT   Information Technology
LEA   Local Education Authority
MDF   Mutual Development Fund (of FEU/TA)
MSC   Manpower Services Commission (*now TA*)
NAFE   Non-Advanced Further Education
NCRVE   National Center for Research in Vocational Education (USA)
NCVQ   National Council for Vocational Qualifications
NEBAHAI   National Examination Board for Agriculture, Horticulture and Allied Industries
NNEB   Nursery Nurses Examination Board
NPS   National Preferred Scheme
NPTC   National Proficiency Test Council
NROVA   National Record of Vocational Achievement
NTI   *New Training Initiative* (seminal document)
NVQ   National Vocational Qualification
PBTE   Performance Based Teacher Education
PGCE   Post Graduate Certificate in Education
PR   Public Relations
TA   Training Agency

Foreword

> The debate on education and training in Britain has too often been concerned with structures and delivery and too little concerned with content and outcomes.

This quotation is taken from the report of the CBI Task Force on Training: *Towards a skills revolution — a youth charter* (July, 1989). The Task force, chaired by Sir Bryan Nicholson and composed of top industrialists, consider 'there is a need for a quantum leap in the education and training of young people to meet both their aspirations and the needs of the economy in an increasingly competitive world.'

The interesting feature of the report in the context of this publication is that the Task Force, in consultation with government agencies, proposes a competence based model of vocational education and training based upon National Vocational Qualifications. They see focusing on outcomes rather than learning processes as providing a clarity and orientation to the programmes which is currently lacking in many forms of provision. Further, by specifying the competences sought independently of the learning process, access to learning through any mode becomes possible. Along with unit credits and credit accumulation, continuing education and training will be made available to sectors of the population which have never participated in the formal system.

The approach to education and training advocated by the CBI Task Force is rapidly gaining ground. The transition towards a competence based model can be traced through a number of government White Papers throughout the 1980s. The *New Training Initiative*[1] in 1981 set out the philosophy and advocated 'standards of a new kind'. This was reinforced in White Papers in 1984[2] and 1985[3] and *Working Together: Education and Training*,[4] 1986, introduced the framework of national Vocational Qualifications to operationalise the new model of education and training. The move towards competence based education and training was further reinforced by *Employment for the 1990s*, 1988[5].

Readers from the world of education may be surprised to learn that radically new models of vocational education and training are being adopted with little debate and with seemingly little research and development. In fact, much research and development *has* taken place, but those doing it are so close to the policy makers and implementors (sometimes they *are* the policy makers and implementors) that the many papers and reports which circulate have seldom entered the mainstream of research literature. The debate has been confined to a relatively small group and has been largely ignored by the educational research establishment.

This book is an attempt to redress this balance and expose the concepts, the models, the research and development work to a wider audience. By doing so, it is hoped that many others will begin to contribute to the growing body of work in this field. This book will be the first of a series of such publications.

The pattern of vocational education and training in the 1990s can now be perceived although many issues remain to be resolved. What will be interesting is the extent to which the concepts and models being introduced will impact upon the mainstream of school and academic education. It is difficult to imagine they will not.

If you have casually picked up this book and are content with the current forms of education and training provision in the UK, I would advise you to stop reading now; you will find this book disturbing. You may never be able to go into a classroom or mark an essay without questioning what you are doing. What I personally find exhilarating about these new approaches to learning is that nothing is taken for granted. Questions are being asked afresh on the purpose of learning, modes of delivery, the nature of competence and assessment — fundamental questions on the way we learn and behave.

References

1   *A New Training Initiative: A Programme for Action, Cmnd 8455*, HMSO, December 1981.
2   *Training for Jobs, Cmnd 9135*, HMSO, January 1984.
3   *Education and Training for Young People, Cmnd 9482*, April 1985.
4   *Working Together: Education and Training, Cmnd 9823*, July 1986.
5   *Employment for the 1990s, Cmnd 540*, HMSO, December 1988.

Gilbert Jessup
Director of Research, Development and Information
National Council for Vocational Qualifications

Chapter 1

Introduction

John Burke

A 'quiet revolution' is occurring in Vocational Education and Training. 'Quiet' because the depth and breadth of change has hardly been noticed outside Further Education, effectively eclipsed by the magnitude of change taking place in schools. That change continues to excite public and media interest. Whilst I do not want to minimize the far reaching consequences and the importance of change occurring in the schools sector, urgent public attention needs to be directed to the vast panoply of change which is occurring or about to occur in what until now has frequently been referred to as the 'Cinderella' of the system, Further Education. And a similar spotlight needs to be focused on the Industrial Training.

Change in further education

The notion of a quiet revolution is premised on change from many quarters. The major factors influencing change in Further Education may be enumerated:

1. Demography — a reduction of 25 per cent in the numbers of pupils reaching school leaving age between 1986 and 1995
2. Legislation — the Education Reform Act (ERA) and the Local Government Act (1988)
3. DES Policy — enshrined in *Managing Colleges Efficiently*
4. New Pay and Conditions — a clearer definition of duties and arrangements for averaging class contact hours
5. Occupational shift — a trend shown by projections for occupations from blue-collar to white-collar work with attendant implications for the range of courses being planned
6. The Single European Market — the recognition of transnational qualifications and the possible sudden demands for English and foreign language training

7   National Vocational Qualifications (NVQs) — the introduction of a coherent system of national vocational qualifications based on the assessment of competency.

Although placed last on this list, the introduction of NVQs is likely to have the most profound and far reaching consequences (cf. Farley, 1988). The revolutionary aspect will have added impact because of the context of change arising from the other factors listed above. In essence, an NVQ is conceived as a statement of competence, clearly relevant to work, that is intended to facilitate entry into or progression in employment, Further Education or training. It is to be issued by a recognized body to an individual. The statement of competence should incorporate specific standards — the ability to perform a range of work related activities — and — the skills, knowledge and understanding which underpin performance in employment.

Change in industrial training

This quiet revolution goes far beyond FE. It embraces Industrial Training and is set to transform it. NVQs are qualifications relevant to employment. They will be awarded for competent performance in work activities and will be assessed where possible in the work place.

In December 1988, the Government issued a White Paper, *Employment for the 1990s*. It stated roundly:

By any measure there is a need for radical reform of our training system. What is now needed is a new framework training and enterprise.

The White Paper enunciated six principles which should guide its approach:

— first, training and vocational education, including management training and counselling for small firms, must be designed to contribute to business success and economic growth;

— second, employers and individuals need to accept a greater share of responsibility for training, and its costs, while Government have a role in setting a framework and in funding the training of unemployed people;

— third, there must be recognised standards of competence, relevant to employment, drawn up by industry-led organisations covering every sector and every occupational group, and validated nationally;

— fourth, the training must provide young people and adults with the opportunity to secure qualifications based on these recognised standards;

— fifth, responsibility for delivery of training and enterprise must, as far as possible, be devolved to local areas where people work and are trained.

It is there that we need to bring together private and public investment to meet the skill needs of business and individuals;

— sixth, enterprises, individuals and local communities must be able to shape arrangements, programmes and opportunities to their changing needs and circumstances.

The Government's aim, it is said, was to provide, in a new partnership with employers, the establishment of such a training system. The intention was to 'facilitate access to relevant training and vocational education throughout working life for every member of the workforce, at every level from entry to top management'.

The role of the NCVQ

Some two years earlier following the publication of the White Paper *Working Together — Education and Training*, The National Council for Vocational Qualifications (NCVQ) had been set up with the following remit:

1 to secure standards of occupational competence and ensure that vocational qualifications are based on this;
2 to design and implement a new national framework for vocational qualifications;
3 to approve bodies making accredited awards;
4 to obtain comprehensive coverage of all occupational sectors;
5 to secure arrangements for quality assurance;
6 to set up effective liaison with bodies awarding vocational qualifications;
7 to establish a national data-base for vocational qualifications;
8 to undertake, or arrange to be undertaken, research and development to discharge these functions;
9 to promote vocational education, training and qualifications.

A timetable for achieving these aims was set up with the requirement that the system should be in place by 1991.

The new approach to vocational education and training fostered by the NCVQ and supported by the Training Agency (TA) is the subject of this book.

Research in competency based education and training

With the imminent widescale introduction of National Vocational Qualifications and in view of the mounting interest of Professional Bodies, one might have surmised that Competency Based Learning (CBL) would have assumed a prominent and important focus for research and debate in British universities. This is not the case. A large number of research and development projects externally funded by the NCVQ and TA have been and are currently under way in different universities and polytechnics but there is little evidence to suggest that HE has generally engaged itself in this sphere of research. Whilst there are isolated examples of CBL research undertaken by academics in some universities, this work appears to have had very limited impact on outside publics.

Virtually all lecturers in universities are expected to undertake research as part of their normal work contract. Choice of research is normally governed by personal expertise or interest, although in some communities a specialized area may develop on a collaborative basis to reflect the particular strength or expertise within a department. In view of the commitment that some education departments have to curriculum development in FE, the technicalities of assessment, the issues of access and progression and, indeed, vocational education, it does seem odd that so little appears to have been published other than externally funded project research.

The explanation for this apparent lack of interest may lie in the way most academics approach a new subject. They read the literature and attend conferences. Until very recently they have had little opportunity to do either.

In the first edition of *Competence and Assessment* Gilbert Jessup wrote of 'a new discipline' centered on the assessment of competence. Although there is a long tradition of research in CBL in America, the underlying conceptual base has been considerably modified and developed in the British research which has informed the development of NVQs. This work has circulated in manuscript form among the small network of consultants and researchers commissioned by the NCVQ and TA but largely, has remained unpublished. When, therefore, the University of Sussex approached the NCVQ to help fund a conference aimed at the HE research community, Gilbert Jessup endorsed the project and further suggested that the papers and proceedings should be published by an independent academic publisher.

As a result of this initiative two-thirds of British universities and a number of polytechnics sent delegates to a three-day symposium on Competency Based Learning held in Worthing in mid-March 1989. A wide range of papers were presented dealing chiefly with substantive issues in assessment and their application to the NVQ programme, the new structure of vocational education and training and the implementation of NVQs in FE.

The book

Historical background

The first paper in this volume provides an historical backdrop. In my view it is essential for anyone coming new to the study of Competency Based Education and Training

(CBET) to locate the context in which these ideas first arose and to see how they have developed. Although CBET is a relatively new focus for research and development in the UK, it has a long history and literature in the USA. Eric Tuxworth locates its origins and reviews its development by carefully relating the American experience to current developments sponsored by the NCVQ and the TA.

Technical issues

The next three papers examine technical issues bound up in the concept of competence. Bob Mansfield points out that the model of development underlying the British approach to Vocational Education and Training reverses previous approaches. The efforts of Industry Lead Bodies (ILBs) are directed towards the formulation of 'clear and precise statements'; these are the 'Occupational Standards' which describe what effective performance means. This stands in contrast to earlier approaches which concentrated on the design of curricula to meet *assumed* needs. He examines the differing consequences of basing standards on a concept of competence which may be either broad or narrow. He concludes that what is required is a broad concept of competence to drive standards and associated assessment and learning systems.

Alison Wolf addresses herself to the vexed question of identifying and assessing knowledge in a competency-based system. She argues that there is no necessary bifurcation between competence and education. Competency based learning is perfectly compatible with the learning of higher level skills, the acquisition of generalizable knowledge and understanding and the development of broad based courses. Her contribution is particularly useful in view of the decision taken recently to extend the NVQ framework above level four. Detailed negotiations are proceeding on a purely voluntary basis with many professional bodies, but there still appears to be wide-spread apprehension that the forms of assessment devised for lower levels within the framework would be inappropriate at higher levels. As they stand, they would. Alison suggests there is scope for developing performance criteria which take account of the deeper and more sophisticated knowledge component embedded in higher level assessment.

Lindsay Mitchell examines the way in which occupational standards are defined and assessed; she, too, examines the role of knowledge in standards. She notes that although the model is still very much in a developmental stage, assessment processes devised for NVQs fundamentally call into question much previous practice. She identifies two key purposes of assessment in the NVQ model: to recognize achievement which has already taken place, and to infer an individual's future performance in the areas of competence certified. 'These fundamental purposes of assessment signal up the aims of the new system. Assessment in vocational qualifications is not for selection of the best for whatever purpose, or for determining in any direct way who has the potential for development in a particular direction. Vocational qualifications may inform these aspects but they are not their main purpose and should not be allowed to influence the developments to the detriment of the key purposes'.

The response of the NCVQ, the TA and the FEU

Having traced the historical development of CBET and analysed some of the issues which arise out of the concept, we move on to consider the way in which three main agencies, The National Council for Vocational Qualifications, the Training Agency and the Further Education Unit (FEU) are contributing and responding to the development of a coherent national framework.

Gilbert Jessup presents a model of vocational education and training which is now emerging clearly from the research and detailed negotiation which is taking place between the many diverse, interested parties with a stake in the enterprise: education, training, examining bodies, both sides of industry, the professions and government. He indicates the main features of the model with specific reference to the qualification framework: The National Record of Vocational Achievement (NROVA) which will provide the structure in which vocational education and training will operate. He makes the very cogent point that the new form of competence based qualifications 'lead rather than follow education and training'. By spelling out what candidates are required to be able to do for the award of an NVQ and stating the criteria by which performance will be assessed, the process of assessment is demystified, probably for the first time in the experience of most candidates and most potential employers. 'In doing so, the statement of competence also sets clear goals for education and training programmes. The specification of competence plus performance criteria provide the operational realization of the new kinds of standards'. At the end of his chapter, Gilbert Jessup outlines a number of challenging research and development issues which might be addressed by the research community.

Graham Debling provides a timely overview of the role of the TA with a detailed examination of the Standards Programme. The concepts of standards and competence are analysed. He explains the role of the ILB, and the development of standards is discussed. He stresses that 'the standards relate to the needs of employment and that employers [should] have a sense of ownership of such standards such that they recognize them and take responsibility for the modernization and utilization'. In the second half of his chapter he addresses a wide range of issues including the risk of defining standards in a narrow way, the place of knowledge and understanding in assessment, the implications for assessment practice, future developments and progression.

Geoff Stanton examines the curriculum implications which arise out of the new approach to Vocational Education and Training (VET) in the UK. He reiterates Jessup's point that statements of competence in the new model of VET are independent of any course or programme of learning. Indeed, 'it is increasingly common for a learner to require their learning in more than one location and under the auspices of more than one agency'. He goes on, 'there is a sense in which [the programme] is only really owned by the individual learner. In this model assessment has become part of the learning process. This has crucial implications for college staff in Further Education. There is a shift in role from teaching to tutoring functions. Their expertise in needs analysis, devising individual programmes, and evaluation has become more crucial than their ability to present material to a class'. This theme is developed drawing on the FEU model of curriculum development and a comparison of the old model of VET with the competence based model.

Implications for FE

The next section goes on to examine the implications for FE *in situ*.

The first chapter, by Jenny Shackleton, describes and analyses an agenda for organizational change which is actually underway at Wirral Metropolitan College where she is Principal. She presents a rationale for a new approach — achievement led institutional development — emphasizing that personal achievement is the core of the college mission statement. She goes on: 'For achievement and institutional development the curriculum has to be redefined in terms which can be directly recognized by the learner and engaged with directly by him or her without mediation or interpretation'. In the present context of competency based education and training, the achievement led institutional development facilitates delivery of NVQs by distinguishing assessment and certification from courses and teaching but has certain implications for delivery. She lists a number of prioritized tasks which should facilitate the implementation of NVQs.

My own chapter focuses on the attitudinal and organizational changes encountered in an ethnographic study of FE colleges involved with the Accreditation of Prior Learning project and the early implementation of NVQs. I stress the importance of obtaining reliable feedback of what is actually going on and the nature of problems and opportunities as perceived by participants involved in planned change. The history of curriculum change in the schools throughout the 1960s should forewarn us about the importance of implementation strategy, as many initiatives floundered because there was not an adequate understanding of the problems and concerns of those who were attempting to manage it 'on the ground'. While some difficulties are identified, I am optimistic about 'the extraordinary release of enthusiasm and directed effort which occurred when [APL coordinators] were given responsibility and a stake in developing the responsiveness of the college'.

Ian Haffenden and Alan Brown are likewise concerned with implementation issues. In a project sponsored by the FEU, they studied 36 FE colleges in England and Wales so as to investigate key aspects in the implementation of competence based curricula in four vocational areas in FE. They focus on a number of issues including: perceptions about the nature of competence, implications of NVQs for curriculum development, staff development and institutional development and assessment.

Competency and teaching

There is growing interest among different professions about the possible application of NVQs to higher level qualifications. Michael Eraut draws on the distinctive approach to teacher training developed at the University of Sussex to compare and contrast approaches to vocational training which are competency based. He notes that a large proportion of the course is carried out as on-the-job training, that competence is assessed by direct observation of job performance and that this assessment constitutes the largest and most essential part of the teaching qualification. Other common features are the heavy involvement of employers, the rigorous process of external approval and evaluation and the use of assessment criteria, although these do not amount to competence statements in the NVQ sense.

He examines a range of non-practice based components which at first appear incompatible with the NVQ model. He suggests these divergencies may be more apparent than real and may eventually be resolved as the problems and requirements of higher level accreditation are accommodated within the developing NVQ model. A notable feature of his paper is the advocacy for a wider concept of competence which recognises grades of competence on the lines of the Dreyfuss model of skill acquisition.

The response of higher education to competency based approaches

The final chapter in this volume was written after the Symposium by Tim Oates of the Further Education Staff College. In the course of the conference many issues were raised in the small discussion groups. Rapporteurs were attached to each group. They in turn discussed with Tim the topics which had aroused interest and debate. He has based his chapter on these debriefing sessions, and additionally he has located their concerns by reference to a framework and context of various seminal documents which gave rise to both the NCVQ and the directed interest of the TA.

One of the intended outcomes of the conference was to stimulate interest and debate in these issues. The conference was conceived not only as a platform for imparting information but also as a genuine two-way forum for exchanging ideas and experiences. Contributions from the floor were an important part of the process. We hope, therefore, that Tim Oates' careful presentation will encourage focus for research and development in the emerging shape of Vocational Educational and Training in the 1990s.

References

DES (1986) 'Student Number Projections for FE: Projected numbers of students in maintained colleges studying on non-advanced courses England 1986–2000', London, HMSO.

DES (1987) *Managing Colleges Efficiently: A Report of a Study of Efficiency in Non-Advanced Further Education for the Government and the Local Authority Association*, London, HMSO.

DES (1988) *Education Reform Act*, London, HMSO.

DOE (1988) *Employment for the 1990s*, CM540, London, HMSO.

FARLEY, M. (1988) 'The Education Act: A second order issue in Coombe Lodge' *Report*, 20, No. 11, pp. 711–720.

Chapter 2

Competence based education and training: background and origins

Eric Tuxworth

Terminology

Confusion often arises over the use of the term 'competence' to indicate a capacity in an individual and a 'competence' as an element of a life role or an occupation. NCVQ refers to 'Units of Competence' and 'Elements of Competence' thus tending to avoid the use of coined terms; NCVQ also refers to 'general' and 'specific' competence. This brings some (welcome) definition to the terminology for future development. In reporting the earlier developments, the coined terms 'competences' or 'competencies' are often seen to be applied in the US (and some UK) literature to describe discrete elements or activities. Where it has been necessary to use this terminology 'competences' is preferred.

Early US sources show Performance Based Education in some cases as an alternative to Competence Based Education. Thus, early articles refer to Performance Based Teacher Education (PBTE). There are conceptual differences in the views of some writers, but this chapter takes the terms as being virtually synonymous, since competence based curriculum design demands performance based assessment. Competence based education and training (CBET) is therefore used as the preferred term for this chapter, to allow for potential applications across the spectrum of post-secondary education and training. Standard English spelling is used, including quotations, rather than a mixture of UK and US conventions.

The development of CBET in the USA

The purpose of this chapter is to review the background of the competency based movement in education and training (CBET) — mainly as it has developed in the USA

— and to relate earlier aspirations with current trends in the UK. The literature on CBET is extensive, though much of the early work was either redundant or ephemeral. The references used are necessarily selective and include some sources which are best accessed through data bases such as ERIC.

The competency based movement, under that label, has been around for 20 years or more in the USA. Its origins can, however, be traced further back to the 1920s, to ideas of educational reform linked to industrial/business models centred on specification of outcomes in behavioural objectives form. From the mid 1960s onwards the demand for greater accountability in education, for increased emphasis on the economy, and towards more community involvement in decision-making gave a great impetus to the concept of CBET. Although it would be an exaggeration to claim that it has been universally adopted in the USA, there is considerable evidence that the movement has had pervasive effects in many parts of the diverse system of that nation.

It is widely agreed that competency based education has its roots in teacher education (Burke *et al.*, 1975; Elam, 1971; Houston, 1980). Later developments extended applications of the idea to elementary schools, to minimum competency standards for high school graduation and to vocational education. There has also been some interest in the professions — particularly in the health related field. Examples of such applications will be discussed later in the chapter but much of the conceptual/theoretical background arises out of early work done in teacher education.

CBET and teacher education

The 1960s were tumultuous times in education in the USA. Extensive demands for curriculum reform, large investment of federal funds in curriculum development and a concurrent dissatisfaction with teacher training were features of the climate when CBET emerged. Calls for greater relevance in the training of teachers (Conant, 1963; Koerner, 1963) and for a more visible accountability to the taxpayer were prominent.

The genesis of CBET, as a distinct response to societal changes, was fuelled by the US Office of Education in 1968 when it gave ten grants to colleges and universities to develop model training programmes for the preparation of elementary school teachers. These models had certain characteristics including 'the precise specification of competences or behaviours to be learned, the modularisation of instruction, evaluation and feedback, personalisation, and field experience' (Swanchek and Campbell, 1981). The models concentrated on pupil achievement and, as Swanchek and Campbell note: 'for many it easily and simplistically followed that there must be a connection between teacher competence and pupil learning'. Moreover, it followed from this that only competent teachers must be allowed to enter the profession and that teacher preparation and certification should be centred on producing and verifying competence. Politicians and State Departments then pressed for certification policies which were intended to effect school improvement through the reform of teacher education. There were also many within the teacher training system who supported reform and were keen to establish a clear cut movement for change. To assist the educational community to evaluate the potential of competency/performance based teacher education, the American Association of Colleges of Teacher Education published a 'state-of-the-art' paper. This served to clarify and establish the characteristics of PBTE (Elam, 1971).

Thus, by the early 1970s it seems that competency based teacher education had become almost a self-sustaining movement, apparently carrying a great deal of face validity as far as some administrators, politicians and state certification agencies were concerned (Lindsey, 1976). Teacher over-supply made the quest for quality more urgent and permitted a greater stringency in applying certification procedures. CBET was seen by some State departments as the means of creating and enforcing the standards so long talked about, but, until then, not politically acceptable or enforceable in a period of teacher shortage and institutional unrest (Hertzberg, 1976).

Hasty mandating of CBET as a required approach to teacher training and certification created a strong reaction from many higher education institutions. There were those with philosophical objections, (Smith, 1975; Broudy, 1981) and others who were more concerned with the pace rather than the direction of change (Swanchek and Campbell, 1981; Spady, 1977). Apart from the threats to institutional autonomy and academic freedoms there were other, practical, issues to be faced, since the mandating of CBET as a sole system for the education and training of teachers has profound implications for administration, resources and teaching methods.

The rhetoric of CBET outpaced implementation in the early 1970s; it was an untried system, albeit with a rational appeal, but still unproven. There was little or no research evidence to show superiority over other forms of teacher preparation. A number of reviews of the existing research on the relationships between teacher behaviour and pupil performance showed little evidence of positive, causative links (Huff, 1976; Heath and Neilson, 1974). The lack of a sound research base was, justifiably, seen as a serious drawback; though the same charge could have been made and upheld in regard to more conventional kinds of teacher training.

Reactions against hasty mandating and over-zealous promotion of CBET tended to slow down the pace of change. Legal suits (e.g., in the State of Texas) showed it to be unconstitutional to mandate a single form of teacher education. States were therefore constrained to take a more consultative stance and to work with, and through, the universities and colleges to develop systems acceptable to administrators, politicians and teacher educators. The reaction of HE institutions to the challenges posed by CBET was, of course, varied. But, with substantial federal and state funding available for research and development (and earmarked for CBET) many university and college departments embraced the concept and set about the redesign of programmes.

The US Office of Education continued to support the promotion of CBET through a National Consortium of Competency Based Education Centres (Burke *et al.*, 1975). The consortium did valuable work in coordinating activities across the nine major centres engaged in USOE funded development work and assisted the dissemination of the concept. Burke *et al.*, note that 'One of the continuing problems faced by institutions attempting to re-do their teacher education programmes in the direction of more competency based activities is the general lack of definition and criteria for just what constitutes a competency based teacher education programme' (p. i). The National Consortium of CBE Centres therefore set out to develop a set of 'Criteria for Describing and Assessing Competency Based Programmes'. These criteria still look surprisingly fresh in regard to current trends in the UK. They are potentially applicable across the fields of education and training so are reproduced in Figure 2.1 in a short format (the extended format includes an evaluation instrument based on the criteria).

Figure 2.1 Criteria for Describing and Assessing Competency Based Programmes
(Source — Burke et al., 1975)

Competency Specifications

1 Competences are based on an analysis of the professional role(s) and/or a theoretical formulation of professional responsibilities.
2 Competency statements describe outcomes expected from the performance of professionally related functions, or those knowledges, skills, and attitudes thought to be essential to the performance of those functions.
3 Competency statements facilitate criterion referenced assessment.
4 Competences are treated as tentative predictors of professional effectiveness, and are subjected to continual validation procedures.
5 Competences are specified and made public prior to instruction.
6 Learners completing the CBE programme demonstrate a wide range of competency profiles.

Instruction

7 The instructional programme is derived from and linked to specified competences.
8 Instruction which supports competency development is organised into units of manageable size.
9 Instruction is organised and implemented so as to accommodate learner style, sequence preference, pacing and perceived needs.
10 Learner progress is determined by demonstrated competence.
11 The extent of learner's progress is made known to him/her throughout the programme.

12 Instructional specifications are reviewed and revised based on feedback data.

Assessment

13 Competency measures are validly related to competency statements.
14 Competency measures are specific, realistic and sensitive to nuance.
15 Competency measures discriminate on the basis of standards set for competency demonstration.
16 Data provided by competency measures are manageable and useful in decision making.
17 Competency measures and standards are specified and made public prior to instruction.

Governance and Management

18 Policy statements are written to govern, in broad outline, the intended structure, content, operation and resource base of the programme.
19 Management functions, responsibilities, procedures and mechanisms are clearly defined and made explicit.

Total Programme

20 Programme staff attempt to model the attitudes and behaviours desired of students in the programme.
21 Provisions are made for staff orientation, assessment, improvement and reward.
22 Research and dissemination activities are an integral part of the total instructional system.
23 Institutional flexibility is sufficient for all aspects of the programme.
24 The programme is planned and operated as a totally unified, integrated system.

It will be noted that compliance with all of the criteria in Figure 2.1 would demand wholesale system revision. Not every institution was ready and willing to adopt the whole system; indeed many felt that the major aims of CBET could be met without serious disturbance to existing schemes. Consequently there has been a great deal of adaptation of the concept, often to the despair of the more committed developers. The early and influential work of Elam (1971) did in fact produce a conceptual model which defined essential, implied, and related desirable characteristics of CBET. This model, shown in Figure 2.2 has been widely used to explain CBET in relation to vocational education and is perhaps more acceptable to institutions wishing to develop CBET in a gradual or incremental way[1].

Figure 2.2 Characteristics of CBE Programmes (after Elam, 1971)

Essential Elements

1   Competences are role derived, specified in behavioural terms and made public.
2   ¬Assessment criteria are competency based, specify mastery levels and are made public.
3   Assessment requires performance as prime evidence but takes knowledge into account.
4   Individual student progress rate depends on demonstrated competency.
5   The instructional programme facilitates development and evaluation of specific competences.

Implied Characteristics

1   Individualisation of learning.
2   Feedback to learners.
3   Emphasis on exit rather than admission requirements.
4   Systematic programme.
5   Modularisation.
6   Student and programme accountability.

Related Desirable Characteristics

1   Field setting for learning.
2   Broad base for decision making.
3   Provision of protocol and training materials.
4   Student participation in decision making.
5   Research oriented and regenerative.
6   Career continuous.
7   Role integration.

Figure 2.2 may give rise to the thought that many of the listed characteristics have appeared as innovations of recent years without the CBET label being attached. The negotiated curriculum, self-paced learning, modules, profiling, work-based and task-based learning have all been popular themes amongst innovators in the UK. The crucial difference is that many of these innovations have been grafted on to existing subject based curricula without being committed to outcomes stated in terms of competence, or to *ab-initio* work in defining the elements of competence.

The wider application of CBET

To continue the account of developments in the USA; it is something of an irony that the application of CBET to vocational education and training in general had to be led by teacher training. There were those who thought that vocational education had always been competence based (Broudy, 1981) but this was an outsider perspective. In fact in the USA, as in the UK, the vocational curricula were usually devised by teachers for institution based education, often placing more emphasis on book knowledge than on direct knowledge of practice. There was persistent dissatisfaction in industry with the relevance of college based courses. The CBET movement appeared, however, to offer a new approach to the design and implementation of vocational education and training — particularly in the opportunities it offered for a much closer cooperation between the education/training function and industry, business and the professions.

Federal funding was widely used to stimulate change and development in the devolved systems of the States but the National Centre for Research in Vocational Education (NCRVE) at Columbus, Ohio, took a leading role in federally funded developments over a twenty-year period. Much of that development centred on the production of Performance Based Teacher Education Modules (Hamilton and Quinn, 1978). The original set of 100 modules was designed for 'mainstream' vocational educators but has since been extended to cover special/exceptional needs, basic skills, instructional management, implementing CBE, educational administration, adult education, industry training instructors and career education. These modules have been widely marketed and sold in the USA and elsewhere in the world (AAVIM, 1988). A review of this particular modular system was undertaken for the Further Education Unit in 1981 (Tuxworth, 1982), with the general conclusion that some of the modules were suitable for use in an adaptive mode but that care was needed in selecting and using them. Evaluation of the use of these modular learning materials, both in the USA and in the UK shows some potential for misuse (Adamsky, 1981; Tuxworth, 1982).

In considering CBET it is necessary to draw differences between the **concept** of CBET, **systems** for applying the concept and **materials**, usually in modular form, which are used for instruction/learning within given systems. Figures 2.1 and 2.2 go some way in delineating the concept but extend to guidelines for delivery systems and, to some extent, assessment of performance. Systems in the USA have been developed on a state-wide or regional basis (Ballard, 1986; Glenn, 1986; Blank, 1987). More usually, however, the delivery systems are institutionally and locally centred. There are some notable examples of fully functioning CBET delivery systems in certain institutions in Florida for example (Tuxworth, 1988). But even with a state-wide CBET policy there are wide variations within, and between, institutions in the take up and development of the concept (Blank, 1987).

CBET in the UK

In the UK there was patchy and desultory interest in CBET until the early 1980s, when the basis of a firmer training policy was laid by a series of White Papers (DOE, 1981; DOE and DES, 1984; 1985; 1986). The emphasis on competence as the necessary outcome of training was clear and it was not long before the notion was applied to some stages of education. Other associated reforms were indicated in vocational education and training (VET), e.g. more flexible programmes, certification related to performance rather than time-serving and better access to VET through modular programmes.

The UK approach to CBET, at least as far as the NCVQ is concerned, is expressed in their *Criteria and Procedures* (NCVQ, 1989). There is, within this guidance, no prescription of delivery systems nor of assessment methods. The concept is, however, established; together with principles for the derivation and expression of competence standards and performance criteria. It has to be said that much remains to be done to apply the NVQ Guidance in order to achieve the main aims of NCVQ, particularly in relation to higher levels of occupations/professions.

CBET: For and against

CBET is not without its critics, who often focus on two major points.

1   That the conception and definition of competence is inadequate — the competent person has abilities and characteristics which are more than the sum of the discrete elements of competence derived from job analysis ('the whole is more than the sum of the parts'). Some proponents are seen to pursue a reductionist approach and 'literally analyse competence to bits' (Wolfe, 1980).

2   There is a lack of research evidence that CBET is superior to other forms of education/training in output terms. Face validity is acknowledged to be high and it is easy to show content validity. What is more problematic is predictive validity (Pottinger, 1980); but this is not peculiar to CBET.

The first objection, i.e., of an inadequate conception of competence is often related to the methods of analysis used to derive elements of competence. There are two major approaches to this, which have developed separately and are often seen as mutually exclusive. The first is based on functional analysis of the occupation/profession and its necessary duties and tasks. This usually yields an extensive list of competence elements grouped under major duty areas or functions. Performance criteria are usually developed to indicate minimum or normative competence levels. Directly related knowledge and functional attitudes and values may be incorporated in competence elements and performance criteria. The methodology of occupational analysis involves consultations with role holders and their supervisors to establish a provisional list of competence elements. This should be verified by a larger sample of the target population — perhaps by Delphi techniques (Norton, 1985; Mainframe, 1987; Tuxworth and Ciechanowski, 1987). One product of this type of analysis is a competence map used to develop individual training programmes and assessment profiles. Such maps have been widely developed in the USA and have been prepared for some uses in the UK (Tuxworth, 1982; Mainframe, 1987).

The second approach to competence analysis is more concerned with identifying the characteristics of superior performers in the occupational role. This tends to yield fewer and more generic characteristics or, as they have been termed, 'soft skills'. The origins of this approach are shown in the work of McLelland and others at the McBer Corporation and Harvard Business School (Klemp, 1977; Spencer, 1983). A form of critical incident analysis is used to elicit the characteristics from a selection of role incumbents, with emphasis on those who are identified as highly successful performers. These methods have had some influence in management education in the USA and UK; Figures 2.3 and 2.4 show lists derived for management training (USA) and Senior Civil Servants (UK).

Figure 2.3 The Competency Programme of the American Management Association (Source: Evarts, 1987)

GOAL AND MANAGEMENT ACTION CLUSTER	— deals with the manager's initiative, image, problem solving skills and goal orientation.
	* EFFICIENCY ORIENTATION * PROACTIVITY * CONCERN WITH IMPACT * DIAGNOSTIC USE OF CONCEPTS
DIRECTING SUBORDINATES CLUSTER	— this involves a manager's freedom of expression both in terms of giving directives and orders, as well as giving feedback to help develop subordinates.
	* USE OF UNILATERAL POWER * DEVELOPING OTHERS * SPONTANEITY
HUMAN RESOURCE MANAGEMENT CLUSTER	— managers with these competences have positive expectations about others, have realistic views of themselves, build networks or coalitions with others to accomplish tasks

and stimulate cooperation and pride in work groups.
* ACCURATE SELF ASSESSMENT
* SELF CONTROL
* STAMINA AND ADAPTABILITY
* PERCEPTUAL OBJECTIVITY
* POSITIVE REGARD
* MANAGING GROUP PROCESS
* USE OF SOCIALISED POWER

LEADERSHIP CLUSTER — this cluster represents a manager's ability to discern the key issues, patterns or objectives in an organisation, and to then conduct himself or herself and communicate in a strong fashion.
* SELF CONFIDENCE
* CONCEPTUALISATION
* LOGICAL THOUGHT
* USE OF ORAL PRESENTATIONS

A SUMMARY OF THE CLUSTERS AND COMPETENCES IN THE COMPETENCY PROGRAMME OF THE AMERICAN MANAGEMENT ASSOCIATION

Note that the competence analysis and specification above was based on the methodology of 'soft skills' developed by the McBer Corporation of Boston, Mass. The specification is obviously not in the form preferred by NCVQ. The issue is whether, if such generic competences are held to be valid, they can be related to a functional analysis. Duties and tasks would need to be identified to provide units of occupational competence. Competence elements and performance criteria would then need to incorporate suitable manifestations of the generic skills above.

Figure 2.4 Summary of Competences for Senior Civil Servants (Source: Coster 1987)

Example 6 COMPETENCES FOR SENIOR CIVIL SERVANTS

CORE COMPETENCE AREAS — MANAGEMENT OF RESOURCES/ORGANISATIONS
MANAGEMENT OF STAFF
KNOWLEDGE/UNDER-
STANDING OF WORK CONTEXT
MANAGING OWN WORK
INFORMATION TECHNOLOGY
MORE SPECIALISED
KNOWLEDGE/EXPERTISE

IMPORTANT COMPETENCE — REPRESENTATIONAL/
    AREAS   PRESENTATIONAL SKILLS
                                  WRITTEN/ADMINISTRATIVE
                                  SKILLS
                                  POLICY MANAGEMENT
                                  ECONOMICS
                                  ACCOUNTING AND FINANCE
                                  QUANTITATIVE SKILLS/
                                  STATISTICS
                                  LAW
                                  INDUSTRIAL RELATIONS

'IMPORTANT AND DIFFICULT ACTIVITIES' RELATED TO COMPETENCE ARE HIGHLIGHTED AS:

1   Keeping up-to-date with developments in own area of work/expertise.
2   Allocating priorities to your own work/managing time.
3   Motivating your staff.
4   Coping with tight deadlines.
5   Adapting an organisation to meet changing needs.
6   Understanding and interpreting the needs of 'users' or (customers).
7   Assessing the strengths and weaknesses of your staff.
8   Assessing policy options.

CBET and the professions

The impact of CBET on the professions in the USA has been variable. With some risk of indulging in dangerous generalisations it would be safe to say that professional and occupational licensing has been affected in only a superficial way. The tendency is still to base occupational licensing on tests of knowledge plus some evidence of experience in practice. In reporting a wide-ranging survey, Pottinger, (1980) was pessimistic about the state of competency based licensing at that time '... more than 2000 occupations are currently regulated in some way, yet ... the credentialing systems usually lack a research base for choosing indicators of competence, for designing measures (of competence), or for demonstrating a relationship between the requirements for obtaining a professional credential and the competent discharge of one's professional duties' (p. 136).

The health related professions in the USA, from physicians through to care assistants have, however, been prominent in applying competency based notions to both initial training and continuing professional development (Norman, 1985; Neumann, 1987; Hart *et al.*, 1986; AACPM, 1982; ADA, 1987). In the case of some of the national professional associations, competency based specifications are issued as *guidelines* for accredited institutions. In other cases quite sophisticated national tests have been developed to assess knowledge directly related to specified dimensions of competence (NABP, 1988; Saxton *et al.*, 1985). There is also evidence of the extension of CBET to health related professions in the UK. The requirements for the licensing of nurses, for example, are based on a schedule of competences (HMSO, 1983). These rules are carried into effect through curricula devised by approved schools of nursing and validated by one of the four national Boards (e.g., ENB, 1987).

Conclusion

This has been, necessarily, a superficial review of the development of CBET with many issues left unexamined. The CBET movement in the USA has been internalised in some quarters but has still to be assimilated in others. The genesis of the CBET movement in the UK is more clear cut — with an obvious political commitment to the notion. The movement in the UK is now quite strong but a great deal of development work is needed. This must be accompanied by research to assist the improvement of system design and implementation: there are substantial opportunities for people in the higher education system to guide and influence the way CBET develops. In particular, there is a need for refinement of the methodologies of competence analysis, of exploration of the potential application of CBET to professions and in evaluation of pilot and operational schemes in both summative and formative ways. Improved methods for the assessment of competence, with the assurance of validity, reliability and cost effectiveness are no less important here, or problematic, than in more traditional spheres. In addressing these opportunities there are some benefits to be derived from the rather chequered development of the CBET approach in the USA and some costly mistakes may be avoided by study of that system.

I would like to offer some propositions for further thought.

(a) There is only limited use in universal definitions of competence, though these may help to establish the framework for more detailed work: each occupational/professional field needs to develop its own conception and working definition. Some fields are more process than product based and may often be context dependent. Competence in many cases is neither value-free nor independent of the context of its application (see Wolfe, 1980).

(b) CBET does not diminish the importance of knowledge and understanding; it does however change the grounds for its justification.

(c) Methods of occupational/professional analysis should be sophisticated enough to give a multi-dimensional view of competence. There is a strong case for 'triangulation' in analysis to avoid a simplistic representation. There has been a tendency to 'tunnel vision' in some examples from the USA with examples which are too rigidly anchored to task analysis. Any model of competence should incorporate both the analysed functions of the occupation and the characteristics of highly competent role holders.

(d) CBET analysis, specification and delivery systems should take account of current occupational needs but still allow for role development and role extension. There is a tendency for some methods of analysis simply to confirm the status quo. The training specification or curriculum which arises from occupational needs should allow for growth and for transfer.

(e) CBET has great potential in continuing professional development (CPD), particularly where it is necessary to ensure that professionals maintain and adapt their competences to new conditions. Licensed occupations (and others) need to maintain competence through CPD and regular performance review.

(f) The notion of 'minimum competence levels' is useful for certification purposes but carries some risks if these are the only standards available. Many organisations depend on high level performers for their success. We should be looking for ways of cultivating excellence in occupational competence and the recognition of enhanced performance.

(g) Whilst a national framework for vocational/professional qualifications has many implications, it does not demand nationally standardised arrangements for the delivery of CBET. But the concept cannot easily be assimilated to conventional courses of a monolithic kind. There has to be change in a number of ways, which may have quite radical effects on course design and implementation.

(h) The providers of education and training have a great deal to do to improve access, to extend opportunity to a wider range of learners and to develop more flexible learning resources. We can make more use of experiential learning, credit accumulation and transfer; these changes are not dependent on CBET but may be greatly assisted through it.

(i) There is a need to continue to find ways of engendering and assessing basic skills (generic competences) through well defined vocational education and training.

References

AACPM (1982) *Competency Task Index for Podiatric Medicine — Final Draft*, American Association of Colleges of Podiatric Medicine.

AAVIM (1988) *Catalogue of Competency Based Teacher Education Materials*, Athens, Georgia, American Association for Vocational Instructional Materials.

ADA (1987) *Accreditation Standards for Dental Education Programmes*, Chicago, Ill., American Dental Assocation.

ADAMSKY, R. (1981) *Does Performance Based Teacher Education Really Work? (Case Studies)*, Columbus, OH, National Center for Research in Vocational Education.

BALLARD, J. B. (1986) 'Arkansas' PBTE and CBAE Professional Development Programmes' in Harrington and Kalamas (Eds) *Achieving Professional Excellence — Conference Proceedings*, Columbus, Ohio, National Center for Research in Vocational Education.

BLANK, W. (1987) 'A statewide system of competency based instruction', in *Journal of Industrial Teacher Education* 24 (4), pp. 36–46.

BROUDY, H. (1981) *Towards a Theory of Vocational Education*, Occasional Paper No. 73, Columbus, Ohio, National Centre for Research in Vocational Education.

BURKE, J. B., HANSEN, J. H., HOUSTON, W. R. and JOHNSON, C. (1975) *Criteria for Describing and Assessing Competency Programmes*: Syracuse University, NY, National Consortium of Competency Based Education Centres.

CONANT, J. B. (1963) *The Education of American Teachers*, New York, McGraw-Hill.

COSTER, P. (1987) 'The Civil Service Senior Management Development Programme' in *Management Education and Development*, 4 (2) pp. 60–64.

DOE (1981) *A New Training Initiative; A Programme for Action*, Cmnd. 8455, London, HMSO.

DOE and DES (1984) *Training for Jobs*, Cmnd. 9135, London, HMSO.

DOE and DES (1985) *Education and Training for Young People*, London, HMSO.

DOE and DES (1986) *Working Together: Education and Training*, Cmnd. 9823, London, HMSO.

DHSS (1983) *Nurses Manpower Planning: Approaches and Techniques*, Approval Order, Stat. Inst. No. 873, London, HMSO.

ELAM, S. (1971) *Performance Based Teacher Education — What is the State of the Art?* Washington, DC, American Association of Colleges of Teacher Education, Dec, 1971.

ENB (1987) *Annual Report, 1986*, English National Board for Nursing, Health Visiting and Midwifery.

EVERTS, H. F. (1987) 'The competency programme of the American Management Association', in *Industrial and Commercial Training*, 19 (1), pp. 3–7.

GLENN, J. W. (1986) 'Statewide Delivery of Teacher Education in New York State' in *Achieving Professional Excellence — Proceedings of National Conference on Performance Based Approaches to Training*, Columbus, Ohio, National Centre for Research in Vocational Education.

HAMILTON, J. and QUINN, K. (1978) *Resource Person Guide to Using PBTE Materials*, Athens, GA, American Association for Vocational Instructional Materials.

HART, I., HARDEN, R. and WALTON, M. (Eds) (1986) *Newer Developments in the Assessment of Clinical Competence*, Montreal, Heal Publications.

HARRINGTON, L. and KALAMAS, D. (Eds) (1985) *Achieving Professional Excellence — Proceedings of National Conference on Performance Based Approaches to Training*; Columbus, Ohio; National Centre for Research in Vocational Education.

HEATH, R. and NEILSON, M. (1974) 'The Research Base for PBTE' in *Review of Educational Research* 44, 4, p. 475 ff.

HERTZBERG, H. (1976) 'CBTE — Does it Have a Past, or a Future' in *Teachers' College Record*, 78, 1, pp. 1–21.

HOUSTON, R. H. (1980) 'An analysis of the performance-based teacher education movement' in Fardig, G. (Ed.) *Prospects of Performance-Based Vocational Teacher Education; Proceedings of National Invitational Conference at Orlando, Fla., March, 1980*, College of Education, University of Central Florida.

HUFF, S. (1976) 'Credentialling by tests or degrees?' in *Harvard Educational Review*, 44, 2, pp. 246–69.

HUFF, S. (1980) 'The assessment of occupational competence — Sect. 6. A synthesis of issues', Boston, Mass. McBer Corporation. (ERIC Ref. ED 192 170).

KLEMP, G. O. (1977) 'Three factors for success in the world of work: Implications for curriculum in higher education', in Bermilze, D. (Ed.) *Relating Work and Education: Current Issues in Higher Education*, San Francisco, Jossey-Bass.

KOERNER, J. (1963) *The Miseducation of American Teachers*, Boston, Mass, Houghton Mifflin.

LINDSEY, M. (1976) 'CBTE and certification in New York State: An overview' in *Teachers' College Record*, 77, 4, pp. 505–16.

MAINFRAME (1987) *One Day Dacum: A Handbook*, Haringey Education Authority, The Mainframe Project.

NABP (1988) 'NABPLEX: A candidates review guide to examinations', Park Ridge, Illinois; National Association of Boards of Pharmacy.

NCVQ (1989) *National Vocational Qualifications: Criteria and Procedures*, National Council for Vocational Qualifications.

NEUMANN, L. M. (1987) 'Long term continuing education for dentists' in *Journal of Dental Education*, 51, 8, pp. 492–6.

NORMAN, G. R. (1985) 'Defining competence — A methodological review' in Neufeld and Norman (Eds) *Assessing Clinical Competence*, New York, Springer (pp. 15–35).

NORTON, R. E. (1985) 'New developments in performance based teacher education' in Harrington and Kalamas (1985) *op cit.*

POTTINGER, P. S. (1980) 'The assessment of occupational competence — Part 3', in *Competence Assessment for Occupational Certification*, Boston, Mass., McBer Corporation. (ERIC Ref. ED 192 167; Feb. 1980).

SAXTON, D. F., PELIKAN, P. K., NUGENT, P. M. and NEELMAN, S. R. (Eds) (1985) *Mosby's Assess Test — A Practice Exam. for RN Licensure*, Princeton N. J., Mosby Systems.

SMITH, R. A. (Ed.) (1975) *Regaining Educational Leadership*, New York, John Wiley.

SPADY, W. G. (1977) 'Competency based education: A bandwagon in search of a definition' in *Educational Researcher*, 6, 1, Jan. 1977.

SPENCER, L. (1979) *Identifying, Measuring and Training Soft Skill Competencies*, Boston, Mass., McBer Corporation.

SPENCER, L. (1983) *Soft Skill Competencies*, Edinburgh, Scottish Council for Research in Education.

SWANCHEK, J. and CAMPBELL, J. (1981) 'Competence/performance-based teacher education: The unfulfilled promise' in *Educational Technology*, June, 1981, pp. 5–10.

TUXWORTH, E. (1982) *Competency in Teaching*, London, Longmans Green, (for Further Education Unit).

TUXWORTH, E. and CIECHANOWSKI, A. (1987) 'Competences of tutors and trainers — A research report' (Unpublished) summarised in *Instructional Competences* (1987) — City & Guilds, London.

TUXWORTH, E. (1988) 'Open entry to mastery learning?' in *Competence and Assessment* No. 4, April, 1988, pp. 6–7.

WOLFE, D. M. (1980) 'Developing professional competence in the applied behavioural sciences', in *New Directions for Experiential Learning*, 8, pp. 1–16.

Other Sources

ADAMS, K. (1981) *Does Performance-based Teacher Education Really Work? Case Studies of a Model Curriculum for Vocational Teacher Education*, Columbus, Ohio, National Centre for Research in Vocational Education.

AQUINO, J. (Ed.) (1976) *Performance-Based Teacher Education: A Source Book*, Washington, DC, American Association of Colleges of Teacher Education.

DUBRAVIC, V. (1986) *Assessing Vocational Teachers; R&D Series No. 262*, Columbus, Ohio; National Centre for Research in Vocational Education.

MEDLEY, D., SOAR, R., and SOAR, R. (1975) *Assessment and Research in Teacher Education: Focus on PBTE*, Washington, DC, American Association of Colleges of Teacher Education.

NCRVE (1985) *Prepare to Install Competency-Based Education, Modules LT-B-4 for Vocational Education Administrators*, Columbus, Ohio, National Centre for Research in Vocational Education.

NCRVE (1986) *Implementing Competency Based Education, Modules K-1 to K-6*, Columbus, Ohio; National Centre for Research in Vocational Education.

Note

1   It differs from the later version shown in Figure 2.1 in one crucial respect. Characteristic No. 1 allows 'theoretical formulation of professional responsibilities', which may allow some to avoid the stricter disciplines of professional role analysis.

Chapter 3

Competence and standards

Bob Mansfield

Introduction

UK Vocational Education and Training is based on a model of development which reverses previous approaches. Rather than design curricula to meet assumed needs, representative occupational bodies identify 'occupational standards' which are clear and precise statements which describe what effective performance means in distinct occupational areas. The standards are then used to develop 'new' vocational qualifications and the assessment which underpins them; plus learning programmes which deliver the achievements identified in the standards.

This chapter argues that occupational standards are based, implicitly, on a concept of competence, which may be either narrow or broad in focus. The consequence of 'narrow' or task based standards will be a standards framework which will not meet the needs of the modern economy — we need, instead, a broad concept of competence to drive standards and associated assessment and learning systems.

Competence and standards

The concepts of competence and standards are the keystones of Vocational Education and Training (VET). If we are clear about what we mean by competence, we can derive associated standards which describe what competence means in specific occupations and work roles. Standards, thus developed, are incorporated into vocational qualifications, and inform the programmes of learning which deliver the standards. Assessment processes are used to match the performance of individuals to the standards.

This whole process is the basis of VET policy — to drive the system from the starting point of competence and standards. This process replaces what is imagined to be the former situation — where learning and assessment drives the system, based on curricula which are descriptions of what people *ought* to know or be able to do.

This chapter makes three points:

- Views of competence vary — for some it is a broad concept which is to do with occupational roles. For others it is narrowly focused on the routine aspects of work activity, and veers towards the 'inputs' of knowledge, skills and understanding' which are attributes of individuals. A crucial issue is which view of competence is consistent with the strategic aims of the economy?
- Our view of competence structures the way in which we design standards. Consequently, some standards are very narrow in focus, whilst others are more broadly based. This in turn directly affects the structure of vocational qualifications and associated processes and delivery systems.
- The training infrastructure is based, in the main, on the narrow view of competence and standards. This drives the development of standards and associated assessment systems.

Models of competence

The VET world uses at least six models of competence. These are reproduced in Appendix 1 in diagrammatic form. All but two are based on inputs, i.e., they are based on assumptions about aptitudes, knowledge and skills which individuals possess. Some models specifically refer to knowledge, skills, attitudes, and related concepts like personal effectiveness which are assumed to 'broaden' the concept of competence. These models assume that competence is an individual attribute. This view is prominent in the extensive American literature on the competency based movement, and management development.

Two of the models in the diagram are based on outcomes — that is, they describe aspects of work roles which are not confined to descriptions of individual knowledge and skills. The first was produced by the IMS team which developed the occupational training family approach[1]. This was the first model of competence in work roles to have an impact on VET.

The second is the job competence model developed in 1985 by Mansfield and Mathews[2] and which has been used to inform an approach to personal effectiveness and the other YTS outcomes which has been endorsed by the Training Agency. The job competence model is shown in diagrammatic form in Appendix 2.

Both of the 'outcome' approaches have common features:

- they are based on descriptions of work role outcomes — they do not describe knowledge, skills or any other individual attributes;

- they are broad based in that they include considerations of the interaction between the 'technical' role and the organisational environment (and the wider occupational environment);
- they are dynamic in that they are able to incorporate changes in work organisation and technology since they act as a framework for identifying specific skills which contribute to the outcomes;
- they are both concerned with (and can accommodate) concepts like adaptability, versatility, change, creativity, innovation — as well as routine activities.

What all six models share is that competence is about performance. They differ in that the 'input' models tend to see performance in discrete elements (skills, tasks, etc.) or the 'content' of performance, whilst the two 'outcome' models describe whole work roles or elements of roles, or the 'outcomes' of performance. So, an input approach would tend to describe the routine activity of photocopying as:

operate a photocopier (a description of a task and implied skills)

whereas an output approach would describe the same event as:

reproduce copies of documents and information (the outcome of the activity).

Note that the latter description is not an individual attribute. It could equally well apply to a department, an organisation or an occupation. As such it is a more sound basis for developing national standards.

The two models of competence — individual attributes and outcomes are illustrated in figure 3.1.

We would argue that the case for the outcome approach is becoming more and more apparent. The economy needs adaptable and flexible workers, supervisors, trainers, bureaucrats and managers. The need for routine, technical task skills is declining and as our economic aims become more strategically focused (rather than concentrating simply on internal efficiency), we need this holistic work role approach even more. This is a concern for the public infrastructure — and many progressive employers are also recognising that the narrow specific approaches to job training are far from adequate to meet their future strategic needs.

We suggest that competence should be described in general terms as[3]:

being able to perform 'whole' work roles
(perform — not just know about — whole work roles, rather than just specific skills and tasks);

to the standards expected in employment
(not just 'training' standards or standards divorced from industrial reality);

in real working environments
(i.e. with all the associated pressures and variations of real work).

Figure 3.1 The Content and Standards Routes to Competence

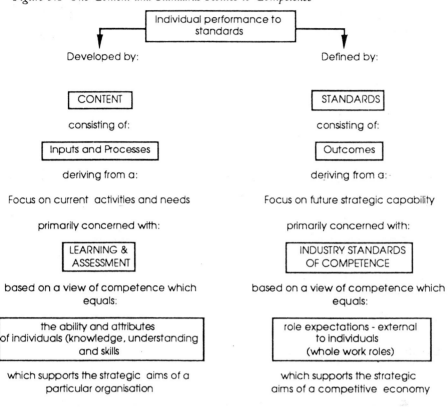

A common reaction in VET and general education has been to apply a 'deficiency' model to definitions of occupational competence which centre on the procedural and routine. This involves accepting the premise that routine occupational skills and tasks are the basis of vocational training and standards, and adding additional elements to make up the 'deficiency' of the narrow and mechanistic tasks and skills. The additions are usually constructs of one sort or another — like personal effectiveness, the ability to transfer, innovation and a host of other vague and unassessable characteristics.

The additions may be learning inputs — in the 1960s they were called general or liberal studies, in the 1980s they are more likely to be referred to as 'social and life skills'. These worthy inputs and processes may well enhance learning processes but they remain inputs and processes. It is a cornerstone of our approach that the view of competence must in itself incorporate the broader aspects of the work role which these constructs and inputs try, unsuccessfully, to capture. We would further argue that the two outcome models described above are precisely designed to incorporate these deficiency constructs.

Models of standards

The development of national standards is driven by the model of competence adopted by the lead body which is responsible for standard setting. Lead bodies with a narrow input view develop standards which are descriptions of tasks and skills with an emphasis on procedures (where flexible responses might be more appropriate).

Standards are, in our view, the means by which the model of competence is specified in the current occupational context. Standards are driven by an explicit or implicit view of competence — an explicit view would be one underpinned by one of the six models identified above. More often the model is implicit — and implicitly to do with tasks.

Many standards in existence at the moment are actually driven by assessment or learning considerations. In other words, standards are seen as being those aspects of performance which can be assessed in work activity (the basis for Caterbase) or the learning programme which will result in effective performance (partly the basis of ABCTG standards). Whatever the apparent justification, we would argue that a view of competence does (and should, explicitly) drive the standards model, with learning and assessment deriving directly from the standards. This relationship is shown in figure 3.2.

Figure 3.2 Deriving Standards

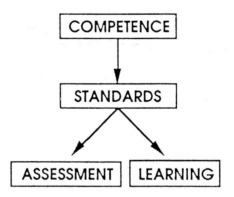

Standards describe competence in such a way that it can link with performance — they are benchmarks derived from concepts of competence against which performance is measured and matched. Standards also draw attention to the characteristics of the work role which should be matched to models of competence. It is here that the relationship between standards and competence is clearest. For example, in a published set of national standards[4] there is a considerable discussion of standards, but no benchmarks are given:

'standards to be achieved are 'in-built' within the actual activity'

Yet most of the 'activities' are stated with no evaluative clues as to what the standards are — for example:

follow a laid down procedure for dealing with client's complaints

Some evaluations are available — but significantly, these are only included in the activities that deal with product outcomes. Another clue to standards can be found in the assessment formats included with the standards. At the end of each activity assessment is the question:

were the above procedures completed in a commercially acceptable time?

Another published set of standards describes the 'minimum standards to be achieved'[5] thus:

as per the objectives (which describes knowledge and techniques)
all health and safety procedures and practices followed without deviation
accurately in accordance with laid down criteria
consistently having performed the complete activity on at least... occasions
at the following accepted and expected levels of productivity (time scale)...

Examination of numerous standards reveal that standards are generally conceived as being to do with:

- following procedures (at all times)
- dimensional accuracy
- accuracy/correctness in respect of laid down procedures
- time taken
- quality specifications

There are other criteria given (like the number of times an activity should be performed) but these are assessment criteria — not standards. The main point is that these standards all refer to product outcomes — the outcomes of tasks and discrete activities.

But some work roles contain little in the way of tasks (shop workers, managers, trainers, designers), and those that do also require the other work role aspects described above. To set standards at the task level means that associated qualifications only accredit and test tasks, and learning programmes are designed to teach them. Important though technical competence may be, we surely do not need another universally endorsed report to tell us that the routine task skills are not a sufficient base for a competent work force.

An alternative way of seeing standards as described in a paper 'Describing the new standards'[6], which is the basis of Technical Advisory Group Guidance Note Number 3 — *The Definition of Competences and Performance Criteria.* These standards are very similar to the standards 'keywords' which can be found in the occupational training family work learning guides, in *Training for Skill Ownership*.

Narrow versus broad views of competence

Our training infrastructure is based, in the main, on the narrow, task-based view of competence and standards. This approach dominates two critical arenas, i.e.:

- standards setting and the development of vocational qualifications
- delivery of accreditation and assessment systems.

Standards setting

This is evidenced in some of the examples described in the sections above, which apply to standards setting, and may be clearly seen in most of the NVQs which have been accredited to date. For example, the ABCTG standards are delivered by an RSA certificate[7] which has an assessment format based on tasks. The RTITB modules which form part of an NVQ are based on skills and tasks — the assessment record is headed 'Task, Operation or Procedure'.

The narrow task approach derives from the early development of the standards model which took place within YTS contexts. YTS occupational areas are primarily foundation or entry level occupations — Levels 1 and 2 in NCVQ terms — and can be more or less adequately described in terms of tasks and routine activities. However, as the 'level' of complexity and responsibility of the occupational role increases, the inadequacy of a task and task analysis approach becomes clear. The crucial and integral aspects of competence to do with system management and coordination, the management of uncertainty and change and the interactions with the wider environment are almost impossible to pick up with routine task analysis.

As the standards development programme moved away from foundation level jobs and work roles, so the inadequacy of the task model became clear. This is not to suggest that task analysis is appropriate for 'lower level' work roles however. There are fundamental reasons why a task approach is not adequate for any standards analysis.

Task analysis was derived primarily to support work measurement systems which were designed to remove the unpredictable and unfamiliar aspects of job and tasks for the purpose of being able to exert greater external (management) control over the work process. Often tied in with payment systems, work measurement through task analysis allowed work study engineers and production system designers to 'design out' of the work process the 'process skills', which are now so valued by employers as the economy goes through radical changes which have fundamentally changed work structures and processes.

Task analysis is appropriate for its purpose — it can measure and atomise work activities for work measurement and specific skills training. For deriving standards — which are work role expectations — it is not an appropriate approach. Other analysis approaches are in the process of development which look directly at expectations and job 'purposes' related to broad work role functions. The most prominent method is called 'functional analysis', which should not be confused with the functional job analysis approach used by Fine[8], nor the descriptions of 'job functions' used widely in American literature.

Assessment methods

Assessment methods used in current VET are centred around skill tests (which tend to be routinized) and tests of routine knowledge. HCTB is a notable exception with a work based assessment format (of tasks). HCTB contains some interesting references to work role characteristics in the module descriptions — but these are not assessed, although they are an assessment criterion. Less 'official' assessment methods, like work based accreditation, have been strongly supported and encouraged in YTS, yet these are often little more than task descriptions with a checklist box against them and can be extremely reliable.

Identifying knowledge elements is sometimes thought of as being the way in which additional work role characteristics like dealing with the unexpected, and responding creatively to contingencies can be accommodated. There is no such guarantee. Most knowledge testing is as proceduralized as skill testing. Knowledge testing is a complex and 'political' issue, often bound up with status claims and professionalism[9].

Recent debates with the VET research community suggest that knowledge is being increasingly seen as an assessment issue — with knowledge testing acting as a 'fall back' position when performance assessment or evidence is not available.[10] Yet employers who appraise and assess staff performance tend to concentrate on work role characteristics like making creative contributions, contributing to the improvement of systems and management of complex work roles. Many of these systems are crude and technically invalid — but employers are becoming clearer about what they want from people — and it is not a battery of over assessed skill tests.

There is a clear need to review the approach to assessment taken in VET. Recent research reports[11] are highly critical of current approaches and methods, identifying wide ranging shortfalls in validity, often justified by the search for a spurious reliability.

Summary

A VET system based on a narrow view of work roles will be tainted throughout its infrastructure. The public and private sectors of the infrastructure must turn **commitment** to a broad view of competence into the **means and the competence** to deliver it. This is not done solely by tinkering with processes or by making statements of intent. It involves embedding a work role model, and associated employment expectations, into the very heart of the system — into the definition of competence and standards.

Work roles are not a bundle of tasks or routine procedures. To base standards development methodology on this premise creates problems at all levels because our expectations of the infrastructure are fixed by the narrow model.

VET delivery agents are capable of analysing a task to within an inch of its life[12], yet the aspects of the work role which are increasingly valued in the economy — adaptability in the face of change, management of roles and systems, taking responsibility for contingencies, standards and output, creativity, flexible responses to new market demands — remain worthy aims which everyone routinely salutes and does little about.

The standards development programme has now incorporated this message and the broad approach. Lead Bodies are now advised to take a broad view of competence (as exemplified by the Job Competence model), and are encouraged to use a 'holistic' analysis to derive broad work role functions[13]. Assessment technology is taking on the challenge of validly assessing the less tangible aspects of competence. Our future economy needs and deserves no less.

Terms and Abbreviations used in the text:

ABCTG	The Administrative, Business and Commercial Training Group (Lead Body for this area)
ET	Employment Training (launched September 1988)
HCTB	Hotel and Catering Training Board
IMS	The Institute of Manpower Studies
Lead Bodies	Industry Lead Bodies define standards on behalf of an industry or industry sector
NCVQ	The National Council for Vocational Qualifications
NVQs	National Vocational Qualifications (vocational qualifications which meet the NCVQ criteria)
RSA	The Royal Society of Arts
RTITB	The Road Transport Industry Training Board
Technical Advisory Group	A group of specialists, Examining and Validating Bodies, NCVQ and TA staff which develops guidance for Lead Bodies on the design of standards, assessment and the development of vocational qualifications.

Training Agency   Formerly the Manpower Services Commission and the Training Commission. Now an agency of the Department of Employment

YTS   The Youth Training Scheme.

Notes

This chapter is based on two previous papers written since July 1988. The papers were entitled *Competence and Standards*, originally written as a policy document for the Training Commission Advisory Group on Content and Standards, and *Supply and Demand Led Training*, which is from the BSD Research and Development Series. *Competence and Standards* was designed to isolate a number of key issues in VET relating to VET delivery within Training Agency programmes, consequently, many of the examples are from standards associated with YTS and ET. However, it is fundamental to the arguments presented in this chapter that the approaches advocated apply equally to all NCVQ levels and levels beyond level 4 (management and professional).

1. *Training for Skill Ownership*, Hayes, Fonda *et al.*, IMS/MSC 1982.
2. *The Job Competence Model*, Mansfield and Mathews, FESC 1985.
3. This definition has been adopted by the Training Agency for ET programmes — see *Designing Competence Based Training Programmes. ET Quality Note 3*. Training Agency 1989.
4. Published by the Hairdressing Lead Body.
5. Published by the Retail Consortium, 1987. We understand that recent versions have contained more precise standards in the form of performance criteria.
6. *Describing the New Standards*, Mansfield. SASU/MSC 1986.
7. The RSA Certificate in Office Procedures. NCVQ Level 1.
8. See Fine, S. 'Functional Job Analysis: an approach to a technology for manpower planning', *Personal Journal* Nov. 1974, pp. 813–18 and Mansfield, B. 'Functional Analysis — A personal approach', *Competence and Assessment*, Special Edition No. 1, 1989.
9. See Alison Wolfe *Underpinning Knowledge and Understanding* a report to NCVQ 1988.
10. This issue is discussed in a number of internal TAG papers, and by Lindsay Mitchell in 'The Identification of Knowledge' in *Competence and Assessment* — Winter 1989. A more extensive debate is to be provided in a forthcoming

publication which summarizes the issues raised in the 'Knowledge Symposium' sponsored by the Training Agency in February 1989.

11 In particular, the two SED/TA reports, *Insufficient Evidence* — the report of the competency testing project, Mitchell and Cuthbert, 1989 and *Credit where Credit's Due*, the report of the Accreditation of Work Based Learning project, Miller *et al.*, 1988.

12 I am grateful to David Mathews for this scornful turn of phrase, which is less amusing than it might be because it is so near the truth.

13 This approach is explict in *Developing Standards by Reference to Functions*, TAG Guidance Note 2, July, 1989.

Appendix 1

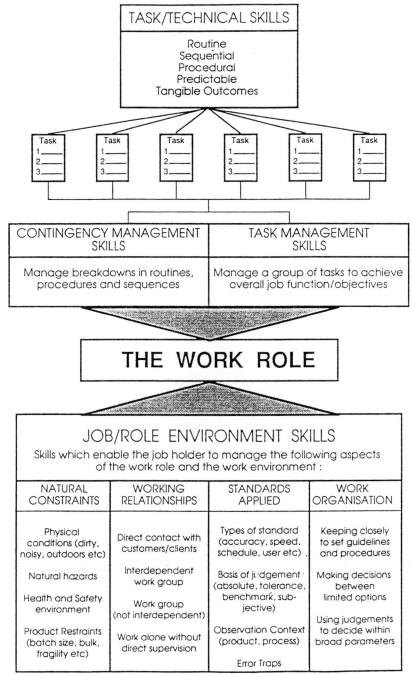

© Bob Mansfield and David Mathews - 1987

Appendix 2

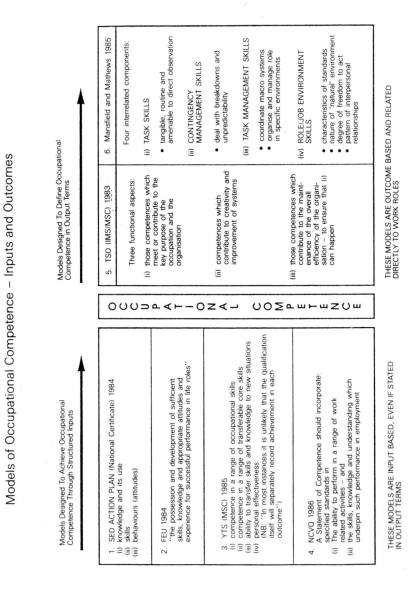

Models of Occupational Competence – Inputs and Outcomes

Models Designed To Achieve Occupational Competence Through Structured Inputs

Models Designed To Define Occupational Competence in Output Terms

OCCUPATIONAL COMPETENCE

1. SED ACTION PLAN (National Certificate) 1984
 (i) knowledge and its use
 (ii) skills
 (iii) behaviours (attitudes)

2. FEU 1984
 "the possession and development of sufficient skills, knowledge and appropriate attitudes and experience for successful performance in life roles"

3. YTS (MSC) 1985
 (i) competence in a range of occupational skills
 (ii) competence in a range of transferable core skills
 (iii) ability to transfer skills and knowledge to new situations
 (iv) personal effectiveness
 (NB: "In most instances it is unlikely that the qualification itself will separately record achievement in each outcome")

4. NCVQ 1986
 A Statement of Competence should incorporate:
 (i) The ability to perform in a range of work related activities – and
 (ii) the skills, knowledge and understanding which underpin such performance in employment

THESE MODELS ARE INPUT BASED, EVEN IF STATED IN OUTPUT TERMS

5. TSO (IMS/MSC) 1983

Three functional aspects:

 (i) those competences which meet or contribute to the key purpose of the occupation and the organisation

 (ii) competences which contribute to creativity and improvement of systems

 (iii) those competences which contribute to the maintenance of the overall efficiency of the organisation – to ensure that (i) can happen

6. Mansfield and Mathews 1985

Four interrelated components:

 (i) TASK SKILLS
 • tangible, routine and amenable to direct observation

 (ii) CONTINGENCY MANAGEMENT SKILLS
 • deal with breakdowns and unpredictability

 (iii) TASK MANAGEMENT SKILLS
 • coordinate macro systems
 • organise and manage role in specific environments

 (iv) ROLE/JOB ENVIRONMENT SKILLS
 • characteristics of standards
 • nature of 'natural' environment
 • degree of freedom to act
 • pattern of interpersonal relationships

THESE MODELS ARE OUTCOME BASED AND RELATED DIRECTLY TO WORK ROLES

©Lindsay Mitchell 1988

Chapter 4

Can competence and knowledge mix?

Alison Wolf

Introduction

This chapter[1] is concerned with the role of 'knowledge' in competency based education and training. Competency based programmes are often perceived as generally (and indeed necessarily) occupied with discrete objectives of direct and limited vocational relevance. Such an approach is then contrasted with the more general concerns of 'educational' programmes. However, while this contrast may reflect some of the practice which is labelled as 'competency based', it is not inherent in the approach.

In discussing how 'knowledge' may be viewed from a competency-led perspective, I hope to show that there is no bifurcation between competence and education. The approach is perfectly compatible with the learning of higher-level skills, the acquisition of generalizable knowledge (and understanding), and with broad-based courses. I also make some suggestions about the ways in which tutors can identify, validate and update the content — including specifically the 'knowledge' content — of competency based courses. However, my particular concern is with how we actually measure or assess aspects of competence.

The chapter falls into two parts. The second section is directly concerned with the practicalities of unwrapping knowledge requirements from *standards of competence*: that is, from the statements which define the output or objectives of a learning (or teaching) process. However, before moving to such concrete issues, the paper also discusses, in the first section, what exactly it is that we mean by 'knowledge' or 'knowledge and understanding' (NCVQ guidance refers at all times to 'knowledge and understanding' rather than to 'knowledge' alone). Some such definition of terms is vital. Just as we cannot train effectively to standards if we do not know what those standards are, so we can hardly define or measure the associated knowledge and understanding without knowing what sort of thing 'they' may be.

It is also important to define, or rather circumscribe, the area of discussion. I am arguing that there is no contradiction between adopting a competency-led approach and teaching generalisable and higher-order skills. However, the *process* of defining 'standards' is obviously very different when one is relating them directly to occupational activities than when one is not. Philosophy degrees arguably develop very *useful* competences, but one would hardly look to an industrial lead body for assistance in defining them, any more than one would involve such a body in course design. In this chapter, therefore, I will be confining my discussion to cases where the utilitarian justification for developing a competence is direct and obvious.

What do we mean by competence, knowledge and understanding?

The essence of what we mean by competence is apparent from the previous remarks. We are talking about the ability to *perform*: in this case, to perform at the *standards* expected of employees. Thus, the standards incorporated in a statement of competence are there to specify the nature of the particular, performable occupational role or roles.[2] Such roles can be relatively narrow and highly specialised — for example, a pastry cook — but one can also be talking about occupational roles which encompass a wide range of specifics, such as systems analysts, production engineers or statisticians.

However, for the purposes of this discussion, one very important point is that, in every case, *competence is a construct*, and not something that we can observe directly. If we are going to assess and train people explicitly in terms of competencies (non-explicitly, we have always done so anyway), we will have to develop observable measures and use them to collect evidence that can 'support an inferential leap from an observed consistency (in the evidence) to a construct that accounts for that consistency' (Messick, 1975). It follows that, if we do not have very clear ideas or hypotheses about the construct, we are not likely to develop very good measures.

It is at this point that definitions of competence tend to assume substantive importance: less because they are particularly specific in themselves than because they tend to indicate what sort of measures those in charge of the definitions will accept. (Most of the situations in which people are serious about measuring competency tend to be overtly vocational, so this usually means the people who control licensing and qualifications . . .). An important difference is between definitions which deal only with outputs, i.e., behaviours in which competence may be said to inhere, and from which it can supposedly be inferred directly, and those which include inputs: the component parts of which, it is hypothesised, competence consists.

In developing competence-based vocational training and qualifications in this country, most of the emphasis has been on 'output' measures. It has also been policy to encourage the direct assessment of 'performance', ideally in the workplace, as the preferred measure of competence. Overall, this has given many people the impression that 'competencies' refer only to very specific practical activities.

However, it can also be helpful to think of definitions of competence which are concerned with inputs — albeit inputs which turn out to be complex constructs themselves. Thus, if we look at the NCVQ definitions, we find both 'skills' and 'knowledge and understanding' mentioned as underpinning performance (and competence). They can thus be seen as 'inputs' which actually inhere in any competence which people achieve and show. For some reason, in the current debates, 'skills' don't seem to cause people any conceptual problem[3]. 'Knowledge and understanding', however, do.

Knowledge and understanding

Rather than get involved in an ultimately sterile debate about where 'knowledge' ends and 'understanding' begins, I intend here to treat them together.

I emphasized earlier that competence is a construct. So, too, are knowledge and understanding, and so are skills. Thus, we can actually agree that knowledge and understanding contribute to competence, while being unable directly to observe or measure *any one of these three*.[4] If we decide that it is relevant to assess knowledge and understanding separately as part of a training programme, we will be doing so at one remove. We cannot open up someone's head and measure directly the knowledge it contains, any more than we can measure their competence.

A large amount of blood has been shed, in the school as well as the vocational sector, over the question of whether or not there is value in learning 'bucketfuls of facts'. (The phrase is from the ill-fated Higginson report on the reform of 'A' levels.) This debate is not unrelated to the equation of 'knowledge testing' with measurement of factual recall, often of the most fragmented kind — and with the prevalence of just such tests in the vocational sector. However, what we should be talking about when discussing the relationship of knowledge to competencies is something much wider than factual recall. It is what much of the literature on medical competence (e.g., Forsythe *et al.*, 1986) refers to as 'cognitive abilities'.

Conceiving of knowledge as a randomly arranged store cupboard full of facts completely violates what we know about the structure of the human mind. As Taylor (1964) pointed out in his critique of stimulus-response theory, even an action as 'simple' as a laboratory rat's pulling a lever to get food actually requires us to posit some sort of intentionality, and the organising of stored 'factual' information so that the correct pieces are brought into play.

This is even more true with human behaviour. If you think about 'routine' tasks, what is striking about them is how different they actually are in many ways. Yet we recognise them as 'basically' the same, and apply the appropriate knowledge and behaviour, with a few more or less marginal changes; whereas a computer would be completely at sea. Contemporary psychological theory sees human beings as creators of mental 'models' or general 'schemata' which they apply to particular circumstances, and modify with experience, or as 'hypothesis testers'. (See for example Jeeves and Greer, 1983; Snow *et al.*, 1980; Sternberg, 1986). This approach emphasises that 'knowing' something involves knowing when to access it, and being able to do so when appropriate — even if that is only in an examination room.

In a discussion of 'The Assessment of Dynamic Cognitive Structures', (1982) Messick has written:

> At issue is not merely the amount of knowledge accumulated but its organization or structure as a functional system for productive thinking, problem solving, and creative invention . . . .The individual's structure of knowledge is a critical aspect of . . . achievement . . . .A person's structure of knowledge in a subject area includes not only declarative knowledge about substance (or information about *what*), but also procedural knowledge about methods (or information about *how*), and strategic knowledge about alternatives for goal setting and planning (or information about *which*, *when* and possibly *why*) . . . .Knowledge structure basically refers to the structure of relationships among concepts. But as knowledge develops, these structures quickly go beyond classifications of concepts as well as first-order relations among concepts and classes to include organized systems of relationships or schemas.

Another way of putting this is to say that, *whenever* we learn something specific, we also learn something general. It is also why our brilliant offspring, having learned to identify dogs at an unparalleled early age, then insist — often very vigorously — that pigs and cows are 'dogs' as well.

The point of this brief excursion into cognitive theory is to demonstrate that the sort of knowledge required for vocational learning or 'competence' is not in some way *different* from that learned in other parts of life, or education. Conversely, one cannot say that some sorts of knowledge are generically unsuitable for competency-based learning. People may need to grasp more or fewer general principles, or deal with a wider or narrower set of applications: but any sort of knowledge involves general schemata of some sort. What we have here is a spectrum, not a dichotomy between general cognitive skills (learned in 'education'?) and narrow vocationally relevant 'facts' (learned in 'training'?).

The case of the child learning to categorise also highlights another very important point. It is that a great deal of knowledge — including abstract, generalisable knowledge — is *acquired through experience*, just as much as 'skills' are. Michael Eraut has discussed the issue in detail on a number of occasions (e.g., Eraut, 1985). What is important is to emphasise, again, that we do not have a dichotomy between competencies (or knowledge) which are, or are not, appropriately acquired 'on the job', but simply variations of degree. ('On the job' in this context should be read as including authentic simulations and applied tasks). It is also important to remember that 'practical experience' does not mean getting your hands dirty.[5] Competency based learning has been bedevilled by the idea that it only works for manual skills: but experience is just as relevant, and just as practical, when concerned with predominantly cognitive activities. School-based subjects also suffer from this curious misperception. In maths GCSE investigations, 'practical' has become equated with making models.

Recognising knowledge requirements

I stressed above that, if you are devising measures for a construct, you had better be fairly clear about what that construct is. In this case, the knowledge which goes to make up an occupational competence is unlikely to be 'just factual'. You certainly need facts. They are the skeleton of the sort of structures Messick is discussing: the basis on which, whether involved in clinical diagnosis or saving curdled mayonnaise, one selects a subset of possible hypotheses to 'test' or act on.[6] That is why, for example, all the research on clinical reasoning (e.g., Elstein *et al.*, 1978; Arkes and Hammond, 1987; Forsythe *et al.*, 1986) finds information a necessary condition of competence. Equally, however, tests that measure only factual recall are inadequate measures of knowledge and unlikely to provide much evidence of occupational competence. Eraut (1985) makes similar points about 'professional' knowledge.

Suppose we take as an example an occupation in which I have been assured that there is 'very little knowledge base', namely, catering: and use, as a specific case, baking. Actually, I think there is a very great deal of knowledge involved in baking, although much of it may never be made explicit. It follows that if we measure competence in baking — directly and via outputs, or more indirectly, via its component parts — then we are going to have to measure quite a lot of 'knowledge and understanding'.

A competent chef will need to know not only that specific items are baked, but also what that means in terms of equipment, where in the oven to place things, how to adapt when faced with an unfamiliar oven or range, and so on. Moreover, there quite quickly comes a point at which we go beyond Messick's *classifications of concepts* to his *organized systems of relationships*. In the case of baking, it is such 'schematic' knowledge which enables chefs to substitute items for each other, improvise in the face of missing ingredients, know how far they can depart from an original recipe without disaster striking, and, ultimately, create new recipes. What is also true is that very little of this 'knowledge' takes the form of identifying ingredients from the names of dishes (a mainstay of traditional multiple-choice catering tests); and that most of it could be inferred directly and quite easily from measures of the overall 'baking' competence *if* one observed a chef for long enough. (See Michael Eraut [1985] for a very useful discussion of practice-created knowledge).

The fact that knowledge requirements like this can be so unrecognised is, I think, related to two factors. The first is that we only recognise as knowledge things which we had to learn consciously and with difficulty. A prime example is calculus, which a computer can be programmed to do quite easily; as compared to face recognition which it can't. Much of the knowledge related to baking is learned best through practice, rather than being codified: and so falls at the face recognition end of the spectrum. Second, and compounding this, is the association of 'knowledge' with what gets tested in traditional factual tests. (Conversely, we also get plenty of situations where a large knowledge base is recognised and identified. However, because we don't refer back constantly to its applications, we don't teach or assess it in the most appropriate way).

The need for breadth

Before turning to how we might actually unpack appropriate knowledge from a competence statement, there is another important point to be made, which is very relevant to the practical issue of developing measures for an underlying construct. It is that, as this discussion will have implied, *'knowledge and understanding' are likely to be highly contextualised — and so, correspondingly, is competence.*

This means that it is difficult to infer from a single measure, or even quite a number of measures, just how far competence extends. In the case of underlying knowledge structures, these may be more general, or less. The chef who bakes a perfect chocolate sponge may or may not be able to create one with lemon flavour; diagnose the problem if it rises faster on one side than another; or estimate the best way to cook such a recipe in an unfamiliar solid-fuel range. This is, of course, the whole 'transfer' issue.

The difficulty of generalising about 'skills' or competencies is something of which, in education, we should all be aware: for example, from the Assessment of Performance Unit surveys, or reviews of profiling developments. (See also, for example, Wolf and Silver, 1986, and Wolf, 1989). However, just as we do not always pay enough attention to the issue, so, too, many competence-based systems treat competence as though it 'inheres in individuals and generalizes across situations' (Forsythe *et al.*, 1986). In fact, this is rarely the case with vocationally-related competences any more than with, for example, general mathematics skills. The literature on clinical (diagnostic) competence is the fullest available, and recent studies (Forsythe *et al.*, 1986; Elstein *et al.*, 1978) indicate that in fact what happens is that particular doctors are good at diagnosing particular types of case. The importance of context when 'unpacking' knowledge and understanding for assessment purposes is that *we can only infer breadth of application from breadth of evidence.*

'Unpacking' knowledge and understanding

Examining what we mean by the 'knowledge and understanding' relevant to a competence makes it clear that:

i   Knowledge and understanding are not divorced from performance. It is more appropriate to see *behaviour* (or 'performance') as deriving from *knowledge* structures.

ii Knowledge and understanding are constructs which have to be inferred from observable behaviour, just as much as competence itself.

iii Knowledge and understanding are often and/or best learned 'in use'.

iv Knowledge is highly contextualised. To infer knowledge with confidence, especially when it has broad applications, one needs breadth of evidence.

In this section, the paper turns to what all this may imply for the practicalities of standard-setting and devising competency-based programmes. And for this, two diagrams are helpful.

Figure 1:

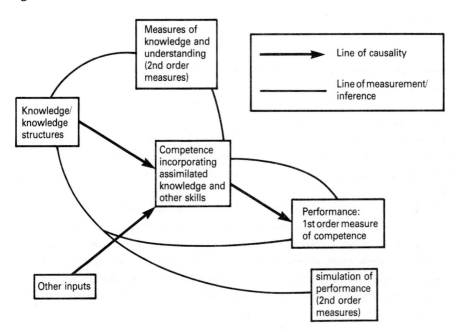

Figure 2:

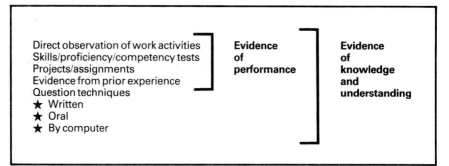

The first of these (figure 4.1) emphasises what was said above: namely that knowledge and understanding are themselves constructs which are assumed to contribute to competence. They can be inferred from measures of competence: or they can be inferred from direct measures.[7] Since we are ultimately interested only in the competence, it might seem perverse to opt for direct measures of the contributing constructs. At the same time, however, *the difficulty of making correct inferences without large amounts of evidence, and the fact that direct measures of competence are themselves highly contextualised, mean that we may find it very hard to acquire adequate evidence by focusing on competence alone.*

Figure 4.2, which is taken directly from TAG note 5,[8] illustrates this point very well. Following the basic Training Agency/NCVQ model, it identifies 'performance' as the best possible measure of competence. Taking any of the extant meanings of competence, this must obviously be right.[9] We also find other tests, which are definitely indirect measures of actual performance, classified as providing evidence of performance: and, even more germane here, *all measures* of competence, whether at one or two removes, shown as providing *evidence of knowledge and understanding.*

What this also suggests is that the question of how one actually deals with knowledge and understanding in a competence-based system is essentially a pragmatic, case-by-case affair, dependent on the type and amount of evidence available from various sources. The more evidence we have which comes from direct measures of competence (or 'performance'), the less we need other indirect measures, which look only at the knowledge and understanding elements. However, we can also only know whether we have got enough evidence from other means if we specify — and unpack — the competence statements themselves adequately, so that the knowledge structures which inhere in them, and in the performance criteria, are very clear. It is here that the contextualised nature of knowledge and understanding is so important: because *if the competences and performance criteria are provided in a decontextualised form we will not know whether we have enough evidence or not, nor what that evidence should be.*

Recontextualising competence

The more general and generalisable the competencies one deals with, the more important explicit contextualisation becomes. This may seem counter-intuitive. However, with narrow competencies, which are used only in a very few, very well-defined contexts, the interpretations and judgements of those involved in teaching or assessing generally coincide. Widen the range of application, and the population involved, and people are increasingly likely to make very different things of what seems to you crystal-clear.

'Range statements', a term currently being used by working groups within NCVQ and the Training Agency, can help by defining the boundaries within which a given standard and performance criteria should operate. At one and the same time, they make it clearer to assessors how adequate their more direct (or 'practical') evidence of competence is, and how far the required underpinning knowledge needs to extend. For example, an element of competence in the new Retail Certificate deals with receiving and directing visitors. Performance criteria are of the type 'Appropriate questions asked to establish purpose of visit', 'Visitor directed/accompanied to correct location'. As the element stands, this could be satisfied, presumably, by either regular direction of a stream of salesmen or regular direction of the personal friends of the proprietor.

However, in fact, a retailer had better be aware that certain visitors (notably health and standards inspectors) have complete right of entry, instantly. A range statement would include reference to this 'contextualisation' of the general competence. In other words, *underlying knowledge and understanding are 'unpacked' by further elaborating upon the nature of the integrated competence itself,* so that it is clear that it is integrated knowledge (or correct 'knowledge structures') that we are after.

Anyone with previous experience of the criterion-referenced test movement will recognise in 'range statements' the idea of 'test domain' in a new guise: and of course exactly the same problems could arise. If you try to make range statements (or specifications of test domain) so specific that you are certain that assessors following them will produce effectively the same measures, you are set for grief. It is instructive to quote James Popham (1984, p.39), the Grand Old Man of competency testing on this point.

> Once upon a time, when I was younger and foolisher, I though we could create test specifications so constraining that the test items produced as a consequence of their use would be *functionally homogeneous*, that is, essentially interchangeable. But if we use the difficulty of an item as at least one index of the item's nature, then it becomes quite obvious that even in such teensy behaviour domains as measuring the student's ability to multiply pairs of double-digit numbers, the task of $11 \times 11 = ?$ is lots easier than $99 \times 99 = ?$. About the only way we can ever attain functional homogeneity is to keep pruning the nature of the measured behaviour so that we're assessing ever more trifling sorts of behaviour. That would be inane.

It seems likely that testing of the National Curriculum is going to get caught in this trap, as it attempts to generate standardised items which are 'fair' to boys and girls, different ethnic groups, etc. However, competency-based systems do not need to do so. We should not pretend that performance criteria, with or without range statements, can be used to generate functionally identical assessment procedures. It makes much more sense to see the assessment of competence as involving alternative ways of amassing adequate evidence using a collection of different sources: with testing of knowledge and understanding supplementing and covering different contexts from those on which direct performance evidence is available. Indeed, thinking about assessment in these 'evidence accretion' terms is crucially important to the whole competency based approach, because it avoids the problems of Popham's type of criterion-referenced testing. It is also, of course, very close to the way in which many educational judgments are already reached in practice, especially at postgraduate level.

Thus, we can envisage that some assessors will accumulate one set of evidence: others, other sets. Some aspects of the competence, where it is easy to collect evidence, will 'suffer' from over-kill, so that one can make inferences with a high degree of confidence, while in others, the opposite may be true. The particular make-up of assessment 'bundles' will differ from case to case: but if the performance criteria and contexts are specified well, and we have some reasonable evidence on all counts, then we can — still treating the case in probabilistic terms, which is actually all one can ever achieve anyway — be fairly confident that we do indeed have adequate evidence on the basis of which to infer competence.

Once again, a figure may illustrate most clearly the situation. This one is borrowed and adapted from the report by Robert Wood and his colleagues on assessing performance in the workplace (Wood *et al.*, 1988, p.25). Both examples in figure 4.3 show ways in which evidence of the same competence has been collected, given the same performance criteria and range statements. In both cases, having sampled, more or less directly, well over half of the underlying competence, one can start to make fairly confident statements about the assessee.

Figure 3:

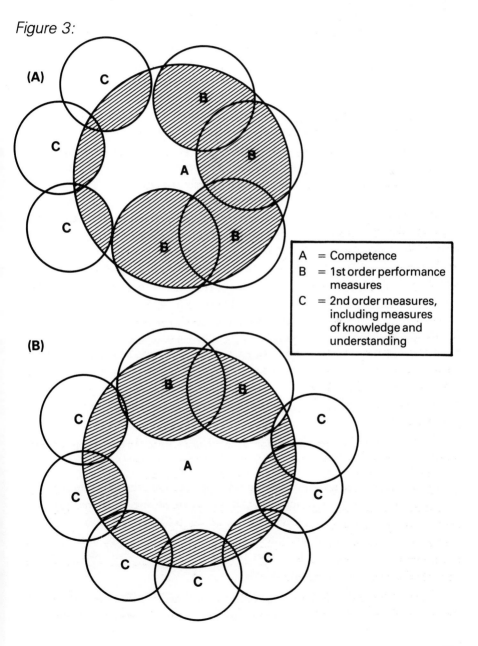

A = Competence
B = 1st order performance measures
C = 2nd order measures, including measures of knowledge and understanding

Thinking in terms of 'evidence accretion' does presuppose that assessors feel confident about exactly what domain concerns them, and therefore about using different measurement mixes. I mentioned earlier that, as a rule, competencies are easier to work with — i.e., to train for, and to assess consistently — the narrower they are, and the fewer people there are involved. This is not, however, just because of the intrinsic nature of more general competencies. The problem is rather that the tutors responsible for delivering them are less likely to have shared ideas, experiences, and understandings.

School experience is relevant here. Coursework assessment by teachers works well to the degree that the teachers involved have clear, shared models of what is 'appropriate' for given subjects and levels. (Shared textbooks, and the continued existence of examination 'anchors' also help maintain this subject-based community). They may do so for very general skills — such as some of those involved in writing — and not for quite narrow ones which are new to the syllabus. Similarly with vocationally related competencies: some narrow ones may be more problematic than some more general ones. Contingently, this is rarely the case.

If we had a very well developed system of integrated apprenticeships, and a corps of trainers who had experienced the same system and internalised its standards, the problem would be minor in scale. We might be able to get away with the same lack of specificity as apparently serves the West Germans. However, we do not. (See Wood, 1985). We are creating new occupational standards as much as specifying them, and that means creating agreement on the range of contexts and knowledge too. All this depends, obviously, on getting the specifications right. Range statements are a way into the knowledge structures which inhere in performance because they recontextualise competencies, but we still have to get statements which cover all the *relevant contexts in which knowledge — and competence — inhere.*

Heuristics versus algorithms

Unfortunately, I believe that this is more an art than a science. To quote Popham again (1984, pp. 39–40):

> At no point in the test development process for criterion-referenced measurement is it more apparent that we are employing art, rather than science, than when the general nature of the behavioural domain to be tested is initially conceptualised . . . .I have been completely unable to reduce the process to a form that is directly teachable — complete with practice exercises, etc. — to others.

My own experience, when running projects that involved developing workplace assessment materials is similar: but I think we can indicate where it is most likely that *performance evidence will be inadequate*, range statements *especially important* and/or inferences about competence unsafe without a *wide range* of verified application. We can also provide some heuristic devices for those involved in unpacking.

Situations in which it is especially likely that direct performance measures will not be adequate, are discussed in some detail elsewhere (Wolf, 1988). This argued that separate consideration and assessment of knowledge and understanding will be desirable when, and to the degree that, occupations are characterised by *unpredictable situations* and/or *a huge range of different situations*. This is because, the more these characteristics apply, the more likely it is that adequate collection of evidence will force one — for practical reasons — to use second-order measures. In the first case, one will want to be very confident that the performance one observes directly (which will almost certainly include application of knowledge, selected from a large base) indeed reflects the 'correct' structures or schemata. In the latter, one will simply be unable to observe many of the situations one would like to see enacted. Competencies characterised by either or both are prime candidates for 'second-order' measures of competence involving separate assessment of knowledge and understanding.

When it comes to identifying in detail what the underpinning or inherent knowledge may be, the available processes which can readily be adapted are Delphi; Dacum; Critical Incident Survey; and Behavioural Event interviews. (See Miller *et al.* [1988] *Credit where Credit's Due* for a full discussion). It is my impression that a large part of the work on standards to date has used some approach which is closest to Dacum or Delphi, both of which involve brainstorming and consensus building by groups of experts. However, in this case, where 'unpacking' knowledge may also involve quite detailed contextualising, I would argue strongly for a 'critical incident' approach. Because it asks people to describe specific and notable examples of good or bad practice which they have observed, it is particularly likely to throw up contexts other than the most routine ones (which are also the most likely to be covered by workplace assessment). I must also admit to a particular fondness for this approach because, when unwrapping the particular area of vocationally required mathematics (see Wolf, 1986), I have found the best starter of all to be 'Tell me about any recent disasters you have had'.

This advocacy of a 'critical incident' approach also reflects my doubts about trying to apply any very detailed algorithm for knowledge specification across the board. I suspect that anything which is generally applicable will also suffer from the same problems as the decontextualised, generic competencies at which we so often arrive. That is, it will have to be so general that it can happily be interpreted in a whole range of completely different ways by its users. Worse, if the instructions are very detailed, they will probably simply never be read. That was certainly Popham's experience with test writers and teachers. It has also been mine with trainers and workplace supervisors.[10]

In discussing how we might go about 'unwrapping', and what it is that we want to unwrap (and measure), I have not addressed the issue of validation. I noted above the observed tendency of techniques such as Delphi and Dacum to produce consensual lists of competencies which have been detached from their contextual anchors. This sort of abstraction makes it easy for other people to agree that the consensus-builders have got it right, because the whole thing remains dangerously detached from actual applications. Just such concerns underlie the insistence of mathetics on prescribing 'synthetic' behaviours (practice) before 'analytic' (theory) for learners and 'mathe-maticists' (Gilbert, 1969). However, there is an equal danger that we may create 'consensual' range statements that are just that: *created* by the group *ab initio*.

We have to build in some form of further validation process (see Wolf, 1988), and I hope that future research will address what that might be. We also need a great deal more work to develop assessment measures that really are concerned with knowledge structures, or with 'knowledge and understanding' as they inhere in competent behaviour.

Notes

1 This chapter is based closely on a paper given to a Training Agency symposium on the identification and assessment of underpinning knowledge and understanding, January 1989.
2 Miller *et al.*, *Credit Where Credit's Due* section B.1.1. provide an extensive discussion of the literature discussing 'competence'.
3 Although to the degree that they are seen as actually synonymous with competence, they reinforce the limited view of what 'competency-based' training is.
4 Messick notes that 'a construct is defined by a network of relations that are tied to observables and hence are empirically testable. The measures are the observables, and the construct is invoked to account for relationships among them', (Messick, 1975, p.955).
5 This may be a particularly British hang-up. 'I'm a practical man myself' translates as 'I possess useful manual skills which I learned on the job, and I don't think much of you supposed intellectuals'.
6 As so often, educational debates at present seem to involve two equally untenable positions. One side argues for 'processes' as though they were free-standing, and the other for 'facts' as though they were enough on their own.
7 Of course, they are not the only contributing constructs. Psycho-motor skills, 'metacognitive' skills of the most general type and attitudes would also have to be in the figure if we were attempting a fully specified model of competence.
8 Guidance Note 5: Assessment of Competence. Training Agency: Technical Advisory Group.
9 However, it is here treated as itself a construct so that actual work activities are described as providing 'evidence of performance', a rather curious turn of phrase. Recent NCVQ discussion papers, by contrast, refer more straightforwardly to 'performance evidence'.
10 See Wolf and Silver (1986) and Wood (1985). Also Popham, op. cit. p.34 'as we ladled in additional spoonfuls of specificity, we were simultaneously reducing the likelihood that our item writers . . . would ever pay (any) attention'.

References

ARKES, H. and HAMMOND, K. (Eds) (1987) *Judgement and Decision-making: An Interdisciplinary Reader*, Cambridge; Cambridge University Press.

BARON, J. B. and STERNBERG, R. J. (Eds) (1987) *Teaching Thinking Skills: Theory and Practice*, New York: W. H. Freeman.

DORE, R. and SAKO, M. (1989) *How the Japanese Learn to Work*, London, Routledge.

DOWIE, J. and ELSTEIN, A. (1988) *Professional Judgement: A Reader in Clinical Decision-making*, Cambridge, Cambridge University Press.

ELSTEIN, A. S., SHULMAN, L. S. and SPRAFKA, S. A. (1978) *Medical Problem-solving: An Analysis of Clinical Reasoning*, Cambridge, Mass., Harvard University Press.

ERAUT, M. (1985) 'Knowledge creation and knowledge use in professional contexts' *Studies in Higher Education*, 10, 2, pp. 117-33.

FORSYTHE, G. B., McGUGHIE, W. C. and FRIEDMAN, C. P. (1986), 'Construct validity of medical clinical competence measures: A multitrait-multimethod matrix study using confirmatory factor analysis', *American Educational Research Journal* 23, 1, Summer, 1986, pp. 315-36.

GILBERT, T. F. (1969) 'Mathetics', in *Review of Educational Cybernetics and Applied Linguistics*, Supplement 1.

JEEVES, M. and GREER, B. (1983) *The Analysis of Structural Learning*, London, Academic Press.

MESSICK, S. (1972) 'Beyond structure: In search of functional models of psychological process', *Psychometrika* 37, 4, pp. 357-75.

MESSICK, S. (1975) 'The standard problem: Meaning and values in measurement and evaluation', *American Psychologist*, Oct., 1975, pp. 955-66.

MESSICK, S. (1982) *Abilities and Knowledge in Educational Achievement Testing: The Assessment of Dynamic Cognitive Structures*, Princeton, NJ: Educational Testing Service.

MILLER, C., HOGGAN, J., PRINGLE, S., and WEST, G. (1988) *Credit Where Credit's Due*, The Report of the Accreditation of Work Based Learning Project, Edinburgh, SCOTVEC.

POPHAM, J. (1984) 'Specifying the domain of content or behaviors', in BERK, R. A. (Ed.) *A Guide to Criterion-Referenced Test Construction*, Baltimore; Johns Hopkins Press.

SCOTVEC (1988) *The National Certificate: A Guide to Assessment*, Edinburgh; SCOTVEC.

SNOW, R. E., FEDERICO, P. and MONTAGUE, W. E. (Eds) (1980) *Aptitude, Learning and Instruction*, Hillsdale, NJ, Lawrence Erlbaum Associates.

SNOW, R. E. and LOHME, D. F. (1984) 'Toward a theory of cognitive aptitude for learning from instruction', *Journal of Educational Psychology*, 76, 3, pp. 347-76.

STERNBERG, R. J. (1986) *Beyond IQ: A Triarchic Theory of Human Intelligence*, New York, Cambridge University Press.

TAYLOR, C. (1964) *The Explanation of Behaviour*, London, Routledge & Kegan Paul.

WOLF, A. (1986) *Practical Mathematics at Work: Learning Through YTS, R & D Series No. 21*, Sheffield, Manpower Services Commission.

WOLF, A. (1988) *Assessing Knowledge and Understanding*: A paper prepared for the National Council for Vocational Qualifications.

WOLF, A. (1989) *Learning In Context: Patterns of Skill Transfer* (forthcoming).

WOLF, A. and SILVER, R. (1986) *Work-based Learning: Trainee Assessment by Supervisors, R & D Series No. 33*, Sheffield, Manpower Services Commission.

WOOD, R. (1985) *Assessing Achievements to Standards*, unpublished report for Quality Standards Branch, Manpower Services Commission.

WOOD, R., JOHNSON, C., BLINKHORN, S., ANDERSON, S. and HALL, J. (1988) *Boning, Blanching and Backtacking: Assessing Performance in the Workplace*. A report to the Manpower Services Commission, St. Albans, Psychometric Research and Development Ltd.

Chapter 5

The definition of standards and their assessment

Lindsay Mitchell

This chapter is designed to look in brief at the technical issues in the development of standards and their assessment. It follows occupational standards through from their definition to their assessment and examines the current thinking on the role of knowledge in standards. It will be seen that the model is still very much in a developmental stage at the time of writing and that the assessment which is envisaged for National Vocational Qualifications (NVQs) fundamentally calls into question much previous practice. The aim of the conference from which this book derives, was to open up the debate to others and particularly those in the further and higher educational world. It is hoped that the issues put forward in this chapter are considered by those at the conference and those reading this book, and that some will join the debate and consequently aid the process along.

A shift in direction and focus

In the past, and still often in the present, education and training have tended to play the leading role in defining the manner in which the needs of employers can be met through training. As the information available was often not in a form which assisted this process, the task was difficult. Vocational qualifications, where they existed for occupations, were reflections of the content and structure of educational and training courses and there was an implicit hope, sometimes founded sometimes not, that at the end of the education/training process individuals would have become occupationally competent, or at the least be 'educated' to take their part in work.

In fact in many respects little was said explicitly about competence; rather, it was assumed that there was a community of understanding as to its nature and content.

This at its extreme came down to the notion that if things went wrong, the individual learner was somehow at fault. They had failed to grasp the essence of the occupation or were unable to integrate sufficiently the learning with the demands of the workplace. The inputs to the learner, or the relevance of these to the demands of employment tended not to be questioned in a manner which could lead to their resolution. With the publication of the New Training Initiative (NTI) (MSC, 1981) this argument was seriously addressed and implicit in that document was a suggested way of meeting the shortfall.

What NTI and the developments which have stemmed from it have done is effectively turned the model on its head. Instead of education and training being the driving force behind qualifications and consequently determining the nature of the competence that was to be trained for and accredited, it was suggested that the whole process should start from the other end. That is, that 'standards' of competence should be set for each occupational area and that these would drive in the future the vocational qualifications and the learning routes which help individuals achieve that competence. The White Paper *Working Together — Education and Training* (DOE, DES, 1986) stated it thus:

> vocational qualifications should reflect competence and be a means of ensur-
> ing a more competent workforce, better fitted than now to meet the
> challenge and the changing demands of employment . . . with stan-
> dards . . . not based on a narrow interpretation of competence.

As long as the standards can, and do, reflect a broad view of competence and do not end up making the work force less rather than more competent, the argument has great credibility. It does however place a tremendous degree of faith in the ability of standards to deliver all that is required of them and, due to the manner in which standards are the explication of competence for a particular occupational area, will make it all the more obvious should they fail to deliver. (For a full discussion of the expression of competence in standards see Chapter 3).

The specification of standards

Standards are external reference points to individuals as they are descriptions of what any individual would have to do in order to demonstrate competence in meeting a particular outcome. In our work we have found it useful to refer to standards using the sociological concept of work role to emphasise that it is an expectation to which any individual is required to perform; it is not a characteristic or trait of a particular individual, which is the flavour of much work on competence. (See Mansfield and Mathews, 1985; Mitchell and Mansfield, 1988).

In 1981 when the New Training Initiative was produced, it spoke of standards but did not say what they were. (It is also interesting to note that NTI did not mention the term competence as such). Following gradual developmental activity from that time onwards and particularly focused in the gradually developing Youth Training Scheme, a structure emerged which for those working in the field it is hard to remember was ever a matter for debate. The nature of the structure depends on a number of factors, not least among them that there should be clear expressions of standards against which individuals are to be judged (assessment) and additional system requirements chiefly focused on opening access to all individuals, and crediting the achievement of them, where it is due. The similarities between this work in its aims and objectives and that of other similar moves in education such as the National Certificate and Standard Grade in Scotland, and GCSE in England and Wales, will be familiar to many readers and do not need to be covered here. What is of more importance is to pull out how this system differs from others and the radical manner in which it has upturned previous practice.

The structure of units, elements and performance criteria by which standards are (or are to be) expressed is probably now familiar to all those with connections to any of the Training Agency programmes, those in industry who have responsibility for education and training, and to those in colleges connected with vocational education. It is also the format which all vocational qualifications will have to take at some time in the future. The structure exemplified by one unit, an element and its performance criteria is shown in Figure 5.1.

This example from the work undertaken by the Association for Dental Surgery Assistants (ABDSA) shows the expectations of anyone working in the area of 'sterilising dental surgery instruments and handpieces'. ABDSA has produced 12 units in total of which 8 are fairly specific to working in Dental Surgeries and four are of a more general nature such as 'contribute to the administration of the organisation'.

Functional analysis: an approach to the identification of standards

In practice at the start of the work in defining standards, there was some debate within the field as to what it was that standards should capture, whether it was possible to reflect a rounded view of competence within standards, and if so how. Much of the initial work focused around the use of task analysis with many viewing standards as dependent on, or comparable with, training and/or assessment.

This debate culminated in the decision by the Training Agency, with feed in from the National Council for Vocational Qualifications, that 'functional analysis' should be recommended as a method to those involved in the development of standards. The reasons for this were many of those mentioned by Bob Mansfield (see Chapter 3): that the focus of the standards was becoming too narrow, that the analysis methods being used, while entirely suitable for the purposes for which they were designed, were not

Figure 5.1

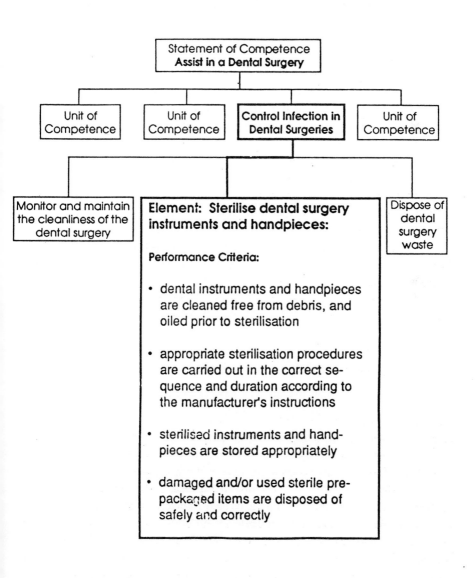

Standards - Elements of Competence and Performance Criteria

Statement of Competence
Assist in a Dental Surgery

| Unit of Competence | Unit of Competence | **Control Infection in Dental Surgeries** | Unit of Competence |

Monitor and maintain the cleanliness of the dental surgery

Element: Sterilise dental surgery instruments and handpieces:

Performance Criteria:

- dental instruments and handpieces are cleaned free from debris, and oiled prior to sterilisation

- appropriate sterilisation procedures are carried out in the correct sequence and duration according to the manufacturer's instructions

- sterilised instruments and handpieces are stored appropriately

- damaged and/or used sterile prepackaged items are disposed of safely and correctly

Dispose of dental surgery waste

capable of describing standards as the expectations of employment, and concern regarding the level of detail to which most of the work was leading. For example, at some points it looked as though each candidate would need to be issued with their own wheelbarrow to take around with them the activities related to their particular occupational area!

Functional analysis has been developed over time and through close experience and involvement with standards development by a group of researchers, developers and trainers at Barbara Shelborn Associates. (It is not to be confused with the Job Functional Analysis of Fine in the USA as it focuses on the outcomes and expectations of work rather than the way in which activities may be grouped to form particular work functions). Functional analysis has the advantages of focusing on outcomes rather than specific activity (and thus grouping a number of activities in a common purpose with the same standards) and of capturing the 'non-technical' aspects of the work role to forge a clearer link with the expectations of employment. Such a focus on outcomes is also likely to give a longer shelf-life to standards and reduce the amount of detail in the system.

Functional analysis considers the expectations in employment as a whole in that it proceeds from the top downwards, breaking the work role for a particular occupational area into purposes and functions rather than by looking at what is 'about' in the field and gathering activities into groups. It is therefore essentially integrative and should at the end of the day be able to provide NCVQ with an occupational map across the whole economy. The work we have carried out in the Building Society Sector provides an example of this approach. Through discussion with representatives of the sector their key purpose was defined as:

- provide financial and direct investment services to individual and group (non-corporate) customers.

For the cashier/customer adviser which was the area of focus of the work this broke down into a number of units, two of which are:

- provide information and advisory services to customers, and
- set up, monitor and maintain customer accounts.

The initial summing up of the key purpose phrase is not necessarily an easy task as it tends to reflect a departure from the way in which the occupation is traditionally thought of. As a rule, few occupational areas or workers actually think about the key purpose of their organisation or their particular place within it, or consider what they do in terms of the outcomes which are to be met. And yet, it is the outcomes which are able to provide the focus of the standards.

The notion of key purpose bears close resemblance to the notion of mission statements popularised in the States but this has to be treated with care as it tends to lead down the road of seeing the key purpose as 'maximise profit' rather than seeing this as an enabling activity which allows the key purpose to take place. (The maximisation of profit is also a rather crude formalisation of the complex shifts and balances which companies have to make).

Throughout the structure of the analysis until the performance criteria are met, there should be a consistency in expression in words and expression in that what is detailed below a function should follow logically from it, and that the manner in which it is expressed should take the same format. If we continue the Building Society example further and take an element from the first unit given above we can see this in action:

- promote the sale of associated products and services to customers.

The performance criteria take a different form to stress that these are the expectations of which evidence is required to infer an individual's competence. So, for the element given above, two of the performance criteria are:

- customers are informed of the advantages and benefits of additional or associated products and services suitable to their needs/status, when appropriate;
- features, advantages and benefits of services offered are described clearly and accurately.

It is worthwhile remembering at this point that functional analysis is not a method (for the moment at least) which can be taken off the shelf by those with a little time and a handbook and applied at will. The more we use and develop the approach, as at the present time it is little more than that, we are convinced that it is an expert system which requires as good deal of background understanding of the philosophy and developments in standards in order to put it into practice as it is intended. This is not an attempt to mystify it, or to preclude others from using and/or evaluating it, but rather that it carries, at present, a health warning on its ready and immediate use. In many ways this should come as no surprise; the layman does not expect to fully understand repertory grid analysis following one or two brief training sessions and through reading a brief manual. To use any analysis process takes a great deal of work and gradual practice in refining one's performance as one goes along.

This takes us into one of the binds in the system however. The TA and NCVQ have the remit from government to put standards and related vocational qualifications into place up to NVQ level 4 by 1991. (NVQ level 4 is difficult to describe in detail but borders on the professions or sub-professions and would include some degree of supervisory management). In order to be able to meet this remit, it is necessary to have a fairly large number of people working in the field who are able to put the ideas into practice. To do this it is necessary to train people in a short period of time to produce high quality standards, and yet they need the competence to be able to do this, which probably can only be developed over time . . . .Essentially there are no easy answers.

What is certainly needed is a greater number of people to work critically in the area and assist in questioning, developing and evaluating all the work that is taking place and which will have national impact. Without this the impact will be there, but it is doubtful whether the quality will match the expectations.

Assessment

Once the standards are in place, there is the whole question of their utility and effectiveness for the purpose in hand. The discussion here relates to assessment and the manner in which this will deliver vocational qualifications. This is not to deny the process by which standards are to be translated, or can be used, in learning practice, but these issues are dealt with in this volume by Geoff Stanton (Chapter 8) and Jenny Shackleton (Chapter 9).

The key purposes of assessment in the standards and NVQ model are for:

- the recognition of achievement which has already taken place, and;
- to infer an individual's future performance in the areas of competence certificated.

These fundamental purposes of assessment signal up the aims of the new system. Assessment in vocational qualifications is not for selection of the best for whatever purpose, or for determining in any direct way who has the potential for development in a particular direction. Vocational qualifications may inform these aspects but they are not their main purpose and should not be allowed to influence the developments to the detriment of the key purposes. If the qualifications are also helpful in this regard this is a bonus rather than a necessity.

As assessment has shifted from the needs for selection and norming to the requirements for the recognition of achievement, there has been a similar recognition that direct measurement of an individual is not the appropriate model to take. This is partly to do with the fact that we are not concerned with individual traits but in matching an individual's performance against the expectations as given in the standards, but also a recognition that whilst at first sight direct measurement appears scientific, it in fact is not so. This has led to a shift away from seeing assessment in the traditional psychological/scientific light to a consideration of a more legalistic notion which relies on the collection of sufficient evidence of suitable quality for reasonable inferences of an individual's competence to be made.

Assessment is the process of getting hold of evidence by one or a number of means and making judgements of the evidence in order to make inferences about an individual's competence. Assessment, therefore, while based on the idea of competent or not competent, is slightly more subtle than that, in that it is stating that there is sufficient evidence from which to infer that an individual is competent; there is insufficient evidence to infer an individual's competence at the present time although they may well be so; or that from the evidence which is currently available it is unlikely that the individual is competent at present.

Decisions on whether there is currently sufficient evidence will be based on the range of evidence available and the nature of that which is on offer. For example, if much of the evidence consistently meets the standards then there is likely to be little doubt that the person is competent. However, if some of the evidence is way off the standards, the assessor is likely to require more evidence in order to feel safe in the inferences of competence that are to be made. (I am grateful to Alison Wolf for discussions on this topic). It would be very easy to build up a highly sophisticated assessment system which demanded a great deal of evidence on each element of competence, and yet this would be unrealistic in terms of the competence under consideration and the risk of wrongful attribution of competence. For example, few would argue that the amount and type of evidence demanded from a trainee air-line pilot should be sufficiently greater than that of a refuse collector. The criticality of the competence in terms of the risks of wrongful attribution to self or others is likely to be one of the factors which have to be taken into account when the assessment is put into practice for accreditation.

Assessment methods are the means by which we obtain evidence, for example, through collecting evidence that is naturally occurring in the workplace, through setting up particular activities structured within the workplace, through the use of simulations in some form of artificial environment, or through the use of questioning techniques. Figure 5.2 demonstrates how assessment methods inter-relate (Mitchell and Cuthbert, 1989). In practice, assessment systems are likely to have to use more than one of these methods as the evidence available from a sole source will be insufficient for the safe inference of an individual's competence.

Evidence can essentially be of two forms — performance or knowledge. As competence is the ability to perform to the standards expected in employment, performance evidence must be the prime candidate for consideration, with assessment in the ongoing course of work the one that is most likely to offer the highest validity. Performance evidence is unlikely to be wholly sufficient in its entirety, however, as there will usually be insufficient occasions from which to gather performance evidence for the range of situations to which the element of competence applies, or the quality of evidence which performance can give will be insufficient to give safe assurances of competence.

This creates an assessment gap, in the sense that although we would in theory like to infer competence from performance as this is the essence of competence and is likely to have a greater validity for those aspects under consideration in terms of later achievement, we are not able to do so. The gap is filled by the collection of evidence of an individual's knowledge, in terms both of the knowledge content from which they have to draw in order to be able to perform, and of the cognitive processes which are

Figure 5.2

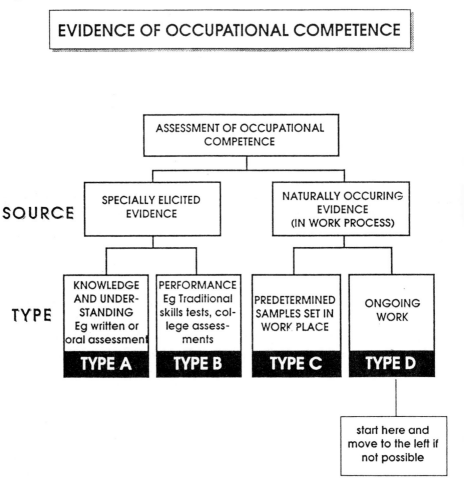

the basis of the performance. The former is relatively simple, although it is probably rather presumptuous for us to think that we will ever be able to specify in full the exact requirements that an individual will need to learn in order to be able to perform. We can make fairly good educated guesses at it however, particularly with the outcomes and the range attached to them specified.

From the work that we have undertaken to date there appear to be four essential ways in which an individual would have to 'work on' knowledge in order to perform an outcome (see Mitchell and Mansfield, 1988). They may have to reproduce the knowledge content such as in answering a straightforward query, select from information available to them in order to produce the correct answer (such as in noting the correct dental shorthand symbol in a chart), produce a solution by weighing and evaluating a number of complex and potentially competing factors to give an optimum solution (such as advising on the most appropriate investment that should be made) or by synthesising knowledge in a new way to produce new meaning or solutions. (I am grateful to Tim Oates for the latter suggestion).

If this model holds this has tremendous implications for the manner in which assessment is to be designed and undertaken. It will involve a careful and full consideration of the evidence that is available on each element of competence for each individual that accesses the system. This will need to look at the range of applications to which an element and its associated performance criteria apply, the knowledge content that an individual is likely to need to be able to perform across these applications and the manner in which they have to process the knowledge within such performance. Our present thoughts are that performance provides evidence of the outcomes of activity and shows whether or not the individual has achieved a particular outcome. Direct questioning of the knowledge base will provide evidence of the content from which the individual is able to perform. What is also likely to be required, especially where the individual has to optimise and synthesise, is evidence of the cognitive process which the individual has to perform. Questioning techniques, as given in the assessment methods, thus have the dual role of supplementing not only the knowledge content but also targeting the cognitive processes as well. For example, it is likely that there will be a need to look more closely at how an individual made a particular decision, through scrutinising the critical decision points, the factors that were weighed, and so on.

This examination of the manner in which evidence can be built up and the exact nature that it can take is still very much in its infancy and needs considerably more thought and evaluation. There are, for instance, lessons that could surely be learnt from the work that has been undertaken in the field of Artificial Intelligence and of professional craft knowledge. One of the problems facing those working in the field is that they are so few, and the demands of time and immediate implementation so great, that the cross-fertilisation from other areas is not as great as it should be. Hopefully the seminar, for which this chapter was prepared, will be the first step in redressing the balance.

References

DOE and DES (1986) *Working Together — Education and Training*, Cmnd. 9823, London, HMSO.
MANPOWER SERVICES COMMISSION (1981) *The New Training Initiative: An Agenda for Action*, Cmnd. 8455, London, HMSO.
MANSFIELD, B. (1987) *Defining the New Standards*, Wakefield, Barbara Shelborn Associates.

MANSFIELD, B. (1988) *Competence, Standards and Assessment*, Wakefield, Barbara Shelborn Developments.

MANSFIELD, B. and MATHEWS, D. (1985) *Job Competence*, FESC, Coombe Lodge.

MITCHELL, L. and CUTHBERT, T. (1989), *Insufficient Evidence? The Final Report of the Competency Testing Project*, Glasgow, SCOTVEC.

MITCHELL, L. and MANSFIELD, B. (1988) *Identifying and Assessing Underpinning Knowledge: A Discussion Paper* (Draft TAG Guidance Note), Wakefield, Barbara Shelborn Developments.

Chapter 6

The emerging model of vocational education and training

Gilbert Jessup

Introduction

A variety of national initiatives and developments have taken place throughout the 1980s to improve and extend vocational education and training (VET) in the UK. These are now being brought together within a new model of VET which is being adopted by the government and promoted through a variety of programmes.

The foundations of the model were clearly laid in *New Training Initiative*, published in 1981, (DOE, 1981). The New Training Initiative set out the objectives to be achieved if the UK was to meet its training needs in a rapidly changing and increasingly competitive economic environment. A key feature of the publication was the introduction of a new concept of 'standards', although the significance of this was little understood by readers in 1981. To quote from the publication, 'at the heart of this initiative lie standards of a new kind' (paragraph 19, page 6).

This chapter indicates the main features of the emerging model of VET with specific reference to the qualification system which will provide the structure in which vocational education and training will operate. The latter point is particularly true in that the new forms of competence based qualifications lead rather than follow education and training. The significance of this statement will become clearer as this chapter unfolds.

The chapter also highlights some of the fundamental research questions that are being addressed in order to implement the new model. The growing body of research and development in this area has wide ranging implications, not only within the vocational field, but also for general and academic education.

The review of vocational qualifications

The model was brought into clearer focus by the *Review of Vocational Qualifications* (MSC and DES, 1986) and more recently in the operationalisation of its recommend-ations by the National Council for Vocational Qualifications (NCVQ). NCVQ was set up in 1986 to create a new framework of National Vocational Qualifications. Criteria have been set (NCVQ, 1988a) which qualifications are required to meet to be incorporated in the national framework. The criteria for National Vocational Qualifications (NVQ) make many aspects of the proposed model explicit. The 'new kinds of standards' advocated in the New Training Initiative are now being put into effect through the introduction of National Vocational Qualifications.

Assumptions and aims

First, there is a growing recognition that to succeed economically in an increasingly competitive world the UK needs a competent and adaptable workforce. Traditional careers starting with a period of initial training, followed by stable employment within an occupation are becoming less common. The pattern in the future will be initial training followed by frequent periods of updating and retraining to cope with changing technology and employment structures.

Second, there is the recognition that the potential of the majority of individuals has seldom been fulfilled in previous generations through their employment. There is a wealth of untapped human potential which, given the opportunity, could be developed and be employed in more creative and satisfying work.

Competence in employment

One of the growing concerns amongst employers has been that much of the provision of VET was not seen as being directly relevant to the needs of employment. Although there were exceptions, it was considered that VET tended to be 'educationally' oriented both in content and the values which are implicit in its delivery. It has tended to concentrate on the acquisition of knowledge and theory while neglecting perfor-mance, and it is performance which essentially characterises competence.

The educational influence is apparent in the forms of assessment adopted in vocational qualifications where written and multiple-choice tests carry more weight than practical demonstrations. Assessment practices such as sampling, providing a choice of questions and adopting pass marks of around 50 per cent, are all imports from an educational model of assessment, which have little place in the assessment of competence. Discrimination between individuals tends to guide the design of assessment instruments (norm-referencing) even when the objectives sought were the standards required in employment (criterion-referencing).

The effect of this bias is not only to reduce the relevance of VET to employment but also to exclude large segments of the population who do not find it easy, or have no wish, to learn in an 'academic' environment. The new VET model is designed for the whole population, and not just the 40 per cent or so who have participated in the past.

Access

Access was a further concern identified in both the *New Training Initiative* and the *Review of Vocational Qualifications*. There appeared to be far too many unnecessary barriers and constraints in gaining entry to VET and gaining qualifications, such as age limits, specified periods of training or experience, specified modes of learning at specified institutions. In many occupations it was practically impossible to gain entry if one had missed out at a particular age. In other areas, many obviously competent people could not gain formal recognition of their competence because they had not come through the traditional qualification route. Barriers to access have presented particular problems to those with special needs.

The NVQ framework and model

The NVQ framework, that is the arrangement of qualifications within a national system, has been introduced to overcome the confusion created by numerous awarding bodies competing in the same or overlapping occupational areas, with qualifications of different size and structure, often without recognising each other's qualifications. This lack of coherence has often created problems in the career progression and mobility of individuals and inefficiencies in the VET provision. Access to higher education and the professions via vocational routes is a further objective sought through the establishment of the NVQ framework.

The framework is being created by allocating NVQs as they become accredited by NCVQ to an area of competence and a level within a unified national system. The framework has until recently been limited to four levels, spanning qualifications from the most basic to those approximating to higher national. In February 1989 however, NCVQ was invited by the Government to extend the framework to make possible the inclusion of qualifications at 'professional' levels. The involvement of professional bodies will be entirely voluntary, so progress in establishing the framework at higher levels may be slow and uneven.

As mentioned previously, the criteria set for NVQs have been formulated in order to achieve prescribed objectives and to overcome the problems identified in past practices.

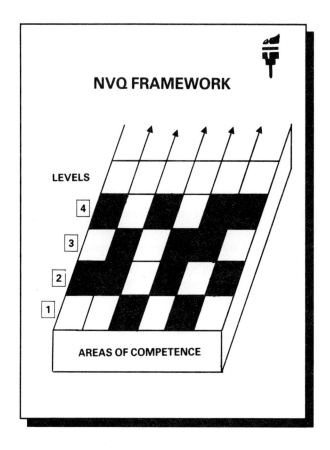

Statement of competence

The key feature of NVQs is that they are based on an explicit 'statement of competence'. NVQs are commonly described as competence based, which of course they are, but this term can mean many things to different people. It needs to be emphasised that NVQs require an explicit statement of competence, that is, a specification written down for everybody to see, in an agreed and recognisable format.

The statement of competence spells out what candidates are required to be able to do for the award of an NVQ, and includes the criteria by which performance can be assessed. In doing so, the statement of competence also sets clear goals for education and training programmes. The specification of competence plus performance criteria provide the operational realisation of the 'new kind of standards'.

This basic concept of a standard is of course not new. Nevertheless, previous initiatives in competence based education and training have tended to be limited to particular courses and programmes. Performance criteria have often been absent.

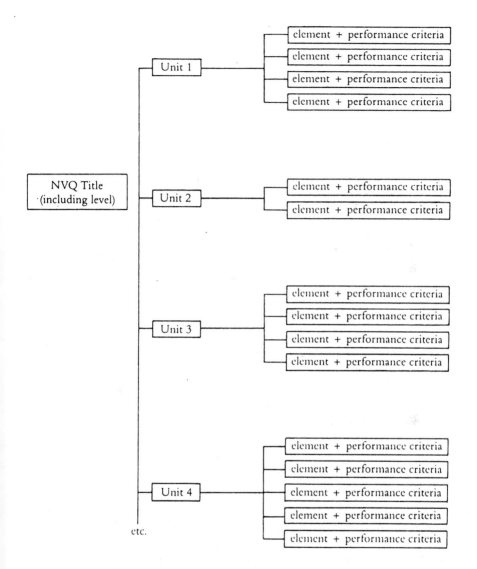

There is little evidence from previous initiatives that the logic of the competence based approach has been thought through, let alone implemented, as a total system as is now happening in the UK.

Employment-led

The NVQ statements of competence are derived, not from an analysis of education and training programmes, but from an analysis of employment requirements. That is to say an analysis of the functions employees carry out, paying particular attention to purpose and outcome. In addition, the analysis is carried out by, or on behalf of, employers and employees in the relevant sector and endorsed by them: thus the term 'employment-led standards'.

Alternative modes of learning and assessment

Statements of competence, derived through this process, are independent of any course or programme of learning. This is an important feature of NVQs which embody the statements. As a consequence of this separation from the learning provision, an NVQ can be gained through any mode of learning. NVQs thus open the way to recognition of vocational competence achieved through experiential learning, workplace learning and open learning and puts achievements via these routes on an equal footing to more formal programmes of education and training. The award of an NVQ is solely dependent upon assessed competence, not the way in which such competence is acquired.

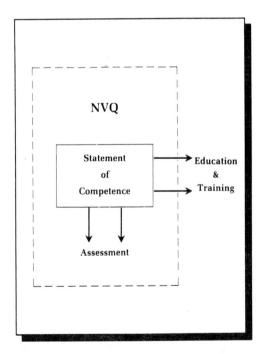

Less obviously, the statement of competence is also independent of the method of assessment. The nature of the competence will indicate the category of evidence required for assessment (i.e. performance demonstrations, knowledge, etc.) but within that category options will exist as to the specific method or instrument of assessment adopted. This legitimises other forms of assessment such as assessment in the workplace and assessment of prior achievement, as well as assessment by more conventional methods. These are all seen as alternative forms of evidence of competence (see NCVQ, 1988b). This further extends access to qualifications and has particular relevance to those with special needs.

Unit credits

Another feature of NVQs which has major implications for the way in which education and training is provided, is that the qualifications will consist of a number of units of competence. Each unit, which represents a relatively discrete area of competence having independent value in employment, can be separately assessed and accredited to an individual. This opens the way to the possibility of credit accumulation towards gaining a qualification.

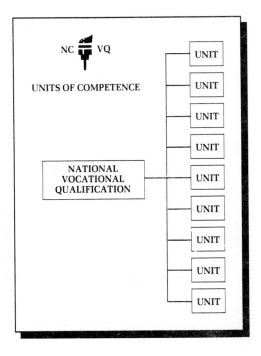

NCVQ has in fact launched a national system of credit accumulation and transfer based upon such unit credits (NCVQ, 1988c). The fifteen major national awarding bodies offering vocational qualifications within NVQ levels I-IV, have agreed to participate and offer their qualifications in the form of units where they do not already do so. A longer-term goal is the recognition by awarding bodies of each others' units for the purpose of credit accumulation towards qualifications. Rationalisation achieved through adopting agreed national standards (statements of competence) for NVQs will facilitate this process.

The credit accumulation system operates through the National Record of Vocational Achievement (NROVA) which was launched by NCVQ in July 1988. It is currently being used on a trial basis in a range of colleges and training centres, and will be introduced more widely from September 1989. It has been adopted within the government's training programmes, ET and YTS (from April 1989), so its widescale use is guaranteed.

To summarise, unit credits and the independence of qualifications (and units) from specific modes of learning and assessment provide the structures which allow access to qualifications in a way which has not been possible in the past. To exploit the full potential of NVQs, vocational education and training, or more precisely the provision of learning opportunities to acquire competence, must be provided in a highly flexible manner. This is currently presenting a considerable challenge to the staff of further education colleges, and those managing training programmes.

NVQ database

Another tool which will be available to support the implementation of the new VET model is a computerised database. The database, which is currently being built up by NCVQ, will contain detailed information on all NVQs, units, and their elements of competence and performance criteria. Related information will include assessment methods and the awarding body for each NVQ and unit. Units and NVQs will be classified according to a number of dimensions of competence and linked to the primary occupations where the competence is practised. While the NVQ framework is being established, comparable data will be held, in so far as it is available, on other national qualifications and the emerging specifications of competence from industry.

The data will be available via local terminals linked to the database which enables an interactive user-friendly dialogue. This will greatly enhance counselling, career planning and the design of training programmes. When established, the database will not only allow individuals and their advisors to inspect the national provision of qualifications, but also the competences required in different areas of employment.

With sophisticated software it will be possible for an individual to generate a profile of their claimed competence, in the form of units of competence, as a starting point to consideration of how they might progress. From the initial profile, alternative menus could be offered of further qualifications which build upon the individual's current competence in a systematic way.

We are also exploring ways in which the qualifications/competence database can be linked to databases of education and training provision (e.g., TAPS, ECCTIS) so once an individual has decided what s/he wishes to pursue, further information can be obtained on where or how the relevant learning opportunities and experience are provided.

The emerging model of VET

NVQs, the credit accumulation system and the database are collectively designed to provide the structures to meet the perceived needs of vocational education and training in the 1990s and beyond.

The model has several characteristics. These are that:

— a comprehensive provision of competence-based qualifications will be available, relevant to all the primary requirements of employment;

— opportunities will be provided for all people post full-time general education to pursue vocational training prior to or during the early years of employment;

— educational and career guidance will be available through a variety of agencies and the NVQ framework/database will provide the language and the means to structure such guidance;

— individual action/learning plans will be negotiated and drawn up following initial assessment and guidance (action plans form the first part of NROVA);

— vocational education and training will be provided in a variety of forms to suit individual needs and opportunities. The modes of learning will include college/training centre tuition, work place/workshop practice, open learning — all available full-time, part-time and in combination to suit the individual learner;

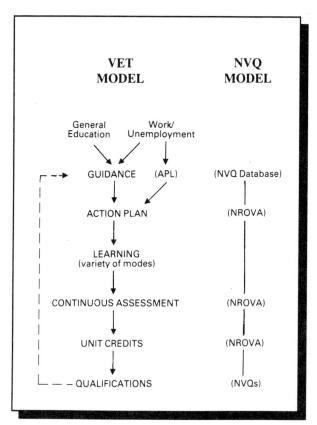

— assessment of competence will normally be at unit level;
— assessment will be continuous and unit-credits may be gained when the individual has met the requirements of a unit (records of continuous assessment form the second part of NROVA);
— individuals will complete programmes of learning and will be awarded the appropriate qualifications (maintained in NROVA);
— the above cycle will be repeated or entered into at various points throughout an individual's career and every encouragement will be given to individuals to continue learning and updating their competence. This will be made easier by virtue of the unit-based credit system and multi-mode learning possibilities to meet individual needs.

The above model of education and training implies that colleges and training centres move towards acting in the capacity of learning resource and assessment centres, providing a variety of opportunities for individuals to learn.

The model is based upon the perceived needs of individuals, employers and the economy. The extent to which education and training providers can meet such needs, and at what cost, is beginning to be explored through a variety of institutional development programmes.

Research and development issues

The current programme to institute the model, as one might imagine, is throwing up a range of technical issues in respect of competence specification, assessments, learning and transfer on the one hand, and institutional and staff development on the other. While a programme of research and development has been building up over the last few years, mainly funded through the Training Agency and more recently NCVQ, and experience is accumulating, many issues remain unresolved or in need of refinement. The following attempts to identify some of the most salient that are exercising researchers working in the programme at present.

A continuing debate exists on an appropriate concept of 'competence'. Competence is conceived as being much broader than specifications of skill as has existed in traditional training programmes. Competence should incorporate all that is required to perform effectively in employment, which includes managing the competing demands within a work role, interpersonal relationships and so on. The Mansfield-Mathews Job Competence Model (Mansfield and Mathews, 1985) perhaps comes closest to what researchers currently seek, but it needs considerable refinement.

Operationalising the concept of competence within a 'statement of competence' gets to the heart of the model and while experience in the area is growing, the principles and methods governing such statements need to be clearly articulated. The programme will succeed or fail depending on how well this objective can be achieved. In particular, the role of 'knowledge and understanding', and more generally the cognitive components of competence, within the statement of competence are currently major issues of debate and the subject of a number of research initiatives.

A new model of assessment is being developed, where assessment is related directly to the elements of competence, and 'sufficiency of evidence' is the key concept (see NCVQ, 1988b). The model needs extensive evaluation.

Assessment in the workplace and a variety of forms of competency testing are being developed and evaluated. Assessment based upon evidence of prior achievements (commonly presented under the "accreditation of prior learning" label) is being researched in major national projects (see NCVQ, 1989).

The role of 'generic' competences, that is those which are common to a wide range of occupations and activities, and their place within the NVQ framework has recently appeared on the agenda as an issue. The debate includes the underpinning competences of number and communication and to what extent they can be expressed as units of competence within the NVQ format. These possibilities have recently excited politicians and employers who perceive them as a way of developing coherence between general and vocational education. The National Record of Vocational Achievement is also seen as an instrument to bridge the educational/vocational divide.

Returning to the concept of competence and the components of competence (skill, knowledge, understanding, etc.), fundamental questions are being asked afresh on the process of learning itself and the generalisability, or transferability, of competence from the place of learning to other contexts.

The need to be explicit about what is learnt and assessed within the emerging model of VET raises fundamental issues which in traditional models of education are perhaps assumed without question and seldom raised.

References

DOE (1981) *A New Training Initiative: An Agenda for Action*, London, HMSO.

MSC and DES (1986) *Review of Vocational Qualifications in England and Wales*, London, HMSO.

MANSFIELD B. and MATTHEWS, D. (1985) *Job Competence — A Description for use in Vocational Education and Training*, Work Based Learning Project, Blagdon, Further Education Staff College.

NCVQ (1988a) *The NVQ Criteria nd Related Guidance*, January, London, NCVQ.

NCVQ (1988b) *NCVQ Information Note 4: Assessment in National Vocational Qualifications*, November, London, NCVQ.

NCVQ (1988c) *Introducing a National System of Credit Accumulation*, London, NCVQ.

NCVQ (1989) *NCVQ Information Note 5: Assessment in NVQs: Use of Evidence from Prior Achievement (APL)*, January, London, NCVQ.

Chapter 7

The Employment Department/Training Agency Standards Programme and NVQs: implications for education

Graham Debling

Introduction to the Training Agency

The Government's Training Agency, within the Employment Department, was formally established in December 1988. It adopted many of the roles of its predecessors — the Training Commission previously known as the Manpower Services Commission (MSC). Its mode of operation and function was spelt out in the Government White Paper, *Employment for the 1990s* (ED, 1988).

The Training Agency was charged with working with employers, the education service, voluntary organisations, training providers and individual trade unions, to improve the training system and to help make the education system more relevant to the world of work. It was to develop the UK training system so that:

— responsibility for training is accepted at a local level;
— access to training and vocational education throughout life is improved;
— recognised standards of competence relevant to work are established by industry-led organisations, validated nationally, and incorporated into vocational qualifications.

The Training Agency's specific aims were identified as:

— to encourage employers to take more responsibility for employee human resource development throughout working life;
— to provide and encourage appropriate training and vocational education for young people, leading to qualifications;
— to help unemployed acquire skills, experience and enterprise;

- to help the education system become more relevant and responsive to changing needs;
- to encourage enterprise and job creation by ensuring needs of self employed and small firms are met.

In common with its predecessors, the Training Agency is to provide programmes and promote initiatives directed at improving the operation of the training market, the effectiveness of the training infrastructure and to help those not currently employed. It is very much concerned with both the volume and quality of vocationally related education and training and in particular the cost effectiveness of learning processes and the relevance of what is learnt.

Introduction to the Standards Programme

Subsequent to the White Paper *Working Together — Education and Training* (ED and DES, 1986) the then MSC was asked to accelerate its work in fostering the development of employment related standards so that they are embedded in National Vocational Qualifications by 1991. The more recent White Paper *Employment for the 1990s* (ED, 1988) emphasised the importance attached to this work. However, the Standards Programme has its roots in the New Training Initiative.

The New Training Initiative, published in 1981, perceived that vocational education and training needed to be more extensive and enhanced if it was to result in the formation of a workforce fully able to respond to the challenges of the late 20th/early 21st centuries. It was recognised that at the heart of the matter was a need for standards of a new kind.

Employment for the 1990s, in describing the new framework for training and vocational education, is more explicit about the nature of the new standards:

Our training system must be founded on standards and recognised qualifications based on competence — the performance required of individuals to do their work successfully and satisfactorily,

and about who should identify the standards:

These standards must be identified by employers and they must be nationally recognised. Thus we need a system of employer-led organizations to identify and establish standards and secure recognition of them, sector by sector, or occupational group by occupational group.

It also expresses the expectation that the standards setting organizations should provide the lead in establishing arrangements for assessing and accrediting learning achievements, have the ability to influence a significant part of the sector and be seen as the body which can deal with Government on training and vocational education matters.

In spelling out the role of what are now known as 'lead bodies' or 'industry lead bodies', the White Paper was recognising the place of such organizations in the new framework. Many of the lead bodies had been in existence for some while and were already heavily involved in the Standards Programme.

The Standards Programme

The Standards Programme is concerned not only with getting a better definition of what should be learnt but also the way that learning or achievement is expressed. It is concerned to foster:

> standards, which as far as is possible, serve both the immediate and long-term needs of industry, commerce and the public sector;
> standards which have currency nationally both within and across occupations and industries;
> standards which are recognised through the award of certificates fostering in the learners a sense of achievement and confidence in the ability to learn;
> standards and associated certification which is valued by all users and in particular employers;
> certification which recognises partial achievement and facilitates credit accumulation, where certification of the individual parts (units) makes sense to, and is valued by, users.

It is perceived that the standards should be expressed explicitly and transparently so that all can see and understand what is expected and what has been achieved, whether learners, those who facilitate learning, those who assess for certification purposes, or those who provide counselling services for the individual. *Of most importance however is that the standards relate to the needs of employment, and that employers have a sense of ownership of such standards such that they recognise them and take responsibility for their modernization and utilization.* Such a requirement can be seen as part of the Training Agency's wider objectives including the fostering of a greater sense of commitment to education and training.

The nature of the new Standards

As has already been said, what is required are standards which are concerned with achievement, relate to effective performance in the workplace, are explicit and transparent, and have credibility in the eyes of users. *The objective is to develop standards which pertain to 'competence'.*

(Further information can be found in the publications of the NCVQ and the Training Agency's technical guidance notes [MSC, 1988]).

Competence

The word 'competence' attracts many different shades of interpretation; not least to facilitate a common approach, a definition has evolved. This definition is not cast in stone, it may still undergo further refinement in the light of experience — refinement rather than major revision.

> Competence pertains to the ability to perform the activities within a function or an occupational area to the levels of performance expected in employment.
> It is a broad concept which embodies the ability to transfer skills and knowledge to new situations within the occupational area.
> It encompasses organization and planning of work, innovation and coping with non-routine activities.
> It includes those qualities of personal effectiveness that are required in the workplace to deal with co-workers, managers and customers.

A competent individual can:

> perform a particular function or satisfy a particular role
> in a diversity of settings,
> over an extended period of time;
> and respond effectively to irregular occurrences in environments having different characteristics.

Certification which attests to competence should infer, with adequate certainty, that the individual is competent as described above. The standards therefore should describe the characteristics of competent performance. As relevant the standards will describe cognitive, motor, inter-personal and personal skills, and require evidence of task and contingency management skills, and suitable responses to and interaction with the different environments. Thus, the objective of the Standards Programme is to foster the development of *competence based standards*.

The competence statements or elements of competence identify the focus of desired achievement, not how one might decide whether or not an individual's performance is satisfactory. To differentiate between satisfactory and unsatisfactory performance, what is required are *performance criteria*. Thus, the new standards are competence based, criterion referenced, explicit and transparent statements which define the expected achievement or learning outcome.

How the new standards are being defined

Reference has already been made to the needs and expectations of employers. Clearly it is desirable, indeed essential, that employers think more accurately about the nature and level of competence they require of their work-force. Further, it would seem reasonable for them to expect National Standards, and National Qualifications, to relate to their needs and for that relationship to be as transparent as is possible.

While one would not wish to detract from the importance of in-company standards, a 'national' standard implies both a level of national acceptance and an as close as possible relationship to the needs and expectations of a specified group of employers nationally.

Realistically there is unlikely to be one single, unanimous view expressed by a pre-defined group of employers. Indeed it is likely that the chance of complete and unanimous consensus grows smaller as the group of employers grows larger and more diverse. Nevertheless, the value of national standards and national qualifications depends directly on the degree to which such standards or qualifications do match expectations. (Further information can be derived from Technical Guidance Note 2, *Developing Standards by Reference to Function*).

Lead bodies

To address these issues, and to foster a sense of ownership amongst employers, the following strategy is being adopted:

a lead body is identified;
it oversees an analysis process directed at defining/elucidating the competence based standards;
as part of this process, the substance and level of the standards are tested by consulting with an as large as possible representative sample of users (employers), and assessment to the standards is piloted to ensure that assessors can interpret them with adequate consistency;
it then promulgates the adoption of the standards as a focus for education and training and seeks the incorporation of the standards into vocational qualifications as relevant.

In identifying a lead body important considerations are that, as far as is possible the relevant group of employers both attributes status to it and has a direct interest in its activities.

To avoid confusion and to support the national dimension, no more than one set of standards is required with respect to any one occupation or activity. This means that there is room only for one lead body. Quite often this is not a problem; the statutory training boards and non-statutory training organizations are charged with this responsibility. However, sometimes there are a number of organizations in a similar field, each of which values its independence. Under such conditions every attempt is made to bring them together into some form of consortium which attracts the designation 'lead body'. Occasionally an organization can not be persuaded to join a consortium, perhaps for reasons of lack of resources or commitment to the work, or an unwillingness to fully cooperate with what are seen as competing organizations. If there is no fundamental difference between the occupations pertinent to the different organizations the work goes on without the disaffected. The standards will be available to the relevant group but they will not have had the opportunity to contribute to their shaping.

There are also occupations which cross most categories of employers, for example clerical, administrative and management occupations. Under such conditions, the Training Agency helps establish a lead body which, as far as is possible is representative of the diversity of employment situations. For reasons of efficiency, there is a maximum size for steering and working committees, etc.; it is impossible to encompass within membership all shades of interest. However, this places an even greater significance on the consultation and piloting stages of the development programme.

As far as professional bodies are concerned, nobody has questioned the right of such bodies to define standards of competence for their members, for the 'professionals' that constitute their membership. Further, where such bodies, by law or practice, in effect provide a licence to practice, there is no question as to their continued responsibility. Also, where the membership is primarily self-employed it would seem that the professional body in essence forms the lead body (assuming that it does in fact ensure that its membership can provide the service expected of it by the customer). However, for some professional bodies, members are employed in diverse situations, perhaps in different sectors of industry, commerce and public service. Under such conditions it would seem that the prime responsibility continues to lie with the employer-recognised organizations.

Consultation

Of course lead bodies are free to consult with, and draw on the expertise of whoever they consider can make a useful contribution. Indeed they may well draw on the standards of competence defined, for example, by professional bodies for their membership. Similarly they draw on the expertise lodged with individuals and groups in education and training, especially where such groups or individuals are held in high esteem because of the quality of what has gone before. To date many lead bodies have included individuals from the further and higher education scene on committees and working parties.

The development of standards

In principle lead bodies can go about the elucidation of the standards in any way they think fit but in practice the ultimate requirements place some constraints on the methodology.

Previously, standards have been of a more global nature and have not been expressed particularly explicitly — Higher Diplomas are of a higher standard than Diplomas almost by definition. Global statements (qualifications or certification) were uniformly attributed to a large population of individuals who had very different competences. Only the most general conclusions or inferences could be drawn from certification. This has been a source of confusion for many users.

An implication of the past state of affairs is that there is very little expertise in defining explicit national standards. Further, the application of a broad concept of competence to standards is new. The Standards Programme is, in effect, an action research programme. To facilitate the work the then MSC established a Standards Methodology Unit within the Occupational Standards Branch. The Unit is charged with stimulating and overseeing investigation work, piloting implementation of good practice, and promulgating recommendations derived therefrom. It publishes research monographs and reports, Technical Guidance Notes, and a quarterly journal, *Competence and Assessment*. It also facilitates dissemination through conferences and seminars, etc.

Its programme of investigatory work is tied to the ultimate objective of the establishment of credible certification. While in the longer term credibility will stem from the technical soundness of the standards and associated assessment practices, and reflect the extent to which the standards match the users' expectations, in the short term credibility will depend more upon public perceptions as to what is happening and the extent to which practices match or contrast with past practices.

Technical credibility will depend upon the relevance of the standards to the expectations of users (both with respect to content and required level of attainment), the validity of the assessment methods, and the consistency of interpretation of the standards by the assessors. Overarching all of this however is the requirement that the whole process is cost effective. There is a need to balance the cost of developing, expressing and implementing the standards (and associated assessment processes) against the cost of failure or added value of the occupations to which the standards pertain.

There is also an expectation that credit accumulation will be fostered. Ideally the analysis process should identify the functions, purposes or roles associated with the occupation under analysis. This should result in the identification of a series of 'units' each of which makes sense in the context of employment, as a free standing unit. That is not to say that learning programmes will automatically be disaggregated into a similar profile of units — for many clients a combination of units will make up a particular learning programme. The primary advantages of the unit structure are that it not only facilitates credit accumulation, it also allows flexibility in the way learning programmes are constructed and it allows rationalization and credit transfer.

Isn't there a risk that the standards will be too narrow?

Any discussion about 'breadth' in the context of standards and qualifications is fraught with difficulties, not least because there are many different interpretations of 'breadth':

(a) It has been used with reference to the range of skills or abilities which have to be displayed, that are encompassed within the standards,
    e.g., are standards about performing specific tasks or do they encompass other matters such as planning, organising, making decisions, taking relevant action without requiring direction, dealing with people, etc.?

(b) It has been used in the context of suggesting that standards and qualifications should separately and explicitly recognise the candidate's ability or achievement in 'core' or 'generic' skills such as communication and number.

(c) Similarly, sometimes it is used to support arguments for the fostering of learning in areas such as communication and number, independent of the needs of occupations.

(d) It has been used in the context of describing the range of vocational or occupationally specific skills which should be encompassed in standards or a vocational qualification.

It has been used in the context of different arguments pertaining to the nature of vocational qualifications:

i.e., vocational qualifications should encompass both employment related standards and other things of significance to the development of the individual. What might be proposed are matters pertaining to use of leisure, role in society, etc.

i.e., vocational qualifications should encompass things not required for immediate effective performance in the related occupation, etc., but which might be desirable to facilitate progression — progression at work, progression academically, or progression to a higher level of award.

and 'breadth' in vocational qualifications should better prepare the individual to adapt and respond to unforeseen challenges in life.

In the context of the Standards Programme, a definition of competence has been adopted which in itself is considered to be 'broad'. As the programme is about developing competence based standards, an indication of the desired breadth can be found in the above definition of competence which reflects much within (a) above.

However, that is easier said than done. In the past, in the context of learning, standards have fallen into one or more of a number of groupings reflecting the purpose or use of the standards:

There are standards which are concerned with recognising knowledge and understanding within a particular discipline. While these standards attached to assessment have attempted to define understanding through the application of such understanding to hypothetical problems they have also depended on, measured and given credit for, demonstrated knowledge.

There are standards which are concerned with competence in generic skills such as communication and number.

There are standards which purport to reflect potential to learn or adapt at some stage in the future.

There are standards which are concerned with the performance of tasks.

Indeed it is believed that earlier attempts to introduce competence based standards as a focus for human resource development failed because the standards were based on too narrow a concept of competence — based on the performance of tasks in isolation from the reality of the workplace.

Traditionally then, the common methods of developing standards have not been concerned with a broad definition of competence. The Standards Programme has sponsored the development of a methodology which, if applied with integrity and a fair degree of commitment to the end objective, should result in standards which do reflect the key elements of competence which contribute to competence in the round. The methodology centres around an analysis of function or key purposes of employment roles, rather than task and the elements of competence and performance criteria reflect the nature and substance of judgments on effectiveness of performance. Whereas task analysis does not reveal associated planning, management and environmental interactions, the suggested form of functional analysis does appear to do so. (The process is described in the *Technical Guidance Note 2 — Developing Standards by Reference to Functions*).

Where does this leave knowledge and understanding?

The term 'knowledge and understanding' in itself has different interpretations: knowledge of facts, an ability to reiterate a theory as evidence of understanding, and/or as referring to complex cognitive processes.

The prime use of the competence based standards and associated certification is as inference of ability to perform effectively in the workplace. Where the skills used in effective performance are totally or primarily cognitive, this will be reflected in the performance based standards.

However, there are situations in which performance manifests itself through an amalgam of motor and inter-personal skills which may or may not depend upon the implicit application of enabling cognitive skills or the drawing on implicit knowledge and understanding. Similarly, a particular cognitive activity might also draw on diverse implicit knowledge and understanding.

It has already been noted that certification can only be based on performance demonstrated during assessment whether on a one-off occasion or over a period of time. However the user, at the simplest level infers that the successful candidate is able to reproduce the performance at some time in the future, probably on more than one occasion. Clearly the user's primary concern is:

> what confidence attaches to the inferences that he or she draws from the certification?

The confidence of the inferences will reflect the extent to which these standards match the future work activity, as well as the accuracy with which the level of expected performance is interpreted.

Issues of context and environment are important — to what extent are the future conditions identical to those which pertained at the time of assessment? Context and environment encompass equipment, systems, working environment (physical and human) as well as the focus of the activity. Significant divergences from the conditions which pertained at the time of assessment can substantially detract from the reliability of inference.

Similarly, assessment occurs over a finite period of time that has much to do with the practicality of collecting evidence and processing it. It is unlikely that an assessment process can require the candidate to address every possible eventuality associated with performance in the work-place. It has been suggested that the best time to finalise a judgement on the competence of the individual is the day of retirement . . . obviously not very practical in the context of national certification of value to users.

Another way of looking at it is that the national standards are about recognising the competence of the individual to perform effectively over an extended period of time, in a diversity of settings relevant to the aspect of competence. The question has to be asked:

> What evidence can be collected cost effectively, which maximises the reliability of inference?

There is no simple generalizable, infallible answer. However there does seem to be three orders of evidence:

first (and most valuable) is evidence of effective performance in a real work setting;

second is evidence derived from a simulation;

third (and often by itself of limited value) is evidence of underpinning knowledge and understanding.

The extent to which evidence, either of one type or a mix of two or three identified above, can provide an adequately reliable inference of ability to perform effectively in the future, depends much on the nature of the future activity. The concern with respect to knowledge and understanding is with respect to the quality of evidence and the extent to which, cost-effectively, it is adequate as a base for inferring ability to practice effectively over an extended period of time and in diverse settings.

In the context of competence based standards, knowledge and understanding have a key place. However, this should be seen as being intimately linked to competence. It is suggested that the identification of relevant knowledge and understanding, and their embedding in the standards can be achieved as follows:

The preliminary functional analysis identifies the separate functions which are likely to form the foci of separate units.

For the individual function, the analysts elucidate the key elements of competence which contribute to the effective performance of the function. The elements of competence are primarily concerned with performance; however, it is possible at this stage that essential knowledge and/or understanding will be identified.

For each element it is then necessary to identify the criteria by which competence is judged. The performance criteria have to pay regard to the nature of the evidence that will be required. It is at this stage in particular that underpinning knowledge and understanding are likely to be revealed.

It is also necessary ultimately to determine if performance in a work or work-related setting provides adequate evidence of the pertinent knowledge/understanding, whether simple questioning in association with performance can reveal adequate evidence, or whether practicalities favour a separate assessment.

If there is a substantial body of knowledge and understanding it may be better encompassed within a separate sub-unit. However, in such a case it is important to remember, and make transparent, that the successful completion of such a sub-unit does not in itself adequately infer competence. Of course, early stages in a learning process may primarily be directed at establishing skills, knowledge and understanding which subsequently will enable effective performance.

What are the implications for assessment practice?

Assessment is about collecting evidence that competence has been demonstrated or achieved. The previous section pertaining to knowledge and understanding has revealed something of the implications for assessment practices.

It is important, of course, that the assessment process is valid. Competence is very much about the process skills — doing, making decisions, solving problems, selecting and implementing strategies, etc. Assessment procedures have to be designed to elicit relevant evidence. Evidence may be of a direct nature, or indirect as is often the case in the context of accrediting prior learning.

An important characteristic of the competence based standards is that they are very explicit. Certification is in effect a form of guarantee that the individual has adequately demonstrated that he or she has fully met the specification contained within the unit — unless specified, there is no scope for sampling.

Clearly there are situations where evidence of effective performance in a work situation, over a finite period of time, has to be sought. On other occasions effective performance in a simulation may provide adequate evidence. Where knowledge is a specific requirement it has to be demonstrated. However, given that the concept of competence is closely related to the demands of employment, evidence of understanding will probably have to be sought through its effective application to real work-based situations or close simulations.

Where written exercises are concerned, it seems unlikely that short essays or simplified problems which in the past have characterised written examinations, will suffice — projects and case studies may better match the requirement. Similarly it is unlikely that the reiteration of facts or theories will be sufficient evidence of understanding — there will be a need to demonstrate an ability to effectively apply that understanding. Multiple choice responses can be used to good effect to test knowledge but again need to be associated with work-related situations if used to assess understanding. (There are interesting examples of multiple response tests being used to good effect in association with interactive video and computer simulations).

Can the standards be implemented very precisely or accurately?

No certification is 100 per cent reliable in its inference.

All standards have tolerances. There is always a possibility that somebody who is on the borderline of competence is judged incorrectly. *All* assessment is subjective at the margins. The issues are:

how precisely are the standards defined?
how well can assessors interpret the standards with adequate consistency?

In the context of criterion referenced standards, enhanced precision is often associated with providing more detail pertaining to the standard and its interpretation. More relevant and apposite detail costs more to establish, and requires more support to ensure adequate interpretation. (There may be little point in producing performance criteria that take an excessive time to read, digest and operationalise, and require more and more extensive assessor training to facilitate adequately consistent interpretation. The result could well be that nobody bothers to read and internalise the standard).

It seems likely that, in the long term, the precision of standards, and the expected consistency of interpretation in the field will reflect something of the importance of the competence in the work-place. This in turn may bear some relationship to the 'added value' or 'cost of failure' associated with the function.

It is important to remember that to date standards have not been defined with anything like the precision encompassed by those currently being developed. Despite the apparent precision associated with marks, say on a scale of 100, it is worth bearing in mind that, as an indicator of effective learning, 50 is not necessarily better than say 49 or 45. Grades are better indicators but even there, for example in the context of the old 'O' Levels, there was only about 50 per cent probability that a candidate got the grade truly deserved, away from the extremes of the scales.

Because the new standards have more explicit performance criteria, it is also easier to identify possible sources of variance in interpretation. Ultimately the question has to be 'does it matter — are the variances in interpretation within acceptable tolerances?'

Shouldn't standards be about other things as well as competence to perform effectively in employment?

It is quite possible that other forms of standards might be required. After all there are many different users of qualifications. It may well be that there are users of certification who want evidence of an individual's ability to handle and apply concepts pertaining to an academic discipline or field of study. (Such standards, however, might be employment-related because the individual aspires to teach or carry out research in the discipline). There are also 'generic' skills such as communication and handling number which can be defined and assessed in a way of value to users of the certification.

Information pertaining to competence in academic disciplines or generic skills may be very relevant as an indicator of readiness (or suitability?) to progress to occupations or learning programmes which draw on such competence. To date, there is no evidence that the methodology suggested for occupational standards could not be adapted to this context, but it has yet to be tried. In addition, it is not clear how far the needs of those concerned with academic progression will correspond with those concerned with progress to a new occupation. Congruence or divergence between the two could only be detected if the standards required were made more explicit.

Certification of vocational, academic and generic standards of the kind above recognises demonstrated achievement, performance or outcomes of learning. As has already been discussed it is possible to draw inferences from such certification as to performance in the future. Evidence of underpinning knowledge and understanding can enhance the reliability of inference to perform effectively in different settings to those featured in the assessment, and infer ability to address situations which did not feature in the assessment. However, the reliability of any inference to perform effectively decreases as the situation diverges from the conditions applicable during the assessment.

There is considerable interest in assessment and certification which, with adequate reliability, says something about potential. Certification which accurately reflects potential might be considered the holy grail of all recruiting officers, whether in employment or education. It is always possible that such assessment and related certification might emerge.

There is also a growing appreciation that knowledge of the personal effectiveness attributes of the individual can be of value in providing a match to the demands of specific jobs and in building effective teams. Such personal effectiveness attributes are more normally profiled rather than pass/fail criteria being applied. Nevertheless there are criteria defined for each element of the profile, used in assessment and providing the basis for certification.

In particular in education, there is extensive interest in these academic, generic, and personal transferable skills. In 1986, the National Advisory Body for Public Sector Higher Education in the UK identified several transferable personal skills needed for general management or professional posts and encouraged higher education to develop them. These skills included communication, problem solving, team work, and inter-personal skills. NAB maintained that these skills could be developed through teaching methods already wide-spread in HE. It was necessary however to make them more explicit and assess them formally. (Transferable personal skills in Employment: The Contribution of Higher Education, NAB, May 1986).

Given the fundamental importance of such skills, the Training Agency is concerned that competence in them be fostered in all the training programmes it sponsors. These skills are also contained within the concept of Enterprise. Through the Enterprise in Higher Education Initiative, the Training Agency is fostering, in the higher education context, their formation, extension and certification.

The Standards Programme also recognises that such skills are considered to be fundamental components of management. Within the programme to develop standards pertinent to management, workers are seeking to establish standards relating to the personal transferable skill domain. However, at the time of writing, in contrast to the context of occupationally specific standards where pass/fail criteria are being established, it seems that with respect to the personal transferable skills domain a profiling approach might be recommended.

How will the new competence based employment related standards be applied in the future?

Reflecting the national characteristic of the standards, they will focus in on the functions of relevance to employment at different sites, throughout the nation. As such it is unlikely that they will comprehensively represent the needs of each employment situation.

Thus, the standards provide a national point of reference. It is likely that individual employers will often supplement such standards with 'in-house' specific requirements to define the expectations of their own work-force. As with any grade or pass/fail criteria, the defined standards represent the minimum for certification. It is possible that individual employers will define their expectations with respect to the minimum, perhaps looking for a higher order of performance. Such standards can therefore provide reference points for human resource development and for recruitment.

Given such explicit statements of needs and expectations, it is easier to judge the extent to which a 'qualification' matches needs. For this to happen however, qualifications have to be equally explicit about standards attained, both with respect to content and level.

Qualifications have to be seen as a form of shorthand. In the context of the new standards, the performance criteria provide the explicit statement of what has been achieved. However, it would not be unusual if, say, five units incorporated about 200 performance criteria. The titles of the five units represent a form of shorthand; the reader who looks no further takes on trust that the standards which pertain broadly meet expectations. If 20 units are combined into a qualification the title of an award is even less informative and so its acceptance by a user is even more an act of trust or faith.

However, the larger a qualification the increased likelihood that the qualification does not match the specific expectations of a particular employer. If a qualification is so designed to meet the needs of diverse employers it risks either matching the needs of none, or of asking the learner to learn a lot more than is required by a specific employment opportunity. While the former can lead to dissatisfaction amongst individual employers, the latter can be wasteful in that learners tie up learning resources (and spend time) learning things which perhaps are never used. Clearly there has to be a compromise.

To return to the first point, the new standards facilitate a clearer judgement as to the extent to which a qualification represents expectations. The quality of *vocational qualifications* can be judged against such standards.

Qualifications may seek to say something about the individual's generic abilities and other matters but the National Council for Vocational Qualifications has clearly stated that they expect National Vocational Qualifications to be employment-related and to incorporate a requirement for evidence of effective performance in work-related situations. The implication is that vocational qualifications in the future should seek evidence of competence within the definition given earlier and, where relevant, require evidence of effective performance in a work-related situation that captures the key characteristics of the work situation.

Will these standards foster the formation of an adaptable, flexible work-force capable of progression?

First, the broad based concept of competence is designed to recognise, and therefore foster the development of, planning, management, personal interaction and problem-solving skills. Such skills are key to adaptability and flexibility.

Secondly, the close link with employment will both motivate many to seek recognition of competence who were not motivated in the past because qualifications seemed to be more about the school room than the reality of life, and it will encourage confidence in ability to learn and therefore adapt. There is considerable evidence that those most willing to learn and adapt to new situations are those whose learning has previously been recognised, i.e., those who have previously gained qualifications.

Thirdly, as already implied, learning directed at the acquisition of competences relevant to particular work-situations provides a sound basis for subsequent learning and progression.

However, this is not to deny that often progression (and adaptation to significantly new activities) may well also require enhancement of generic skills and perhaps ability to handle new and more challenging concepts embedded in new disciplines. Under such conditions confidence to learn, and ownership of learning skills, will be of paramount importance.

What are the implications for education?

At the end of the day this is a question that can be answered only by education. It has to be recognised that education serves a variety of different purposes and seeks to meet the needs of a range of different clients.

Education is very much about developing personal skills, independent of specific roles or occupations, such as the broad intellectual abilities of critical thinking, problem-solving and synthesis, communication and other characteristics of personal effectiveness and enterprise. Education is often concerned with extending capabilities in an academic or a range of academic subjects. However, education is also about preparing individuals for employment and some educational programmes are about preparing individuals for specific employment opportunities.

Education provides a service to many different clients having different needs. Content of learning programmes should reflect clients' expectations and needs:

— An employer seeking a contribution to an integrated programme of education and training for employees will have particular expectations, whether to do with initial formation or continued development.

— On the other hand, the pre-employment student may be looking for a wider base which maximises employment opportunities. Clearly there is a need for a balance between maximising the number of potential employment opportunities (but not meeting the expectations of any one) and meeting the expectations of a specific employer with no guarantee of employment.

— Where a learner is sponsored by the state, either through a government training scheme or through being in receipt of a study bursary, or less obviously be accessing subsidised courses, the sponsoring organization has a right to stipulate expectations.

— Where an adult has a self-identified (and funded) learning need, he or she is the client.

All the above have implications for the way in which programmes of learning are constructed. The establishment of standards of competence pertinent to effective performance in employment and the adoption of more explicit standards pertinent to education programmes, will make more transparent the extent to which education programmes do or do not prepare people for employment.

How and where learning might be fostered

It is likely that many vocational qualifications will be unavailable unless the individual has the opportunity to develop and demonstrate competence in a work related situation which captures the key characteristics of the work place. Providers of institution-based learning will probably have to facilitate work-based learning opportunities on a much larger scale than previously or offer qualifications which only go some way towards being a full vocational qualification.

There are implications for learning strategies. While there is likely to always be a place for traditional didactic teaching it is likely to be unsatisfactory in many instances. Such a teaching approach does nothing to foster problem-solving ability, initiative, decision making or working in teams. It has little to contribute to competence.

There is likely to be a need for considerably more student centred learning, drawing heavily on case studies and simulations.

Curriculum organization

Decisions will have to be taken as to whether a unitary curriculum is offered or an integrated programme which nevertheless facilitates credit accumulation.

Assessment

Assessment methodologies are also likely to change. In the past there has been too heavy a dependence on assessing knowledge. Given the definition of competence adopted there will be a far greater emphasis on the collection of evidence of effective performance in work-related situations. There is also likely to be a greater emphasis on the use of case studies and project work not only as learning strategies but also for assessment purposes. Assessment increasingly will be devised and implemented locally — this will depend on the enhancement of assessment expertise.

Candidates will have a clear perception of what is required of them and the standards to which they must aspire. There may well be a growth in requests for assessment on demand.

Administration

Current administrative infrastructure is predicated on a simple model of operation — for most FE clients there is one entry date, assessment for certification purposes is often associated with a common finishing date. The modular curriculum, a greater diversity of needs and expectations, and the potential for assessment on demand all argues for more flexible administrative procedures.

References

ED (1981) *A New Training Initiative*, London, HMSO.
ED (1988) *Employment for the 1990s*, Cm.540, London, HMSO.
ED and DES (1986) *Working Together: Education and Training*, Cm. 9823, London, HMSO.
ED.TA (1989) *Development of Assessable Standards for National Certification, Note 2 — Developing Standards by Reference to Function*, Sheffield, ED.TA.
MSC (1988) *Development of Assessable Standards for National Certification, Note 3 — The Definition of Competences and Performance Criteria*, Sheffield, MSC.

Chapter 8

Curriculum implications

Geoff Stanton

Vocational Education and Training (VET) in the UK is currently undergoing, or has recently undergone, a number of different but related changes. Although the conventional model used to describe the processes involved in curriculum development remains useful in the new circumstances, the balance of attention which needs to be paid to different processes has changed. The usual methods of describing and implementing learning programmes have, however, had to be changed in order to cope. This chapter explains how and why.

The first paragraph had to be careful to avoid using the term 'course' in connection with VET. A 'course' implies a programme of study with predetermined content and often to fixed length, under the control of a college, certification being dependent upon the extent to which the student achieves sufficient of the objectives of the course. In this case a 'pass' is awarded. Courses are allocated 'levels', and admission to those at a higher level usually requires successful completion of an earlier course. A group (of similar learners) of a given size is normally required for a 'course' to be viable. The present situation in the UK makes all these assumptions questionable.

Firstly, Vocational Qualifications are in the process of being reformed so as to make them 'competence-based'. This means that a qualification is gained (ideally) when the individual is able to demonstrate that their performance meets the criteria for competence laid down by the responsible body. The responsible body is comprised of representatives of employers and employees in the vocational sector concerned. The means by which the competence has been gained is irrelevant.

Secondly, it is increasingly common for a learner to acquire their learning in more than one location, and under the auspices of more than one agency. For instance: an individual on a Youth Training Scheme may be employed in a retail store; be involved once a week in a project in a local college, the data for which has to be obtained by investigating activities in the place of work; and may meet fortnightly in a group led by a youth worker where s/he is encouraged to reflect on and make sense of his or her current difficulties, successes and progress.

The point is that this is a joint programme, not one owned by (say) either the college or the employer, to which the other contributes. Although the whole programme may be coordinated by a 'Managing Agent', there is a sense in which it is only really owned by the individual learners. In these circumstances, their progress has to be carefully mapped or 'profiled'. Since it is progress towards agreed standards of competence, it is possible, and desirable, to involve the learners in negotiation about the route they are taking without prejudicing quality, and it is vitally important to share with the learners the criteria for assessment.

Thirdly, demographic trends, changes in personal life-styles, and a diversification of the economy all further stimulate the need to individualise learning programmes. In the UK we have more people in the working population than ever before, but proportionately fewer of them are 16–19 year old, or male. New client groups with different domestic and other responsibilities both require more varied modes of attendance and have different learning styles. Rapid changes in the labour market, in particular the decline of industries which traditionally recruited large numbers of apprentices, and the growth of 'new' service-based occupations which have no traditional links with colleges, have meant that colleges have to prove their cost-effectiveness to new customers. For many of them, particularly those who are interested in retraining to meet new circumstances, the gaining of a specific qualification is a secondary consideration. The primary requirement is efficient and appropriate learning, and there can be no hiding behind a 'syllabus' in order to excuse tedium or irrelevance.

All of this puts a premium on a provider's ability to 'tailor-make' a learning programme to suit an individual learner or company, rather than their expertise in selecting applicants for their ready-made courses. Schemes are made and kept viable by running sessions on a 'workshop' basis using a bank of learning assignments, rather than requiring a group of (say) fifteen learners to move in step through a taught syllabus. Syllabus topics have been replaced by a checklist of activities and objectives, and schemes of work replaced by profiles and profiling procedures which keep track of an individual's progress.

Assessment has become part of the learning process, with as much emphasis on diagnosis and target setting as on passing and failing. In fact, the concept of an individual 'matching' the requirements of a particular occupation or further learning programme has proved a more precise and helpful approach than did 'failing' someone with 49 per cent whilst passing those with 50 per cent.

Most crucially of all, college staff have shifted their role from teaching to tutoring functions, in the sense that their expertise in needs analysis, individual programme design, and evaluation has become more crucial than their ability to present material in an entertaining manner to a class.

The FEU has, for some time now, adopted the model shown in Figure 8.1 to represent the processes involved in curriculum development. The model (of which this is a simplified version) indicates that all four processes must be satisfactory if a good quality learning experience is to result and be maintained. Traditionally, however, the college lecturer has been largely concerned with the 'implementation' phase, with the needs analysis and programme design phases often being undertaken by other agencies at a national or regional level. (The evaluation and review phase has usually been the most neglected at all levels).

Figure 8.1 FEU Model of Curriculum Development.

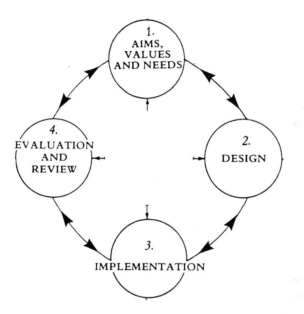

By suggesting that the curriculum needs to be tailor-made for individual clients (whether these are people or enterprises) we are, in effect, arguing that the expertise of the college staff needs to be deployed primarily in phases 1, 2 and 4. Indeed, it may be that after thorough-going and professional analysis and design it becomes apparent that the individual and/or company concerned have resources of their own which will allow them to implement at least part of the necessary learning programme themselves. Even where this is not the case, once the learning targets have been identified and understood it may be that learning can be via access to open-learning materials, whether paper- or computer-based, rather than requiring face-to-face teaching. The learner is, however, likely to need professional help in evaluating the extent to which the designed programme has met the needs as identified, or revealed new ones.

Insofar as this approach is correct, it fortunately implies that it is possible to individualise without a net increase in staff resources. What is the case, however, is that the role of the staff shifts from what we used to call 'teaching' to what we might more appropriately call 'tutoring' (where this term is used in an educational rather than a simply pastoral sense). This shift may not be simply a matter of coping with changing circumstances. Many professionals feel that the technique of working 'alongside' learners in this way is, in any case, a more effective one than the more usual 'presentational' (or even 'confrontational') style.

I say 'more usual', but this is only true of certain contexts. Primary school staff in the UK have long adopted this approach, which is also a feature of recently introduced schemes such as CPVE and YTS, where the participants (at or just beyond the compulsory school age) could not be assumed to be conventionally studious. Training programmes for senior managers or in art and design have also, in effect, followed this pattern, so it is not only appropriate for the low-attainers. The argument is, indeed, that the implementation-centred approach is really teacher-centred, and has been maintained where possible only because it appears to be so much more comfortable for them.

The switch, as earlier described, to competence based qualifications seems likely to further emphasise the need for this approach. This can only be speculation at present, since the new qualifications are only now being introduced, and very few have yet reached their final form. Nevertheless, it is possible to compare, again in model form, the old situation with the new — see Figures 8.2 and 8.3.

Figure 8.2 Model of traditional learning programme.

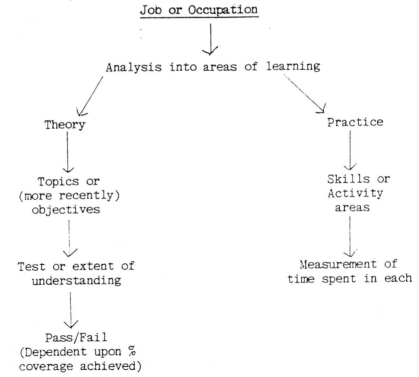

Job or Occupation

↓

Analysis into areas of learning

Theory → Topics or (more recently) objectives → Test or extent of understanding → Pass/Fail (Dependent upon % coverage achieved)

Practice → Skills or Activity areas → Measurement of time spent in each

Although Figure 8.2 is inevitably somewhat of a caricature of the actual situation, it does reveal the greatest weakness of the whole approach, namely, that it is possible to allege and even discover a disturbing lack of connection between the ability to pass the course and competent performance in the vocation concerned. We have only to look close to home for (at least anecdotal) evidence of this. Most of us have not found much correlation between those of our fellow teachers who are the most highly qualified and those who are the most highly competent (however defined). The converse is also true. Some very competent colleagues are thinly qualified, and what is more are not permitted to merely deploy evidence of their performance in order to become more qualified.

The alternative, competence-based model, might look something like that shown in Figure 8.3.

Figure 8.3 Model appropriate for competence-based learning programmes.

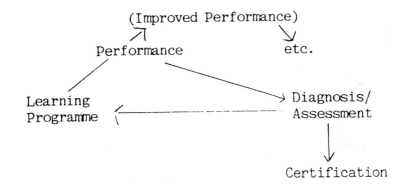

Here, assessment comes before a learning programme can be identified, let alone followed. Further, if assessment shows that the definition of component performance can already be matched, no 'course' is required before a certificate may be awarded. If the performance falls short of what is required, the process becomes a diagnostic one, and the professional skills of the tutor are required in order to identify what learning experiences are most likely to bring about an improvement. It is therefore the learning programme itself which is under test: if after it has been followed in good faith no improvement follows, it may well be the diagnosis or design which is faulty.

Everyday exemplars of this approach are the health clubs which seem to be increasing in number all the time. In this context the reasons for enrolling can be varied. One person might be aiming to go ski-ing shortly, another might be recovering from a mild heart-attack. In either case their present condition will be assessed and compared to the level of performance they wish to attain. Then a training programme can be designed and explained to them. It is noticeable how often this approach proves much more acceptable (and less threatening) to participants than did their 'physical education' lessons at school. The converse is sometimes the case as far as teachers and their managers are concerned, because of the implications for their professional roles and the structure and equipping of institutions. Before leaving this example, it is worth also noting that these individualised learning programmes are not incompatible with group membership. Indeed, the social support given by a group can be all the more freely developed when there is no question of people being held back by others, or pushed uncomfortably fast.

It may be objected that the analogy is a weak one because of the degree of difference between 'performance' in the gym and performance in a vocational role — such as teaching. I would certainly wish to argue strongly that it is the competent performance of a role that should be rewarded by a vocational qualification, rather than possession of given techniques or the ability to perform a series of tasks adequately. I do not intend to go into detail about this here, except to say that most people would accept that there is a crucial difference between a competent worker and a worker with a number of competences, and that the argument applies at all vocational levels, not just the higher ones.

If the 'role-competence' approach is accepted, then I believe that the model described above still has validity in the most sophisticated of occupations/vocations, though the ways in which competence is defined and assessed have to be equally sophisticated. In this chapter, however, I wish to briefly examine the implications for the design and implementation of learning programmes.

Whilst considerable attention is currently being paid to the issues of how competence is to be defined and standards expressed, the matter of how individuals can be helped to become more competent more quickly is comparatively neglected. I also suspect that we shall find that we have a lot to learn about how it can be best done. I hope that in the search for effective methods we shall find that important contributions will come from both 'trainers' and 'educators', and that the self-justifying and self-regarding members of both camps will find their positions increasingly untenable.

I offer a final model (Figure 8.4) which I find useful.

The hypothesis is that competence occurs because of possession of the right combination of facts and skills, on the one hand, and contextual understanding on the other. Without the latter, not only may the individual not know how and when to deploy the knowledge and skills they possess, they may not have the basis from which to further develop and adapt them as circumstances change. Without the former, the understanding is impotent.

In other words, we need neither the uneducated nor the untrained. Nor does either education or training exist in its own right. Both must justify themselves in terms of their contribution to competence. I would guess, however, that because the means by which skills and knowledge are acquired differ from those by which understanding is developed, it would be a mistake to lose the distinctive presence of each item within the curriculum.

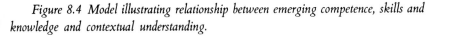

Figure 8.4 Model illustrating relationship between emerging competence, skills and knowledge and contextual understanding.

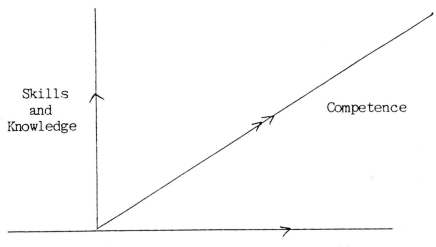

This is *not* to say that they therefore need to be separately assessed for certification purposes. There is another argument to be had about whether the assessment of understanding is required in its own right, or merely to provide further evidence of competence more cost-effectively than repeated observation. I will leave this issue at the point where I emphasise the importance of not confusing curriculum with qualifications, and the criteria for the quality of one with the criteria for that of the other. For instance, the quality of the curriculum will partly depend on expert diagnosis of *learning* needs, whereas the quality of a qualification will partly depend upon the quality of the assessment of the level (of attainment or competence) reached. Similarly, assessment criteria are not necessarily the same as learning stages — but to fully explore all this would require another chapter.

Chapter 9

An achievement-led college

Jenny Shackleton

Introduction

During the last year the Wirral Metropolitan College has been preparing for the numerous changes facing FE by organizing itself behind an approach which it has come to call achievement-led institutional development. Due to the interest stimulated by this activity, this chapter has been prepared setting out its main features.

Achievement-led institutional development

A rationale for a new approach

Despite the commitment and hard work which has gone into college and curriculum development during the last two decades, the results are mixed. There is much good practice, but this may still be vulnerable to changes in funding and staff. FE is still the part of the education system which is least attended to from outside, and least thought through from inside. The plethora of smaller initiatives in further education over the last decade have demonstrated that things can be done differently for small numbers of people, and rounded a few hard edges. However, they have so far failed to deliver their key objectives: increased participation; a more informed and qualified public; greater personal, corporate and public investment in, and support for, learners, education and training.

By and large it is still the case that syllabuses and lecturers constitute the conceptual centre and starting point for colleges; and that students are secondary. The student is still normally required to adjust him or herself to an established curriculum. Whatever the individual lecturer's disposition, a college's organization and structure tends to make this so. Too strong a focus on the teaching role can make the learning process a matter of covering the syllabus; narrow efficiency targets can turn negotiation with students into covert persuasion or pressure.

Nevertheless, the various changes now underway, and the context in which they are occurring, provide a window of opportunity for reviving and developing FE on an exciting new basis. From having operated as a largely once-for-all terminal service within a restrictive array of qualifications, FE now has the possibility of becoming the essential intermediate component of an open education and training system based on unit credit transfer for individuals and institutional honesty.

Education and training is not value-free, and a mature institution is one that is capable of working through and articulating its values and purposes. Given its greater autonomy and lack of shelter in the future, and the requirement to contribute to and win support within its locality, a college has to set out clearly what it stands for and is responsible for. And whatever else it may be there for, a college has as a prime purpose the development of individuals and the certification of achievement. Therefore all of its values and purposes are bound to stem from, and interact with, the learner and his or her achievement.

It is accepted wisdom that everything a college does can be regarded as the curriculum, since everything will have a bearing upon teaching and learning. Achievement-led institutional development takes a similarly holistic view by regarding everything that an institution does as having a bearing upon individual achievement. However, it then goes on to suggest that the curriculum is itself so tied into courses, teachers and teaching, that it should for the present be replaced as the central tenet and starting point by the real thing: individual development and achievement. Thus we arrive at achievement-led institutional development.

Being a strategy, achievement-led institutional development embodies most of what we as a college are thinking and moving towards. As a new mental set it is inherently reforming or corrective in nature. It therefore seeks to dispense with the industrial conservatism which may affect formal and informal relations within a college; with separate and different agreements and conduct for various groups of staff and students; with the teacher as proxy and spokesperson for the learner; and with teaching as proxy for learning. It recognizes that a college as an entity may be less mature than its students and staff as individuals, and may as a result limit and condition its and their behaviour, to the detriment of personal development and achievement.

A college mission

The challenge to be responsive to disconnected external pressures can only be handled effectively by a college which has an understanding of its environment, its purposes and its characteristics. This can be worked through and established by the production of a mission statement, which is by its nature a normative statement.

Personal achievement is the core of this college's mission statement. The document states:

1　Personal achievement is every individual's right, and the College should organise itself behind this right.

2　The establishment of personal achievement is a powerful aid to learning and motivation; it should be seen primarily in these terms, within a framework of standards.

3　The physical, mental and psychological involvement of learners with their own development and achievement, and that of their peers, should be adopted as an organising principle for the College.

4　Personal achievement should constitute the core mission of the College. To encourage the College to be self-critical about its ability and preparedness to support personal growth, positive appraisal measures should be introduced and developed for learning, teaching and learner support.

In keeping with the belief that everything a college does has a bearing upon personal achievement, our mission incorporates five associated and supportive themes:

learner involvement and empowerment
institutional appraisal and self-scrutiny
needs analysis and responsiveness
human resource development
reflective management.

These come together in the mission statement to express an organization with consistent principles and approaches throughout.

Curriculum or learning support

The mission statement and the position it takes regarding the curriculum have an inevitable impact upon the next stage of strategic planning, which would normally be curriculum policy and principles. Currently the widely accepted curriculum principles include access, progression, autonomy, relevance, breadth, balance, differentiation, coherence. Their meaning has been defined through their operation in schools and colleges, and their existence is often much more real to lecturers, teachers and managers, than to the students.

For achievement-led institutional development, the curriculum has to be redefined in terms which can be directly recognised by the learner, and engaged with directly by him or her without mediation or interpretation. Ideally the learner should be as self-directed within a college as he or she would expect to be elsewhere, and as being entitled to receive a range of developmental and certification services according to his or her needs, aspirations and circumstances. This approach when taken forward into actual services significantly expands and diversifies the college offering, making its developmental and certification services the collective responsibility of the whole college in a direct and thoroughly practical sense.

This means that coherence is a matter for the student to determine, and not the lecturer or institution. Coherence emerges through the relationship formed between the student and the various services provided for him or her, rather than in the mind of the provider. Coherence can occur when the institution responds to individual need and circumstances within a progressive system of credits. It is not necessarily the same as curriculum continuity.

Therefore a new set of 'learning (curriculum) principles' has been developed for the Wirral Metropolitan College, the headings for which are as follows:

recurrence
advocacy
flexibility
empowerment
personal achievement
visibility
learning support

Once defined further, these give rise to a series of objectives for college development. As an example, 'personal achievement' has been defined by the following objectives:

1   The motivating effect of personal achievement should be optimised.
2   Programmes should recognize and build upon the learner's prior achievements.
3   Under-prepared learners should have the means of acquiring the essential preliminary achievements for entry to courses and programmes without delay, and where possible as part of course entry.
4   Assessment and reviews of progress should be incorporated in all learners' programmes.
5   The learner should have in his or her keeping an action plan showing, among other things, achievement targets and achievements gained.
6   Assessment should at all times be visible to and understood by the learner.
7   Supplementary and reinforcement learning should be available to assist learners.
8   Learners should be able to test their progress and achievements on demand.

From these, required action and targets can be established, and their attainment monitored.

Action plans and implementation

By embracing the concepts, values and principles of achievement-led institutional development, a college has a means of evaluating and responding to the various national and international developments associated with assessment and certification. By standing behind the student rather than any of his or her proxies a college is able to regard courses and classes as one delivery option among many, and to avoid a psychological dependency upon current ways of doing things. Of course this does not mean that changing is straightforward; most of the parts for the new approach have yet to be assembled and organised into a delivery system. Nevertheless, a strongly communicated vision of comprehensive arrangements to generate and optimize personal achievement enables a college to revitalise its talent and resources and step out of its old skin. For most colleges, change cannot wait until the values and principles underlying them have been thoroughly worked through and subscribed to. An interactive and reciprocal process is needed, which involves rapid practical activity alongside and integrated with the refinement of ideas and communication.

In this College during the last year we have tried to move forward by:

reviewing the college's structure and as a result significantly reducing its lateral and vertical internal divisions;

developing a fuller internal career structure for support staff, who in increasing numbers provide educational services to individual learners;

introducing a 5-year action plan for the College which also provides the basis for the TVEI extension programme (in the College from 1989);

acquiring external funding to reflect, comment and report upon the changes, but not to shoulder the changes, which are being carried through as a priority for the College's substantive budget.

A development team of senior and key colleagues reviews and steers developments, undertakes the most complex activities, sustains networks with other organizations and helps to embed the changes through the staff development programme.

The College 5-year action plan gives an impression of the most concrete and practical steps now being planned and undertaken:

1 To create a College which is strikingly ahead of its current image and activity.
2 To plan and implement an admissions service.
3 To plan and introduce a range of student support services including counselling, study centres, careers centres and work placement units.
4 To plan, introduce and evaluate a universally available core curriculum framework which includes continuing experience and achievement in communication, mathematics, information technology and science.

5 To plan and introduce individual learning programmes for all major vocational routes, based upon learning centres.

6 To plan, introduce and evaluate assessment on demand for the core, individual and open learning programmes, and a selection of vocational competences.

7 To design and introduce a summative assessment and certification service which links with the range of current qualifications on offer, and those which will emerge through NCVQ and SEAC.

8 To plan and introduce an exit and transfer service.

9 To develop the College's marketing practices to include family and weekend learning, summer schools, and assessment and placement services for employers.

10 To exchange and disseminate information and experience for the benefit of the College, its users and clients, and the service generally.

This chapter stems from a wish to communicate and share ideas and practice, not because this college is particularly special or advanced, but because everyone benefits from exchanging and networking.

The link with NVQs and externally sponsored initiatives

Achievement-led institutional development facilitates the delivery of NVQs by distinguishing assessment and certification from courses and teaching. This does not mean that the process of delivery is ignored, though. The achievement-led approach is equally intended to facilitate the educational objectives expressed by the National Curriculum. Guiding principles include:

the power of assessment as a learning tool;
the desirability of introducing a modular curriculum as a means of stretching achievement in all directions;
the importance of designing learning and achievement for long-term economic, social and cultural goals.

This means that the College is seeking to introduce NVQs as a new certification system, and not simply as a set of qualifications. Therefore we are much more concerned to relate to NCVQ's long-term aims than to the present characteristics of individual awarding bodies and conditional awards. The college has therefore prioritized the following tasks for the next 12 months:

1 the establishment of a collegiate admissions service with standard features in respect of information, diagnostic assessment, advice and record raising;

2   the introduction of NROVA for all full-time and as many part-time students as possible, and incorporating a formative record-system for TVEI purposes;

3   the establishment of individual learning workshops for an educational core comprising communication, mathematics, IT and science and technology;

4   the identification of core requirements and achievements within vocational courses;

5   the organization of courses into vocational, generic/core, and integrating components;

6   the establishment of college centres for study, support and assessment.

These tasks are being monitored and supported by externally funded projects. The arrival of TVEI Extension within the College from September 1989 is facilitating these changes in a striking manner.

Further information

Achievement-led Institutional Development is now the subject of a series of college workshops. For further details contact Pip Ellis, Staff Development Manager, on 051-653-5555, or Rhiannon Evans, Head, Learner Services on the same number. Alternatively please write to either of them at the following address: Wirral Metropolitan College, Borough Road, BIRKENHEAD, Wirral L42 9QD.

Chapter 10

Attitudinal change in FE in response to the introduction of NVQ's

John Burke

The research on which this chapter is based arises out of an on-going NCVQ-funded project which focuses on six case study FE colleges. Five of the colleges were chosen because of their involvement with a joint TA/NCVQ initiative on the Accreditation of Prior Learning (APL). The sixth college was included at a later stage because, although it is not part of the APL project, it is involved in a thorough going reorganization into a single coherent institution. The common thread which unites all the case study colleges was their perception as 'pro-active' institutions which were making determined strides to implement curriculum change. It was not the intention to evaluate the APL project but involvement with that initiative provided an initial focus and a point of entry. The time scale for completing this work has had to be revised because of involvement with other complementary research; this report represents a provisional interim analysis. A broader perspective has been adopted in presenting this chapter to include the perspective of some other staff in FE colleges in order to establish the context in which change is taking place.

Situational knowledge

Eraut (1988) proposes a 'map' of management knowledge consisting of six knowledge categories:

Knowledge of people
Situational knowledge
Knowledge of educational practice
Conceptual knowledge
Process knowledge
Control knowledge.

For the purposes of this chapter I would like to focus on situational knowledge, which he explains is concerned with how people 'read' the situation in which they find themselves:

> What do they see as the significant features? Which aspects of a situation are most susceptible to change? How would it be affected by or respond to certain decisions or events?

He points out that much but not all of this knowledge is consciously held, though it is rarely written down. It usually contains strong personal elements. It is affected by the person's role, personality and perspective. It constitutes the work-a-day common sense understanding that arises from living in a situation rather than consciously studying it. It is an insider's perspective often involving some discussion and deliberation but frequently built on intuitive assumptions.

This kind of knowledge is very important for senior managers in any institution but there are difficulties because much of this knowledge reaches a manager second-hand, already shaped and filtered by the perceptions of the informants. In a similar vein, Popkewitz (1984) speaks of 'a conceptual lens' which orients and offers different types of explanation. Theoretical as well as perceptual perspectives may filter different accounts.

But Eraut develops a micro-political strand in his thought:

> Not only are such accounts affected by what informants consider significant but also by what they consider fit to pass on. In particular they will be concerned with how their accounts will reflect back on themselves. Hence there is a tendency to pass on only that information that they think is wanted and to organise it in a way that shows that they understand the senior manager's intention and concerns.

He concludes that little of the information managers gather in this way could be described as objective and much of it may be acquired with a lot of unconscious filtering by perceptual frameworks of which they are only dimly aware.

If Eraut's analysis holds good for an institutional manager, as I concur it does, it is even more true of 'outside' managers and other publics who have a legitimate interest in what is going on in any particular institution, for example an LEA or a funding agency. This is not in any way to attribute bad faith or any intent to deceive but simply to acknowledge in Goffman's terms (1971) the presentation of front.

Interestingly, a facet of the same problem was raised in an interview with a Head of Department at one college. His deputy had just explained in some detail what he perceived as the college's responsive attitude to innovation:

> What is a useful level of analysis of what an institution really is? Because I think N gives a clear picture of the leadership as regards innovation in this

college. You have got to then ask the question: to what extent is that a general picture, to what extent do you need other perspective to get a real picture? The fundamental problem I am raising is when do we know an institution? When we know its senior staff? When you know individual lecturers? When you know its students? — or when you have added up the sum total of everything? And you then get the problem that one glance of N College gives a different picture of the institution than another.

He went on to reflect on the implications for change management:

You could work out a change strategy that was successful in one part of the college but which was unsophisticated in its ability to cope with another department in N College. Because it is a question of 'would the real institution please stand up!'

At another college the APL co-ordinator remarked:

What is N College? It is a phenomenological reality. You reify it when you call it a college.

With a nice feeling for etymology and clearly echoing a persistent theme in his Vice Principal's philosophy, he concluded:

It's a collection of *people* sometimes trying to do very different things, sometimes with very different attitudes.

Ethnography offers a possible way in for an investigation of attitudes which can arise out of and are grounded in the taken for granted knowledge and experience of different members of the institution. Although it has to be acknowledged that various filters will operate in the researcher's selection and organization of material it nonetheless offers a certain scope for reporting the views of different members of an institution without mediating or interpreting meanings.

In the next section, I examine the attitudinal response of different groups within the FE college largely by reference to the ideas which were explored in a series of open-ended interviews and discussions.

Attitudes

Attitudes (cf. Oppenheim, 1966) are usually defined as a state of readiness, a tendency to act or react in a certain manner given the requisite stimulus. When we talk about the 'right attitude' we are usually making value judgements about appropriate behaviour. What constitutes appropriate behaviour will normally depend on the perspective we adopt. I use the word 'adopt' advisedly because in different contexts and at different times it is possible for the same person under different circumstances to evidence mutually exclusive or contradictory attitudes and to vary in the strength of the underlying beliefs or dispositions which support these attitudes. We may also acknowledge a strong link that frequently exists between perceived self interest and varying attitudes. In fact, in my analysis, enlightened self interest is identified as the determining principle which informs the attitudes of all groups encountered in this study.

This chapter proceeds by examining the attitudes of different staff in three membership categories.

(a)   The Principalship (with sub-set APL coordinators)
(b)   Heads of Department
(c)   Lecturers.

These categories are illustrated by transcripts of interviews with individuals from each group which reveal their orientations. They are supplemented in some cases by comments *about* different groups.

The view from the top

All members of the first group exhibited what can only be described as a very pro-active and enthusiastic stance to the NCVQ initiatives. The Vice Principal of one college felt that most good FE colleges could be distinguished in terms of an orientation towards either a 'marketeering approach' or a 'missionary approach'. Thus in his view the principalship had embraced the opportunity to take part in the APL project primarily because of the opportunities it offered for enhancing the reputation and standing of the college and the lead this would give in developing the provision of services within the college, or because of the strong commitment the college leadership felt to the needs of the local community which would benefit very obviously from the increased access and open opportunities. Both considerations would clearly figure in the decisions to take part, but one or other would be much more important. From my discussions and interviews with Principals and Vice Principals I think the distinction is valid. The important point is that irrespective of the impetus, the principalship in all the case study colleges was extremely committed. The main difference in approach lay in the way they sought to motivate their staff. Typical comments from the Vice Principalship revealed these orientations:

> We *are* a pro-active college — a centre of excellence. There is a price to pay — we may make mistakes but we are at the forefront of innovation.

> You know, we're in the front line, we're actually influencing, you know, what is going to be decreed for the system as a whole.

I chose this job because it is in an area of acute social deprivation. I think the APL project represents a crucial change in how you deal with students. So I thought if we start to work with standards in the very early stages to give them [students] a better perception of themselves, we may kick the hell out of the tyrannical exam system. If we can credit learning from other places and if it takes people along the road, or even 25 per cent towards something, then the monopoly enjoyed for years and years stands to drop down a bit.

APL coordination

The APL coordination or project leaders, senior lecturers or principal lecturers, were cast in the role of change agents. They too were extremely enthusiastic, well informed and 'dedicated'. They and their small teams had each put in much work and effort, frequently in the evening and during half term and long holiday periods. Their attitudinal orientation placed them in the same category at the Principalship:

> It has been a lot of hard work. I've got six hours a week I'm supposed to spend on this project. In fact I have spent far more than that.

JB: How much more do you reckon?

> At least twice as much. As I say I came in three days during half term week. It is something I couldn't have done if I hadn't enjoyed what I was doing.

Pro-active involvement

All APL staff I spoke to accepted without demur that they were 'pro-active'. They recognised the description as a just acknowledgement of the huge amount of effort they were currently expending on the project. Staff development was seen as a central focus for much of their work. In one college an especially well thought-out series of residential courses were mounted. Some indication of the coverage may be gauged from the range of outcomes aimed for and appropriately couched in competency statements:

ACCREDITATION OF PRIOR LEARNING

CHECKLIST OF ASSESSOR COMPETENCES

The APL Assessor should be able to:

1 Explain the key principles of Experiental Learning.
2 Differentiate between the broad concept of Experiential Learning and its sub-set Prior Learning.
3 Write competence statements which contain clear action words reflecting the language of the workplace and, where appropriate, indicating the level of performance to be achieved and conditions under which it should be achieved.
4 Convert appropriate syllabuses/courses specifications into a range of competence statements.
5 Design and construct a series of valid, reliable, credible and acceptable assessment techniques appropriate to APL.
6 Consult with prospective APL students, using appropriate counselling skills, in order to ascertain degree of prior learning acquired.
7 Translate prior learning claims into relevant course competences.
8 Design and implement suitable self-assessment mechanisms to support APL students in the identification of prior learning relative to course competencies.
9 Select or design appropriate assessment techniques to be used to verify APL claims.
10 Identify other sources of evidence suitable for the verification of APL claims.
11 Make suitable arrangements for accredited prior learners to receive education/training in non-exempted areas via a mode of learning appropriate to their needs.
12 Complete the necessary Validating Body documentation relating to exemption application for Accredited Prior Learners.

Most (but not all) colleges reported a slow start to the project:

VP: In the early stages of the project particularly in the first couple of months March, April and May when we appeared to be treading water and not making progress because we were chewing the fat on how it should be done. Every now and again people would begin to loose faith and say we are not getting anywhere and I want to say, keep on saying, well hang on a bit we've had a little bit of experience of this before. If it is a genuine research project you haven't got to expect to get far in the first couple of months.

Each Vice Principal appears to have identified closely with the project. This has the effect of giving it prestige and status within the college, a powerful psychological support necessary to get the scheme off the ground.

The Vice Principal of another college gave the following guidelines to support the APL coordinators who had been selected in the first place partly on their ability to negotiate the micro-politics of the institution:

Project Worker Guidelines
1 During the first months do not be afraid of being perceived as 'doing nothing' — time invested in reading about, talking about and learning about the project is invaluable.
2 Identify and prioritise (conflicting) management lines — national, local, college, client.
3 Identify where the power is and make alliances.
4 Demand essential resources — base room, desks, secretarial support, reprographics, filing systems, answerphone, stationery, hospitality.
5 Learn about PR — marketing, positive project promotion. Establish credibility.
6 Have answers ready for the inevitable question from others — 'what's in it for me?'.
7 You will be perceived as a threat — exploit this carefully where appropriate.
8 Guard your autonomy.
9 Be confident — make demands; talk to people — whoever and whatever they are in the institution.
10 Do not be afraid to say 'no' — a project worker will be asked to do a variety of tasks by a variety of people for a variety of reasons.
11 Be self-regulating.
12 Make sure the product is good (this takes time).
13 Remember that other people are as smart, skilled and knowing as you.
14 Remember that you are often in a teaching situation.
15 Prioritise activities to ensure that *change does occur*.

A lecturer in another college reported her uncertainty in the early stages:

> We started off at first with a little bit of a problem because we tended to be going round without any clear objective and the first thing in retrospect was a waste of time realistically because we didn't produce anything but at least we started examining the issues.

Such feelings normally follow any innovative change. Although each college had given firm support from the top and each college received strong support from the centre, feelings of anxiety were exacerbated on this occasion because the EAV bodies were themselves grappling with problems. This was a very unusual experience for most lecturers who were used to clear guidelines from BTEC, CGI and the RSA:

> In fact it also appeared that BTEC and City and Guilds were also on a learning curve because as we did it we began to see things wrong with it. You got the feeling they were doing this because they themselves hadn't any idea of what the problems and issues were.

Worries about change were contained because there was a feeling of collaborative exploration. The various APL coordinators worked to support their teams and there was careful oversight and developmental support from the project centre with regular visits, training sessions and conferences.

However, it must be remembered that this level of support will not be available as NVQs are developed. Of course, many of the problems which arise in a pilot project will have been solved. In my view the commitment and investment of self which characterises the APL project has been very instrumental in its success so far. As we shall see later, the attitudinal response of APL staff generally is unlikely to be matched in the college as a whole without an extensive involvement in staff development.

Heads of department

Attitudes of HODs

The attitudinal stance of most HODs appeared to be governed by their pre-occupation with coping, prioritizing and generally managing their department and the deployment of its resources. In the main they did not appear 'pro-active' either in their own estimation or the estimation of their lecturers. In fact as a group they were frequently described as occupational barriers to change. Their immediate responsibility is for the department and this is where most of their interests lie. Any initiative tends to be evaluated on the basis of its cost or contribution to the department, rather than the college.

Within the traditional pattern of FE college management the Head of Department occupies a very important position in the hierarchy of power and responsibility. Although he or she would usually have a number of wide-ranging responsibilities, control of resources was often singled out as the most jealously guarded perogative of the HOD by all sections of the staff. The multi-disciplinary team who constitute the principalship may know little about the subject base of some departments within the college, and the vice principal with curriculum responsibility will clearly have to lean heavily on some HODs because of the very diverse nature of different departments. The federal organization of the college — frequently with different departments grouped on different sites — means that HODs usually enjoy a semi-autonomous position with a good deal of delegated power, both formal and informal. This pattern is extremely useful for senior management in ensuring a local area of accountability when change is piecemeal. On the other hand, in the eyes of many lecturers the HOD system is a barrier to any institution-wide change precisely because in their semi-independent strongholds they are seen as 'Robber Barons', to use the graphic description of one lecturer. Because they control and have responsibility for resources in many colleges, staff development was locked into the departmental structure.

Even when staff development courses were mounted as a college initiative at times when all full-time staff *could* attend, there was often little incentive for any but the self-motivated members to attend unless there was stong encouragement from HOD. In the sense, such courses were aimed at those already converted. Some lecturers managed to remain optimistic:

> There are colleges I suspect which are much further down the track than we are. Where they have managed to develop staff development courses which are institutionally based and which are working even though they haven't got the most optimal Head of Department — despite the fact that they have departmental structure. Many colleges found they had expertise or they can supplement that expertise if they go across college. And although the HOD may operate as Robber Barons in their own departments there *are* all sorts of strategies for circumventing them.

HODs and organizational change

Staff at all levels I spoke to were aware of the initiative in college-wide institutional change taking place at the Wirral (cf. Jenny Shackleton, chapter 9) and this was being watched with considerable interest, but all the APL colleges I visited were firmly wedded to the HOD structure for the foreseeable future. In fact, one Vice Principal said he was very anxious to increase the strength of the HOD structure as this was the way, in his view, to ensure proper cooperation. If they felt their power was being threatened they were more likely to resist change. At one college, the Vice Principal had instituted a policy of 'right of access' for APL coordinators. HODs are typically very busy individuals but with the prestige of the Vice Principal behind them, coordinators could command their attention for development initiatives which might otherwise flounder or stagnate because of their power to simply ignore or 'react passively' to requests from more junior staff who might be outside their department.

It was interesting to see how different colleges could sometimes react to outside influences in very different ways. The Education Reform Act will affect HODs directly; as a lecturer put it:

With the changes which are happening, the literature is tending to suggest that for NVQs — to undertake procedures like APL — there needs to be organizational change. FE can't continue the way it has. What we have almost done in a college is to say the opposite. To say in this college the department will become even stronger, will become more autonomous even more powerful with the introduction of things with ERA.

They are, as it were, running their own small businesses and we will have to live by those consequences. We are in a department where the HOD is not enthusiastic, not responsive to change. We are in it. We have to take responsibility. It is essentially Head of Department led but departmental people lead that Head of Department. The Head of Department is good because of the *people* in the department.

The changing role of HODs

The same lecturer quoted above developed this theme:

I think HOD roles are changing dramatically. I think that these people are under more pressure than people who are not at that level. They are now having to become 'man-managers'. If they can't guarantee the responsiveness of their staff they have got a problem. So now HODs are like teachers used to be with the new skills like interviewing or profiling and self evaluation — really being managers. *Not* subject experts but man-managers. Now I think that brings in the education dimension that we might be an excellent training institution and the training is excellent, but the educational values, the philosophy that people are involved and that people, other people are trained in the skills [these are the jobs of the HOD].

An HOD in the same college put forward a similar view:

I think there is a bigger backcloth than NCVQ. NCVQ threatens courses and I'm sure there are some Heads who see it as threatening because it is something that has to be coped with and the past is no longer seen as relevant therefore it threatens. But I think the Education Reform Act makes Heads feel more vulnerable in terms of target setting, performance indicators control and evaluation. And I think (it is a value judgement in my part) that the implications of ERA are a bigger backcloth against which you have to measure NCVQ because I think their leadership will be deflected downwards to team leaders because Heads will have a priority concern coping with ERA. Perhaps academic leadership will be managed by Heads, not led, because they have bigger worries in mind. I don't think it is anything to do with philosophy coming to the fore. I think it is to do with pragmatism coming to the fore.

HODs and performance criteria

This pragmatism might be born of financial necessity. A Deputy Head of Department explained the dilemma facing many HODs in view of the new performance criteria. Their view of what was desirable from a curriculum development standpoint was governed by cost management decisions imposed as performance indicators. The pressure to meet these indicators might dictate the kind of response the HOD made to any initiative not in terms of the merits of the proposed initiative but simply as a business proposition:

> The HOD role is changing in a way commensurate with the nature of change in performance indicators. For example, APL current performance indicators; SSR in exchange for FTE. If I have a good healthy FTE it affects the budget I get. It affects my image in the principal's eyes. If it changes to 'cost per successful student' APL allows me to get through programmes very quickly which means I can get more through successfully — depending on how we define success. APL now becomes something very attractive. Therefore I will change to encouraging that. If those indicators stay as they are you have a very different set of questions for APL. What does it mean for my SSRs, what does it mean for my job security and the job security of my staff? As soon as the indicator changes it becomes: 'Right, I want to start doing that straight away'. How do I get my staff to understand it? We are managing against financial performance criteria.

An alternative model of HODs

At another college, the Vice Principal explained a very different model of the HOD:

> The day-to-day running of a department is the responsibility of the deputy head. We did try to change the name but the deputies did want to be called deputy heads. Deputy to us seems to mean you take over when somebody isn't there but we don't see that as their function. The day-to-day running of the department is their concern. They will be responsible if somebody is off sick to cover, etc. They are responsible for time-tabling. They are responsible for resources. The Head of Department has a curriculum and marketing role. They are very much seen as having some responsibility for quality control — for part of the curriculum auditing team. Never auditing

their own department — always doing it for others. It's true to say that of all the changes which have taken place within the college this has been the least successful. HODs find it difficult to adopt a curriculum role. They see power very much in terms of resources. And you know it is a symptom of what is going on in FE at the moment. All our concentration is on resource modelling, getting the Principal lumps of money so he can manage the finances. However, we are in the business of curriculum and it's sad for me that HODs hanker for being able to dish out resources, for being responsible for promotions. And this is one of the major problems. I think there are maybe signs that it is beginning to change . . . I am sure we have got it right.

Both these models may be viewed as attempts to disentangle a mass of responsibilities and prioritise some functions in a formal way. The benefits for the institution are considerable. Managerial accountability is separated from curriculum responsibility but is still located within the Head of Department's province. This diversion should allow a more focused effort in both directions and help alleviate some of the considerable anxiety that exists among many lecturers that HODs are too inward looking and uninterested (because pre-occupied) in changes which involve cross-curriculum activities and the interchange of resources.

Not least of these resources is the experience and expertise which individuals gain by involvement in various projects; all too often in the view of many respondents this expertise is buried within a department. A number of colleges have set up college-wide academic committees to cross fertilize this experience. But even where this is happening the results are not sufficiently disseminated. An example may be drawn from one college where I know this type of committee already meets regularly. Several lecturers who were worried because they knew *of* projects and experiments taking place in different parts of the college but did not really know *about* them. In a sense they felt their department was missing out. Unless some of that expertise was fed back into other departments, some areas of the college would be less able to respond to change. Not realizing it already existed, they suggested that such a mechanism should be set up as so much valuable expertise was currently untapped.

Perceptions of lecturing staff

Pro-active or re-active?

When I introduced myself to different individuals and groups I was frequently asked why I was interested in their college. The standard answer I gave was that they were perceived as being a pro-active institution. The Principalship and APL groups accepted this as an accurate description. HODs were generally pleased that the contribution their college was making had been recognised; they too were prepared to accept that description. Some lecturing staff also accepted the description uncritically but a large number of individuals, in groups or alone, challenged the assertion. One lecturer said:

> Very few colleges are pro-active, I think most colleges are *reactive*. And I think one of the barriers to institutional change is the common perception of 'wait and see'. The Examining and Validating Bodies will eventually — will actually — rewrite schemes in Competency terms. They will then issue guidelines, instructions, goals, profiles whatever it may be to local centres and Moderators will come round and say this is how you fix it in and this is what you do. In the end they will go on pretty well as they are. In other words there will be no institutional change. There will be pragmatic reaction responses to what the EV bodies do. So I think one of the barriers to institutional change is that the EV bodies are seen as the motor for change and that is incorrect. Colleges tend to think 'well, we know a lot about learning and we have always been in the position saying we have never been happy about how we assess the Learners on their particular scheme. We do it because this is what the EV bodies tell us to do'. Learners come here to get the qualification. And we say to them if you want to get the qualification you are going to have to do this, this and this, and this is how we assess it. And I think there is still a tendency for this to happen.

This particular lecturer was very well informed about what was supposed to be happening. He saw himself as a realist rather than a cynic. He welcomed the NCVQ initiative but he had strong reservations about the practicability of the infrastructure changes needed to support it.

This was quite a common perception. The ability of the NCVQ to exert influence at the pressure points which would actually bring about change was mentioned on a number of occasions:

> The changes required for NCVQ do run alongside and complement changes required in FE for all sorts of reasons but there is still a fundamental difference in that colleges . . . . Look, LEAs have power over the change required for local demographic change. They don't have that power over NVQs. . . . The vast majority of staff are going to say it costs too much and we will wait until the EAV bodies take the lead.

Decision about direction of change

Part of the reluctance to engage in 'deep change' was put down to earlier poor experience. It was possible 'to back the wrong horse':

L1   Some colleges have changed. Some may wish they hadn't changed in the way they had.

L2   Tertiary which was the flavour of the month a short time ago now appears less so and the Secretary of State is actually turning down schemes for tertiary which a while ago they would have passed on the nod.

L3   Colleges which dropped their A-Level teaching now wish they hadn't because performance indicators now favour those courses.

These comments expressed the view of lecturers on how senior management would respond. In fact, in every case senior management had declared itself fully committed to change. There appeared to be a serious communication problem or a credibility gap.

Degrees of change

Even when it was college policy to bring about institutional change in order to allow for the full development of NVQs, many lecturers had grave doubts about the eventual degree of change which would occur:

> I think what will happen is departments which start doing NVQs will say: 'Oh good, the rest of the college is going to be doing what we have been doing. We have always done that!'. And that will mean they won't actually feel the need to change. They will carry on teaching the knowledge based things to enable people as they have always done. It hasn't got through yet that there are a few engineering qualifications that have got through that are accredited.

In one college there was evidence that NVQ staff had started teaching without an adequate amount of training:

L: In business studies we've just started the diploma of office procedures which is an RSA and it's got the NVQ's stamp.

JB: Accreditation? It has got the full accreditation?

L: Yes, so staff in our department have started implementing that.

JB: In your department?

L: Yes. So presumably they'll have to use the NROVAs. I don't think they know about this yet. In fact I went to a conference about the NVQ import into it. They know RSA because they always used RSA qualifications so as far as they are concerned they are only now beginning to think of the NVQ implications of it. But apart from that I don't think... [she could think of any other NVQ in college].

In some colleges I visited the situation was demonstrably different. Staff who were either engaged in NVQ teaching or preparing to begin in the next academic year were very enthusiastic. It is important to point out that all the comments reported so far in this section were made by lecturers who were not themselves involved in teaching NVQ courses.

Responses from the limited number of people interviewed who had actually taught NVQs in different colleges tended to be very positive. The fact that they were actually engaged in something new had had a stimulating effect on them. In one college, staff were especially buoyed up by the support they had received in staff development programmes.

Staff development

The need for staff development was recognized everywhere. But again, there was a degree of cynicism about the possibility of mounting *adequate* and *institutional* programmes in some colleges:

L1   There is little evidence that what colleges are doing is developing colleges. Saying: 'In 1991 the chances are likely that most vocational courses we offer will be NCVQ therefore we need to engage in institutional change'. But it wasn't the case. Any change is a spin off, a change implemented in some places. It is a reaction to examining and validating bodies.

L2   I think there is a feeling that to become pro-active is very expensive and it is going to require real institutional change. It is going to require restructuring on a fairly radical scale and that is going to be fairly costly. Teaching staff need updating in the occupational section. If they are going to investigate learning opportunities in the industrial sector to identify methods of assessment, workplace learning; there are implications for time-tabling and there are implications for cost. You can't leave somebody teaching 21 hours and then expect them to spend a day in the workplace identifying them. There are all sorts of things we would like to do and we can't afford them. So there are two hinges for institutional change:

(a)   What are we going to do and how do we do it?
(b)   What is it going to cost?

I think the evidence is: where staff development has taken place is when the EAV bodies have asked for it. For example: in departments of business studies where they have chosen to run RSA level 1 and level 2, NVQs or the City and Guilds level 1 NVQ. That has actually provoked departments to embark on staff development programmes. But again it is a result of EAV bodies saying: from now on you want RSA office procedures; it is an NVQ — it's a new assessment skill. You are going to work out how you deliver it. In that sense it has still been colleges being reactive to Validating Bodies. Wherever it has been colleges undertaking institutional changes — you must know about Coventry — I mean massive institutional change. As it happens that institutional change has prepared Coventry for NCVQ but it took place in 1982 so it took place not as a result of NCVQ. We need similar change.

The reader may infer from many of the ethnographic transcripts produced above that many staff were extremely well informed about what was needed. Among those staff who weren't actually taking part in an NVQ programme there was a good deal of disbelief that colleges would be able to manage the staff training they felt would be essential.

Cynics

If the previous respondents could be classified as hard-edged realists rather than thorough-going cynics, there was a category of cynics which figured in a number of accounts. One Vice Principal distinguished three main groups by their responses to change:

My biggest worry is staff who are cynical. Who say 'we have seen it all before'. So you have got the people who will say they will never change the system and you have got the people who say yeah, they will change the system but only 25 per cent of the people will be involved in NVQs. For 75 per cent of people it will be very much the same where I lecture in groups of 15–18. And there are those who embrace the system and say the whole system is going to change. To be able to deal with cynical people is a major problem.

Anxieties with new practices

Some lecturers who had already started teaching NVQs experienced a range of concerns. The change from lecturing to a whole class, to a more student-centred approach caused practical difficulties and was far more demanding. One lecturer said she felt she might lose the esteem of her colleagues; she might be perceived as taking the easy way out. And there were ethical worries. Was she doing a good job? Were her students benefitting? Did the Vice Principal appreciate her difficulties:

I think they [fellow lecturers] need a change of attitude all round really. From the management point of view I think we need classes to be smaller because when you're going round a class of fifteen all doing different things it is exhausting, far harder than standing up and teaching them all the same thing at the same time. And yet there tends to be an attitude, 'well you're not really teaching them', because say I've got seven of them [business students] I'll give a booklet we've done for teach yourself subjects one, two, three and four would be doing something else and another four would be doing something else and they — well you're not really teaching them are you? They're teaching themselves. And from some of the students you get that as well, 'You haven't taught that, Miss. It's really from the book'. ... And this may have some sort of ethical, moral concerns on both the part of the teacher who is conscientious and wonders 'Am I giving my best?'. And also the students who might think, 'Oh am I getting a thin deal?'.

The Vice Principal would have to sell the idea and you might be able to do that by suggesting he lets people go with smaller classes to begin with because he recognizes that it is difficult to do it this way and he recognizes that people are in fact working hard doing it this way.

Constructing an ideal type to illustrate staff development problems

One of the major problems in dealing with ethnography is the time it takes to review it and the space it requires to present it. It's chief advantages lie in its authenticity, its immediacy and the richness of the data which obliquely reveals far more than the respondent may have consciously sought to communicate by the very way it is expressed. It cannot be validated by replication as in experiments; the chief means of validation lie in respondent validation and triangulation. In the course of gathering data, certain themes emerge as important in the perception of interviewees and this allows for a process of progressive focusing. Eventually various images begin to take shape. These images can then be tested by 'trying them out' in further interviews with either the same or similarly placed persons.

One of the areas of investigation which most interested me was the range of perceptions which individuals held about the possible barriers to the successful implementation of NVQs. I tried to elicit the views of a wide cross section of staff. From various different accounts of the difficulties some individuals would have in adapting to new methods of assessment, a less didactic, more student-centred, flexible approach, it seemed possible to assemble these images and construct an 'ideal type'. Who was the kind of lecturer who would most need support in adapting to a new role involving a genuine change of practice rather than mere outward aquiescence or compliance? This construct is given flesh and blood in a hypothetical case study:

> David Franklin, 45 years old, lecturer in engineering, motor mechanics.
>
> Left school at fifteen, embarked on an apprenticeship at Rolex Engineering. Served apprenticeship, attended one night per week at Technical College to enhance skills. Five years experience as a motor mechanic, gaining sound industrial experience. Applied for job at Technical College, became Lecturer. No formal lecturing training, but knowledgeable and good at job. Successful with his students because he had credibility. Soon absorbed the culture of his department and acquired the necessary teaching skills by association with other lecturers. Head of Department introduced various modifications into department in line with new developments required by EAV bodies.

Something approximating to a personal crisis occurs in 1989 or 1990. New NVQ requires facilitator approach and close liaison with industry.

> David Franklin has a problem because not only does he not possess the new skills required, he harbours secret doubts about his ability at this stage in his life to acquire them. He is uncomfortable about talk of 'new conceptual models' the technicalities of assessment and the implications of 'roll on, roll off' courses. Meanwhile his most secret fears are being realized. He based his legitimacy as a lecturer upon his industrial experience. He has conscientiously updated his teaching as required by his HOD but he must now face the fact that in the last twenty years the skills he acquired as an apprentice, later at college, and subsequently as a motor mechanic are now thoroughly out of date. Whereas in industry he worked as a mechanical engineer repairing engine components, the men now doing his job in industry are working in electronic fault diagnosis. Parts are no longer repaired, new sealed units are replaced. He is hardly in a position to offer expert college advice on assessment and is anxious about too much involvement in liaison.

It should be acknowledged that the biographical sketch is drawn in caricature form rather than as a representative portrait, deliberately emphasizing the most critical points from different accounts.

When I discussed this with a number of different respondents in different colleges most had little difficulty in identifying this man from their own experience *mutatis mutandis*. An HOD in one college offered the following respondent validation:

> Yes, I think that the scenario you presented would be recognized by Heads of Department as being very accurate, very realistic — possibly slightly polarized — but the analysis is thorough and valid and I think they would

empathize with the description and recognize it as a problem or the type of problem we have got to solve. I think unless any mode of change addresses itself to the complexity of these issues it is going to be struggling.

Alternative ideal type

Although most respondents agreed that the tumb nail sketch accorded largely with their experience, one senior manager was more critical. It transpired that his own background was very similar (he had left school at 16 to begin an apprenticeship in electrical engineering):

> Obviously with people like that you have got to find a way of allowing them back to industry. A man of 45 — you are not going to get rid of him. Someone like that — you have got another 20 years to get out of him. These are the people who stay with you — they don't go for promotion, they are not going to go elsewhere so you have got a problem.

However, whilst he conceded that some individuals could fit the scenario he had doubts about its broader applicability:

> I find in the college that the sort of people you describe are very, very much aware of the need to keep themselves abreast of changes taking place in industry and they do that. I find the major problem is not with those sort of people but with people who are, if you like, academics and have been dealing with A-Level people for the last so many years and are now flinding themselves deprived of A-level, say Physics, and eventually end up having to deal with BTEC 1st Diploma and they are the people with a problem.

The main problem, in his view, was that such people had a disdain for the very concept of competence. They were dedicated to a higher ideal of academic excellence. 'Competent' meant merely 'satisfactory'.

Another lecturer in a different college had a similar notion about the degree of attitude change which was going to be necessary. His remarks were framed in a broader context but are particularly apposite at this point:

> It is not just new practices and processes which are required but new concepts. There is a need for much development work to bring about a common perception of shared perspective.

The biggest problem in the perception of many respondents was the groups who would outwardly comply but not effect any real change in practice.

Conclusion

I have tried to focus on the situational knowledge which reflects the different perspectives and concerns of various groups and individuals within the case study colleges. Using a simple axis of pro-active/reactive, the data have ranged through a very broad spectrum of issues to reveal many of the concerns and preoccupations of the different members.

Another way of conceptualizing these data is to see them in terms of Kelly and Rudduck's (1976) distinction between 'dissemination' and 'diffusion', where dissemination is what the curriculum developer intends to happen and diffusion is what actually happens. Some of the themes which emerged may be grouped under different headings to allow for a degree of analysis. For the purposes of this chapter I shall focus on two; others may draw further conclusions from the data presented.

Scope for control

In my view there is a very strong correlation between the degree of power and control experienced by the individual and their commitment and enthusiasm for change. Thus the close identification with both the APL project and the successful implementation of NVQs arises out of an identity between self-interest and the interest of the college on the part of the Principalship. When the college decided to become involved it was their decision. It is part of their responsibility to be aware of 'direction': they form an overview of the needs of the college. This need may be recognized in terms of its expansion, its service to the community upon whose support it depends, or even in terms of the survival of the institution. All sorts of other concerns will be subsumed within these considerations — the progress of welfare of students, the job security of staff, the quality of provision, etc. But the Principalship makes policy. It is in charge — it provides leadership. The perception of these colleges studied as being pro-active is therefore well founded by outside publics, because there are plenty of examples of colleges which are not pro-active where senior management is not prepared to take risks, when the Principal may wish to move in more placid waters and not risk rocking the boat. Indeed this may be considered prudent management.

The APL leaders or coordinators are likewise pro-active. They were largely chosen (even if they volunteered) because they were seen as men or women who were in agreement with the philosophy at the top. They were also seen as individuals with potential for growth and the assumption of management responsibilities. A number of coordinators have received promotion at least partly in recognition of the effort they could be relied upon to make to the success of the project. In return for the opportunity, all APL staff have invested more time and effort than it would be reasonable to demand. They are undeniably pro-active.

Heads of Department are revealed as individuals who are beset with many sometimes conflicting demands. Their primary responsibility and accountability is in terms of the successful working of their department. As frequently pointed out, they have to take a broader view. They may be constrained by more pressing demands which arise out of managerial concerns which push them into making decisions based on pragmatism rather than a commitment to educational philosophy. The question of performance indicators is a simple example. Policy decisions may have to be taken at a higher level than HOD or indeed the Principalship if some of the dysfunctional pressures are to be eliminated; pressures may inhibit their full support for initiatives which currently may not be in their interests to pursue.

When we examine the attitudes of lecturers we see that many individuals rejected the pro-active label. Some found the very notion derisory. At lecturer level individuals are far less in control. Policy decisions may be made above their heads and they have to live with the consequences which may adversely affect their career prospects or run counter to their perceived self-interest. (This perceived self-interest may of course be professionally bound up with the promotion of their students' best interests). It is not surprising that many lecturers should resourcefully employ a range of strategies directed at circumventing imposed changes. The most frequently reported strategy was outward compliance — getting the paperwork right — with very little change in practice. It must be recognized that while management can legislate for change it cannot legislate for attitude and can do little effectively to change practice without a degree of cooperation. This may be withheld if it is not in the perceived best interest of the individual.

Help in changing practice

While some lecturers were undoubtedly cynical in their attitude I encountered a huge fund of goodwill in the colleges I visited. Most lecturers could see that change was inevitable. But many were very uneasy about the degree of change which was possible. The very breadth of possible changed was daunting. What was clearly required was a sufficiently ambitious staff development programme that took account of their needs. These included the development of skills in:

assessment
working as a facilitator rather than instructor
handling (or orchestrating as in primary teaching) individuals or groups at
    different levels in the same classroom or workplace
time management (without normal time-tabling frameworks)
record keeping
team teaching

counselling and guidance
industrial liaison.

But these skills could not be developed in isolation from a deeper understanding of new conceptual frameworks so that there was a shared understanding and common perspective: staff development linked to curriculum development.

There was a clamour for cross-institutional development so that resourcing and expertise could be shared in teaching, devising new materials and leading staff development courses. Much of the expertise to do these things was already in the college, but in many cases not available outside particular departments.

Beyond this there was a need for the kind of psychological support and understanding which had characterised the development of APL. Although this would not be on the same scale, staff would need the assurance that it took time to develop new expertise and that in the early stages progress would be hindered by lack of confidence which should not be confused with incompetence.

If we reflect on the change process we can see that anxieties are well founded. Attitudinal adjustment is important because without the 'right attitude' most people will not attempt to change practice. But actual change in practice is especially difficult to bring about even if people *have* the right attitude.

In the early stages of a career all sorts of difficulties are concentrated simply because of lack of experience. As people acquire experience they learn reliable ways of dealing with common problems. Most people eventually work out a routine so that they do not need to think about every little problem: there is a routinized way of dealing with recurring problems. We call this 'experience'.

When you ask an individual to change his or her practice you are in effect putting them into a novice situation where they may not be able to rely on past experience. In Eraut's memorable phrase, they lose their 'navigation lights'. They may lose all the reliable 'sign posts' they have developed to give themselves feedback on their performance. It is difficult to evaluate progress. It may be difficult to assess results.

In this situation most people feel threatened, and that is a perfectly natural response. They need psychological support because they may expose themselves to error and mistakes and this may be both stressful and discouraging. Without the 'right attitudes' the process is even more difficult, because individuals will not even try to effect changes in practice. As Handy (1976) suggests, individuals often find it hard to escape from the role that cultural traditions have defined for them:

> Role ambiguity results when there is some uncertainty . . . as to what his
> role is at any given time . . . but ambiguity may lead to role stress.

As departmental cultural traditions are so ingrained in many departments in FE this is an especially difficult problem. Without adequate support, the A-Level teacher cited earlier will have real difficulties in adjusting. Handy (1976) lists the four most frequently observed instances of role ambiguity which occur in work situations; each has a bearing on the kind of adjustment which will be required:

uncertainty about how one's work is evaluated
uncertainty about scope for advancement
uncertainty about scope for responsibility
uncertainty about other's expectations of one's performance.

There are, of course, many other kinds of role conflict which may occur, ranging from role overload, to role underload which may affect performance, self concept and morale.

The inescapable conclusion I draw from this brief review is the need for a thorough-going needs analysis as a basis for staff development, which takes account of the different and legitimate self-interests of different groups. There are many different starting points and many different needs. Where serious staff development — especially residential courses — has been undertaken, it has been noticeably effective in the colleges I visited, but there is clearly a need for more and that more should be carefully targeted. Moreover, it should be clearly linked to curriculum development and a coherent policy on resourcing, so that participants may be empowered not only to identify need but to actually implement change.

Some of the problems arose because staff are socialized within a strongly hierarchical and heavily segmented organization; to help offset problems which result from this form of socialization, staff development should be linked to institution-wide provision and, where possible, institutional development. Staff can hardly be expected to teach in an open, flexible, integrated way unless these patterns of organization are mirrored to some extent and valued in the organization and ethos of the college. The cross-institution, participatory mode of working which was encouraged and developed among APL coordinators provides a valuable insight into how the competence and experience of staff may be recognized and harnessed in promoting change. An extraordinary 'release' of enthusiasm and directed effort occurred when they were given a responsibility and a stake in developing the responsiveness of the college.

References

ERAUT, M. (1988) 'Learning about management: The role of the management course' in POSTER, C. and DAY, C. (Eds) *Partnership in Education Management*, London, Routledge.
GOFFMAN, I. (1971) *The Presentation of Self in Everyday Life*, Harmondsworth, Penguin.
HANDY, C.B. (1976) *Understanding Organizations*, Harmondsworth, Penguin.
KELLY, P. and RUDDUCK, J. (1976) *The Dissemination of Curriculum Development*, London, NFER.
OPPENHEIM, A.N. (1966) *Questionnaire Design and Attitude Measurement*, London, Heinemann.
POPKEWITZ, T.S. (1984) *Paradigm and Ideology in Educational Research: Social Functions of the Intellectual*, Lewes, Falmer Press.

Chapter 11

Towards the implementation of competence based curricula in colleges of FE

Ian Haffenden and Alan Brown

Introduction

This chapter is based on research undertaken by the University of Surrey and commissioned by the Further Education Unit; this report is organised on the following basis. Section 1 provides a general context to our work. There is an outline of the project approach, a short background note to our discussions with college staff and other interested parties, a brief summary of the features of the new system of National Vocational Qualifications and our initial delineation of the nature and scope of the change being brought about by the implementation of this new system. We do this by considering the implications of this change for colleges in the medium term.

Section 2 outlines our general findings, as many of the concerns of staff and their analyses of the effect of change were common across sectors. This section is divided into sub-sections on perceptions about the nature of competence; consideration of the implications of NVQs for curriculum development, staff development and institutional development; and assessment.

Section 3 gives sector-specific commentaries, in the four areas: agriculture, clerical, hairdressing and caring. Appendix 2 carries a fuller commentary upon the sector-specific findings.

Section 4 seeks to look forward with the identification of major issues which will need to be addressed. This section contains our commentary upon key issues in curriculum development, staff development and institutional development coupled with a separate sub-section upon the crucial area of work based learning and assessment. It should be emphasised that our reflections are grounded upon what is actually happening in colleges. Thus, for example, Appendix 1 outlines how one group of college staff were involved in framing an embryonic college-wide response to the challenges presented by NVQs.

Section 5 looks at possible ways forward for the Project, especially for Phase 2, and more generally at the process of managing change.

One final comment should be made about the nature of this report. The project is continuing, but it was felt important to produce this report as a means of disseminating and influencing the processes we were scrutinising. To this end then, this report should be treated as an interim report as not all the information collected has been utilised here. Rather, this report seeks to further discussion, both within and outside Phase 2 of the Project, of the implications of the implementation of competence based curricula. This report then is not summative, it is not the end of the process, but rather a stage along the way. We would, therefore, welcome feedback and critical comment from those reading this report. Any such comment could then inform continuing developments.

1. General context

1.1 Project approach

The primary aim of the project was to investigate, nationally, key aspects in the implementation of competence based curricula in four vocational areas in Further Education. The intention then was to investigate the factors affecting the aims, design, implementation and evaluation of competence based provision. The vocational areas were chosen to reflect diversity in the extent to which their provision was already competence based.

In order to achieve the project aims, the researchers intended to interview two sets of people (although there was some overlapping membership): those with an overview of national and/or regional developments and those more directly concerned with provision. The first group were easy to identify using both our own and FEU intelligence, coupled with an explicit snowballing process of asking the first respondents who they considered were the key figures with an overview of developments. Who to contact in the second group (those concerned with delivery) posed slightly greater problems. The methods used to identify the first group could be applied to some extent here also to identify colleges where significant developments were taking place.

However, this brought with it dangers that we would see pockets of perhaps highly unrepresentative individuals or groups of staff, who were aware of the significance of NVQs and were already framing a response. Conversely though, we did not wish to spend a great deal of time at places where we believed 'not much was happening'. In the event, we adopted a strategy which sought to balance contributions from both sub-groups. We interviewed mainly activity managers, but also tutors and those with special responsibilities for curriculum development and/or staff development, in colleges with significant activity in one of our chosen vocational areas. (In agriculture, we also had discussions with those responsible for management of the institution. In other areas, those with institutional management responsibilities were only seen if they were picked up in the national or regional trawl. The researchers made a conscious decision to focus upon those directly concerned with implementation, yet there is a clear need for further work to be carried out on the implications of the implementation of competence based curricula with those with institutional management responsibilities).

At the same time, whenever we were visiting a college to talk about one or two vocational areas, we sought to interview staff from the other areas as well. By this means, it was possible to build a more representative picture in a way which was economic with our effort. The picture of both exceptional and unexceptional practice was supplemented by attendance at seminars and other events directly relevant to issues associated with the development of NVQs and again through interviewing those responsible for regional and/or national staff development activities. Thus impressions and intelligence, again supplemented by close liaison with FEU staff, about 'what was happening on the ground' could be tested and underpinned by interviews with college staff with widely varying awareness, understanding and experience of the implications of the implementation of competence based curricula. A list of colleges and other organisations most directly involved in our research is given in Appendix 3.

The project looked at a full range of curricular issues, although in the interviews particular attention was focused upon perceptions about the nature of competence, approaches to learning and teaching, the role of the 'team' in the curriculum development process, industrial liaison and involvement, assessment, moderation, staff development, credit accumulation, access and progression.

The outcomes of the first phase of the project were to include an analysis of the key issues involved in the implementation of competence based curricula, an identification of the nature and the extent of good practice in this field and the range of staff development and training required for effective implementation.

1.2 Background to responses of college staff

Unsurprisingly, the reactions of college staff in the different vocational areas varied according to the imminence of major curricular change. However, most staff were interpreting the changes mainly in terms of the effect on courses in their vocational area. This tended to produce a response of 'wait and see' what happens to particular qualifications, with the expectation that changes will be mediated by examining and validating bodies. The medium-term implications were acknowledged, but the extent of change within FE over the last decade meant that most staff felt that immediate concerns were the most pressing. Where broader issues were addressed, this was usually because college staff had been involved in national or regional initiatives, pilot projects, etc. It was still relatively unusual for a college to be framing a college-wide response, although this could be seen in embryonic form in some places.

1.3 National vocational qualifications

In the light of partial awareness of developments in this field, it might be helpful to reiterate briefly some of the features of the new system of National Vocational Qualifications. The basic task of NCVQ is to establish a coherent national framework for vocational qualifications and to relate those qualifications to the standards required for competent performance in employment. The NCVQ framework envisages in the first instance four levels to which vocational qualifications will be allocated. The levels of occupational competence will be defined by industry lead bodies. The provision of examining and validating bodies will then be scrutinised and conditional approval will be given to those qualifications which meet the NCVQ criteria. The target date for approving vocational qualifications in all the main occupational sectors is 1991. This means that even in sectors where there is apparently little happening in terms of college activity and course provision at present, further back among EAV bodies, industry lead bodies and NCVQ itself, plans are being made which will have a major impact in the relatively near future.

NCVQ has published full details of the criteria which qualifications must meet to be accredited as NVQs in *The NVQ Criteria and Related Guidance* (January 1988), and FEU and NCVQ, both singly and jointly, publish regular bulletins outlining the latest stage in developments. Briefly, however, an NVQ must embody a 'statement of competence' which has to be achieved to employment led standards before a candidate can receive an award. The work involved in the development of employment led standards varies between occupational sectors depending upon the type and pattern of existing qualifications. Industry lead bodies, some specially devised for the purpose, will play the decisive role in the establishment of agreed standards of competence, with support from the Training Agency.

An NVQ is composed of a number of units of competence, each one of which can be separately recorded and accredited. Each unit is itself sub-divided into elements of competence, to which are attached performance criteria. These criteria indicate the standards of competence to be achieved. NVQs are expressed in terms of *outcomes* and will not mention content, modes of delivery or how, where and when competence is developed.

The most striking features then for the FE system as a whole relate both to the breadth and depth of change which will be required. In terms of the numbers of staff who will be directly affected over the next three or four years, this will have greater impact than the advent of BTEC, YTS and CPVE *combined*. Similarly, the development of NVQs will be more radical in its effect on virtually all aspects of vocational education and training: design, delivery, assessment and evaluation.

1.4 Medium-term implications

That many college courses will seek to link explicitly with occupational competences could mean students spend less time in formal classes in college. Links with work placement providers are then pivotal: even where these are long-established (e.g., caring and agriculture) the nature of the relationship will need to alter to meet new assessment requirements.

College staff may then have much more of a strategic role in the learning and assessment process as a whole. To facilitate the integration of college-based and workplace provision could require college staff to play a major role supporting the provision of work-based learning. Techniques and approaches to assessment will need to be reviewed, but such technical changes will be only one part of a major overhaul of curriculum design and delivery. Provision will have to be made for candidates taking units of accreditation at different times and speeds.

Also, it should not be assumed that individuals will restrict themselves to a single route and again this has implications for how college provision *as a whole* is presented (e.g., the need for a credit accumulation policy).

The new assessment systems will require monitoring, and college staff, because of their key strategic position, can play an important role in supporting and enhancing a system of workplace assessment. Applied to this, however, will be the need for colleges to calculate the real costs of the implementation of such a system.

If colleges do switch from primarily course-production to a much more mixed mode of operation whereby they also provide a much wider range of consultancy services (e.g., training needs analysis, assessment support, training and supporting workplace trainers and supervisors, development of and support for the delivery of open learning materials, etc.), then the staff development to support and deliver such a system will itself need to be comprehensive, including management training.

Colleges will require a strategy to deal with the assessment of prior achievement, and similarly credit transfer can be seen as playing a key part in the system as a whole. (Transfer within a single EAV body's provision should prove unproblematic, but the crux will be how easy it is to transfer between awards by different bodies).

The role of regional organisations in supporting colleges in staff development should be recognised. Regional Advisory Councils, Regional Curriculum Bases, etc. can help staff development not only through the promotion of regional events, but also in coordinating and facilitating transfer of 'good practice' between colleges. There is a wide 'gap' between what is promulgated at national level and the response which is made by individual colleges. To some extent, national organisations (such as

NEBAHAI) have responded with regional seminars, but these are not a substitute for continuing and coordinated action at a regional level. Indeed it could be argued that the most pressing need is not for further development work at national level, although that is clearly also required, but for a sustained programme of staff development in an attempt to close the 'gap'. Without this, there is a real danger that the disjunction between rhetoric and reality will widen still further. However, the most recent LEAs Training Grants circular (August 1988) has cut staff development for colleges by 25 per cent. DES are keen to promote staff development for the (schools) core curriculum and NVQ issues are not seen as a priority area.

This leads on to broader questions about source of funding for staff development: DES, TA, LEAs, national and regional bodies and colleges themselves all have interests and responsibilities in this area. How to coordinate such provision and ensure staff development addresses medium-term (and strategic) issues relating to the implementation of competence based curricula is itself a major issue. Needless to say, the principles outlined above should be applied to any staff development programme itself.

A further major change will come in the interaction between colleges and work placements. The emphasis given to work-based assessment in the new system will necessitate some major changes in role for college staff. The major client groups, delivery mechanisms and models of learning may all require radical reassessment. The changes to the relationship between college tutors and work placements is clearly then of central importance. Some possible ways this relationship may develop are discussed in Section 4.4 on work based learning and assessment.

2 General findings

This section outlines our general findings, as many of the concerns of staff and their analyses of the effect of change were common across the four occupational sectors.

2.1 Perceptions about the nature of competence

Competence was defined broadly within colleges across the four vocational areas. Analysis of the definitions given by college staff provided six distinct categories. Definitions related to:

role
criteria
level of support to the trainee
task
personal competence, and
no explicit definition of competence.

Role related definitions of competence were found in all four vocational areas. There was the tendency here, however, to view competence in fairly limited terms of skill development and proficiency or performance and speed. Two types of role related definitions of competence emerged. The first type were definitions of the form 'able to *operate* appropriately and independently within a limited area of skills', undertaking part of the full role. The second type were in terms of definitions of the role related to a range of 'levels' of worker: craft level, supervisory level, etc. Sometimes role related definitions of competence were seen in terms of the expected role performed by a 'competent mature adult worker'.

Criteria related definitions of competence were viewed in pass — fail terms. The definitions offered here were typically of the form 'can do it/can't do it' or 'can be achieved at will' versus 'has been achieved once'.

The third form of definition of competence offered by college staff (in hairdressing and clerical in particular) in many ways forms a bridge between the first two categories given above. Here, competence was defined in terms of three levels of support. The trainee either could not do the work and required supervision, could partly do the work and was supervised periodically, or could do the work unsupervised.

For some college staff, competence was defined in terms of the task. Trainees were defined as competent if they could work to employer standards for specified tasks.

In addition, those college staff who defined competence in the above ways also held contrasting perspectives as to what was meant by a competence based and competence led curriculum. In the case of competence based curriculum Unit Based Schemes were clear this meant a curriculum based upon the skills and training specifications laid down by the industrial training body, whereas some agricultural departments, for example, saw it meaning a curriculum based on the *existing* standards and tests administered by the National Proficiency Training Council (NPTC). To others, however, it meant any curriculum that was student centred and/or skill based.

Staff ideas relating to what was meant by a competence led curriculum were less clear. To many college staff it raised concerns over the use of *minimum* standards and the division of responsibility between colleges and industry. There was a lack of clear meaning as to what was meant by a competence led curriculum. However, as we will argue later, given clarification the idea of a competence led curriculum could have considerable merit in leading the process of curricular change.

The final two sets of responses given by college staff emphasise the gulf between those au fait with the latest developments and those with only a hazy idea of what is meant by competence.

Some college staff considered that one way to ensure that competence is not seen simply in terms of 'can do' statements could be to switch the emphasis. Thus course teams could be encouraged to view their aim as being to produce *competent people* rather than occupational competence. Personal competence could be then viewed as incorporating learning skills, personal responsibility and personal development. Particularly in relation to young people, for example, it was felt one of the key components of competence should be their ability 'to pick up the threads' in future when their skills required updating. However, how well this fits in with industrial conceptions of occupational competence was felt to vary widely, with perhaps one factor helping to produce such varying responses being size of firm. Larger organisations take the view that they need flexible people, who may be asked to fulfil various roles in future. In such cases, personal competence should increase the likelihood of transfer of skills, knowledge and experience and so reduce training time and effort. By contrast, industries with a large number of smaller establishments may feel that the over-riding need is for people to be able to perform the immediate tasks.

Related to the idea of personal competence is the extension of the can't/can do division to include a further stage of 'will do'. That is, to try to convey the idea that competence goes beyond a technical assessment of whether a person is able to carry out particular tasks and includes a predictive element that they will be able to respond and perform in roles as a whole.

Another extension proposed, notably by Japanese companies working in this country, was that the stage beyond 'can do' was 'can show or teach others'. These skills relate most clearly to the role of the supervisor or work place trainer, but on occasion may also be required of other workers. Again, such a concern reflects the feeling that skills are required of some of the workforce so as to be able to effect quickly a change in the skills of the workforce as a whole. In this view then, personal effectiveness, learning to learn, etc., are seen as integral to conceptions of occupational competence.

In sharp contrast it should be noted that some of those involved in the implementation of competence based curricula treated the issue of competence as unproblematic. Either they responded that they used the definition given (by an EAV body or other interested party), but could not say what this was. They were treating the whole issue as being in the realm of 'common sense' or intuitive understanding and did not probe either their own or others thoughts on this. Hence they had no sense of having to engage with some of the broader issues in order to have to 'work through' how it applied to their area of work. This meant they would be unable to mount a critical examination or evaluation of whether the implementation contradicted in any way the underlying aims and objectives. They were working with a very restricted model of curriculum development, and were perhaps not necessarily expecting that there would be major change in some of their areas of work.

Others were aware of the plethora of opinions about competence and its definition, but they felt that this could be bypassed in that objectives and performance criteria had been spelt out in their area of work and these could then be accepted as given.

In summary, it can be seen that there are widely differing perceptions about the nature of competence. The most coherent and comprehensive view of competence relates to personal competence. The advantages of such an approach are manifold, not least simply because it underlines the centrality of people. The diversity of opinion about competence in itself can be viewed as indicative of the need for a much fuller programme of staff development — not to impose a single understanding of the nature of competence, rather to get broad agreement upon the overall direction the curriculum should take. In this sense, although it may seem a little ·pedantic, it is important that curricula should be *competence led* rather than just be seen as competence based — the latter term being perhaps too passive and reactive, whereas use of the former term could be seen as indicative of curricular change which has *direction* and *purpose*, and is itself *a process* rather than being a state which has or has not been attained. The curriculum should then be *led* by the broadly-defined goal of personal competence.

2.2 Implications of NVQs for curriculum development, staff development and institutional development

Curriculum development

When considering the response of staff throughout a college to the implications of NVQs for curriculum development, it was clear that two factors were particularly significant in raising general awareness. Firstly: if the college was actively involved in national or regional development work. Involvement in pilot projects or other development work often heightened awareness elsewhere in the college, although the extent to which this opportunity was built upon depended largely upon the second factor: whether there was a clear institutional lead in making such connections. The lead could come directly from a clear commitment from college management to the importance of an initiative (this was often a primary factor behind the enthusiasm with which regional initiatives were picked up by different colleges). Alternatively, in some colleges the lead could come from a specialist unit like a Curriculum Development Unit.

Such a unit could have among its functions the gathering of intelligence about significant developments and offering support to departments/sections in working through the implications. This support was particularly welcomed by staff in some vocational areas who had reservations about the initial approach being adopted by their industry lead bodies. The realisation that NVQs did not necessarily mean narrowing the curriculum was often welcomed. Thus a reassurance that the overall goal was 'to prepare people for change' by developing a flexible, adaptable workforce, helped to stiffen resolve for some to resist any temptation to focus exclusively upon a skills-based curriculum. In addition, the support of a CD unit could help staff, in areas where some courses were now competence based, to frame a response which took account of consequent changes: for example, processes to look at prior learning, open entry and exit to courses and orientation phases to facilitate course choice.

A further area where the CD unit could offer support was in the process of bringing about change in the classroom. It was felt that students may sometimes act as a brake on initiatives in that they held a conservative view of the learning process. In such circumstances, unless the tutor feels committed to change there may be temptations to seek to minimize the change to existing practices. The CD unit could help the tutor seek to institutionalise processes, whereby student perceptions of the learning process were aligned with the direction of change rather than operating against it. Thus, if systems are instituted whereby students formulate personal action plans, and are given some responsibility for carrying these out, then this may help break down expectations of students that they should be passive recipients. (This is not to downplay, however, the extent to which such changes have already taken place within schools and FE over the last decade, but rather to acknowledge that there are some areas where traditional attitudes and practices have remained among tutors and/or students).

The effect of the NVQs on course organisation was seen as profound. There was a recognition among many of the more aware tutors that college-wide responses to re-organising the curriculum would be required. For example, the need to secure greater involvement and integration with industry, which in turn would require industry liaison time. Similarly, with the increasing modularisation of courses, staff time on the design, development, production and assessment of materials would need to be allocated. The role of course teams was seen as likely to become more significant in putting such programmes together, providing support and guidance in the lecturer's changing role, including increasing student counselling responsibilities. Indeed, the variety of skills required might mean that rather than individual lecturers being expected to be able to undertake any of these duties, there might be increasing specialisation. In such circumstances, course teams would become even more vital. This in turn would mean that the management of resources within and across teams would need central consideration in the organisation of National Vocational Qualifications in colleges.

Moreover, some colleges are already developing specialised areas to deliver student centred, open learning packages, capable of independent study, to mesh in with NVQ levels of competence. The provision of such flexible learning opportunities were again seen as having major curricular implications, leading to the development of resource areas (and changing the face of conventional library provision).

Additionally, it was pointed out that colleges will need to look carefully at the implications of continuous assessment replacing end of year examinations, standardised courses across departments and the need to reduce staff-student ratios to accommodate changes in style and method of delivery. The structure of courses will then require radical reassessment, not least because for financial reasons pressure will be on to increase rather than reduce staff — student ratios. To some extent it may be possible to reconcile the competing pressures by having fewer formal classes with the teacher operating in a didactic mode. Greater independent learning, coupled with mixing of a number of groups/individuals working in the same room with a tutor acting as a common resource may help offset the cases where a tutor has to work with very small groups or even individuals (although in such circumstances one could question the efficacy of staff — student ratios as a meaningful indicator of efficiency or performance).

The delivery of courses was seen as an area which will be particularly affected by the introduction of NVQs. For example, college staff expect that formal teaching will decline with more practical work and open and individualised learning replacing it. They see their role changing with more administration and assessment together with responsibility for designing and facilitating learning. New skills will be needed to achieve this, including the ability to design and write learning programmes which enable the assessment of competence to a range of specified standards.

To facilitate such changes within the NCVQ requirements will need the creation and maintenance of effective communication channels and structures both within the college and between college staff and their industrial counterparts. College — industry links need to be strengthened and a number of colleges were seeking to achieve this either through the appointment of college — industry link officers with a staff development role or else by encouraging staff throughout the college to build such links.

That such changes would significantly affect access and progression was widely recognised by college staff. There would be an opening up of opportunities for students and this would require more flexible responses to entry, delivery and progression. It was felt that these changes could include the development of more roll-on roll-off courses with students choosing individualised packages from a menu of core and option choices. A pick-'n'-mix arrangement was envisaged by many with modularised programmes, which were student centred and based on flexible and open learning approaches. More open access for mature students was expected and it was felt likely that there would be more intensive cost-recovery short course programmes for industry to generate income.

It was generally thought that to facilitate progression new programmes would have to be modular. As a result, in addition to the changes outlined above, colleges would have to improve internal communications and their marketing policies. Hence not only would improved communications between departments be required but also with college administration. The marketing of courses would need to be integrated on a college-wide basis.

Thus, while college staff could see the necessity to address issues associated with credit accumulation and transfer, to some extent they felt they could not take full advantage of the opportunities for more open access and flexible provision for two reasons. One related to the need for EAV bodies to 'get their act together' in deciding upon parity between different awards and in recognising all or part of each other's qualifications, presumably with the 'encouragement' of NCVQ. The other reason was financial. Such an overhaul would be costly in terms of resources, particularly staff time. Without support, change was likely to proceed piecemeal over a relatively long period of time. The sheer scale of the curricular changes that college staff envisaged as consequent upon the implementation of National Vocational Qualifications should highlight two critical issues.

Firstly, one should recognise that there is a major difference between some (far-sighted) tutors being able to articulate the curricular changes consequent upon the implementation of National Vocational Qualifications and the realisation of those changes. We shall return to this theme in Section 5.2 on the management of change. The second issue concerns evaluation.

College staff said relatively little directly about evaluation, but they were concerned about the wisdom of some of the curricular changes which they saw as consequent upon the implementation of National Vocational Qualifications. In addition, reservations were sometimes expressed about the selection and specification of the competences themselves. The latter is fundamental, given the strategic importance of competence in the new system. Any review of competences, at element and unit level as well as in relation to the role as a whole, should include a *systematic evaluation* as to how they are being developed and assessed both in workplaces and colleges. College staff should then have an opportunity for input, based upon their experience of the operation of the system in practice.

In relation to college based evaluation, some staff mentioned the possibility that a Curriculum Development Unit could play a spearhead role in this by, for example, reviewing local standards of moderation, ensuring college-based materials were reviewed and kept up to date, etc. Otherwise, there was uncertainty about how this could best be achieved.

Finally, although this section has focused primarily upon curriculum development, the artificiality of the tripartite division (although nevertheless useful) can be clearly seen. Time and again curriculum development issues raised here have had major implications for both staff development and institutional development. Indeed, although the starting point for reviewing curriculum development for NVQs may be a consideration of how courses should be structured, delivered and supported, the paucity of such a limited approach should become readily apparent. A more fundamental and thorough-going review is required, involving major changes in each of the three components. It is to the second of these, staff development, to which we now turn.

Staff development

In developing and delivering NVQs, college staff recognised they will need to look at a wider range of teaching and learning strategies than are currently used. For example, the following need be reviewed: team teaching, cross college mixed provision, student centred learning, industrial involvement in the design, delivery and assessment of courses, possibly both in industry and at the college. More guidance will also be required to enable the fuller integration of theory and practice in the development of practical assignments. Each of these may be already taking place to some degree within the college, but the need for them to take place upon a much wider scale was seen as having significant staff development implications. Indeed there was a concern that the experience of existing 'pockets' of 'good practice' might not be translated across colleges, because of a lack of suitable arrangements for cross-fertilisation between departments, across sectors, etc.

College staff in all four sectors considered staff development to be pivotal to the successful implementation of NVQs. However, many colleges also pointed out that the introduction of NVQs was often considered secondary to more immediate problems facing the colleges, the most significant concern being the effect of the Educational Reform Act on college survival and jobs. Thus this wider context will have to be taken into account during the implementation of NVQs as it forms the environment in which staff recruitment and development will take place.

College staff indicated that there would be a need for substantial work shadowing or work secondments to be organised and funded if NVQs were to be effectively delivered. Moreover, improved communications between industry and college are necessary to ensure effective liaison with the workplace and the maintenance of reliable industry based assessment. This theme is developed further in Section 4.4 but it should be noted the staff development required is double edged with both college and industrial staff needing to learn equally from each other, with mutual respect for each others' competences. The introduction of NVQs is also likely to lead to increased use of part-time, untrained staff, with relevant industrial or commercial experiences to share, but perhaps without formal training. This body of staff will thus need training and support.

Another aspect of staff development relates to curriculum design, delivery and assessment, as required for the new NVQs. To achieve this, it has been suggested that a clear structure and programme of continual professional development of staff is required. The content of such a programme would need to be extensive. For example, staff themselves identified the following as issues to be addressed in a staff development programme.

They could be grouped into two categories. Firstly, those directly related to the implementation of competence based curricula. The second set concern wider issues which are clearly affected by and/or made more urgent by the advent of NVQs, but are not wholly attendant on these changes, relating as they do a much broader pattern of change in FE.

The issues which related more specifically to the implementation of competence based curricula were identified as: clarification of the definition of competence and its implications in practice; updating to include more frequent and detailed guidance and information about the implications of implementation; involving the workplace in the curriculum, helping and guiding the workplace in administration, assessment and certification; staff development and support in the theory, planning, course design and assessment of competences.

The broader staff development issues which college staff thought needed to be considered in a wider context included: development of skills relating to team teaching, resource allocation, marketing both targeted at particular new client groups and integrated marketing across departments, use of information technology and approaches to student management, administration and record-keeping. In addition, whole sets of skills would be required to support more flexible learning provision. For example, the ability to create and facilitate specialised areas for individualised open learning; programme design for individualised provision, menu and modular approaches.

Such changes would involve a further shift towards a more student centred approach, with the staff needing to recognise that this can involve a variety of teaching and learning strategies. Indeed it was argued that developing an awareness of the need for contingent approaches to student centred learning, including the setting of an appropriate balance between didactic and more open approaches, could itself be one of the goals of a staff development programme.

Staff development is a broad area and in this particular context, following on from our arguments in Section 2.1, it might be more useful to speak of competence led staff development. (This line of argument was followed by FEU and NCVQ in July 1988 in the promotion of their joint pamphlet *Competence-led staff development*). Competence led staff development would necessitate moving *all* staff from an awareness of NVQs to a more thorough understanding of their implications. Alongside this, however, there will be a need to match staff development with the particular *roles* staff will play in the system.

The breadth and scale of the staff development suggested is vast, although it could be made slightly more manageable if staff development needs were matched to the different role requirements of different groups of staff. However, such an approach would make most sense if it were conducted on an inter-college basis, and this would presumably require a degree of regional coordination. We will return to this issue later. Indeed, staff development as a whole is such a key area that it is a major theme of this report and will be taken further in Section 4.2.

Institutional development

The research indicates that there are major implications for college-wide reorganisation and development as a result of the introduction of a new national system of vocational qualifications. Role changes will be required throughout colleges. The functions of those primarily responsible for organisation and deployment of resources and those primarily responsible for delivery would both need review. Obviously those staff with dual responsibilities would similarly have to reconsider their role within the organisation as a whole. Clearly in such circumstances all staff with a staff development role would also need to review their responsibilities (and the scale of change required would presumably require *more* staff to undertake a staff development role).

Demographic trends coupled with the tighter financial constraints on colleges (see *Managing a Changing FE*, FEU, 1988), are giving great impetus for change. The direction of change is not however the same in all cases. Some college staff considered that their institutions might respond to financial pressure and the degree of change required to implement new vocational qualifications by seeking to expand their A-Level provision. It was felt this route might be both more familiar and financially more secure. For example, the point was made that this might be one means of maintaining or increasing staff — student ratios, whereas changes to vocational qualifications might lead to moves in the opposite direction (that is, although attempts to deliver individualised learning might be worthy and desirable on pedagogic grounds, in the short-term they might prove expensive). Other colleges, however, were being a little bolder and were looking to diversify their provision to new client groups and to include courses that were income generating. These courses are often aimed at local industry and commerce. Further, even to ensure the provision of existing courses the need for a wider marketing strategy is becoming recognised, opening up the colleges to a wider age range of clients per course.

Financial constraints are therefore reinforcing other pressures (including demographic change and the development of new qualifications) leading to changes in the client groups and how colleges will respond to client needs. If the college was seeking a substantial slice of vocational provision (rather than expanding other provision and adopting a 'wait and see' attitude to NVQ developments), then staff argued the need for changes in college organisation becomes clearer. To facilitate both financial and course changes there is a need to move towards less full-time and more part-time courses, credit transfer between and credit accumulation within modularised course programmes, more roll-on roll-off facilities which require more individualised self-instructional materials and open learning approaches. This will result in the need for more individualised student support of an individualised type and possibly more staff per 'group' of students. To enable this and to develop competences effectively and cheaply (as colleges will not be the sole agents involved in the development and assessment of competences) there will be a further need for a greater integration of staff and resources, with the boundaries between departments weakening.

For the above changes to be brought about for all levels of staff will require substantial staff development. It is likely that senior staff will have increased responsibility for staffing, marketing, salary negotiations and resourcing. Moreover, comments were made that the attitudes of many senior staff would need to be changed to enable the rhetoric of student centred learning to become practised in the classrooms. Further the teaching of flexible classes will mean that 'bums on seats' becomes an inappropriate measure of course success.

For teaching staff, role changes have already been outlined above. In short, the effect of institutional changes will bring about an increase in part-time staff, moves towards industrial training as opposed to teaching, with full-time staff becoming course designers, facilitators, material developers and assessors.

As stated earlier, a marked difference was found between those staff who had been involved in working parties, pilot projects or in other ways formally considering implications of the implementation of the new system of National Vocational Qualifications in some way and those who had not. The latter often complained about a lack of information and communication about the implications for courses with which they were involved. (It should be further noted that to a large extent, the responses of those who had so far had little involvement were gleaned from either talking to college staff in other settings — courses, briefings or other meetings — or from ancillary visits. That is, when we visited a college which was 'active' in one sector, we also sought out staff from our other sectors. Thus we were able to ascertain views from staff with a range of experience, without setting up formal visits to people and departments who were largely so far inactive [in our terms]. This clearly gave such departments some exposure to changes taking place elsewhere).

Symptomatic of current concerns about finance, a number of respondents mentioned the tension between the type of changes required and attempts to reduce costs. They recognised that the cost of putting on new flexible learning programmes is likely to be high in a number of respects. There will be significant costs associated with a major staff development exercise to re-orient staff and equip them with the necessary competence. The start-up costs of introducing such programmes are likely to be high (compare experiences of Open Tech; Open College, etc.). The search for greater individualisation or 'tailoring' of learning and the pursuit of greater industrial relevance will also inevitably generate expenditure. Some of the activities undertaken in pursuit of these goals, for example visiting trainees in the workplace, may not be formally recognised. Similarly, the assessment systems required to meet the NCVQ criteria are likely to be significantly more expensive than existing ones in most cases.

The whole issue of costs was one which for many of our respondents 'set alarm bells ringing'. However, most of our respondents were activity managers rather than staff with major financial responsibilities, so this is an area which needs further investigation. The impression given by activity managers was that many of the concerns of those with overall financial responsibility were with developing management information systems which could generate the type of performance indicators mentioned in the Joint Efficiency Study. Many of these indicators were looking backwards to an FE of the mid-1980s or even before. Indicators like staff — student ratios, average class size and exam pass rates will be very clumsy (indeed largely inappropriate) in dealing with the type of FE system required of the 1990s.

In summary then, when considering the implications of the implementation of competence based curricula for institutional development, it is important to look at other factors currently impinging upon colleges as organisations. When this is done, it can be seen that according to one scenario a synergy is developing in the need for colleges to seek new clients (due to demographic change), the increasing emphasis upon adult learning (including both retraining and continuing education and training), the requirement to open up access and delivery through recognition of prior learning and development of flexible learning and the reformation of vocational qualifications and the changes that entails. These changes could mutually reinforce one another in a dynamic way, but it is important that they relate to all college activities. For example, mainstream activities should be flexible, rather than open learning being seen as a bolt-on to existing provision.

2.3 Assessment

Of all the changes National Vocational Qualifications are likely to bring about, it is their effect on assessment that is causing greatest concern. Where some college staff feared the marginalisation of college involvement altogether as a result of increased work based assessment, others clearly saw a new role for them in moderation and standards monitoring.

A related problem was one reflected in a widely voiced concern that workplace assessment was only as good as the workplace. Moreover, it was recognised that staff training in workplace assessment for both college and industrial staff was long overdue. It was felt that at present such assessments are usually a measure of the tasks undertaken by the students as opposed to the competences they use. Thus, it was stressed that whilst paperwork needed to be kept to a minimum, ticking boxes was an insufficient means of recording progress. Some concern was also raised over the possible cyclic nature of a curriculum developed under 'levels' as against the linear and progressive nature of workplace learning. Further concerns related to the extent assessment would cover depth of learning as well as breadth. In addition, college staff were often unclear about whether and to what extent simulation (in the college) would be allowed as a means of assessing competence.

For college staff, the changes in assessment procedures will mean a move from externally assessed courses to more internal continuous assessment and moderation. Staff development was called for to aid the changeover from norm to criteria referencing and assessment on a pass/fail basis. Overall it was expected that the new assessment, especially if it needed to be carried out in the workplace, would lead to a decline in traditional block release. Instead, in order to allow learning and assessment to complement one another, ideally moving in tandem, it was felt that this would be replaced by one or two day per week placements in many vocational areas.

An alternative view was that rather than the 'ideal' requirements of learning and assessment determining the mode, this would be influenced by more practical considerations relating to the ease (or otherwise) of getting work placements, and the preferences of the employers. Indeed the sheer scale of the administrative load in seeking and organising work placements itself could become a major issue. Similarly, college staff expressed doubts over whether it would be possible to find sufficient interested employers/supervisors, etc. to meet ideal requirements of their involvement in the development, assessment and moderation of college based provision.

Besides general worries about how assessment systems would operate in practice, there were also some more technical concerns. For example, whether it would be possible to combine assessment of skills and knowledge and approaches to working related to successful performance of a job (that is, recording responses to deadlines/critical events, etc. and to contingencies) as well as recording the more routine aspects of performance. Would the performance criteria not only be based on outcomes, but also upon the processes by which outcome was achieved: e.g., response to clients/customers, etc.? Thus would statements of competence attempt to deal with aspects of roles not just tasks? Would the assessment facilitate the delivery and development of broadly based competence, such that learners would be fulfilling a variety of roles as well as successfully completing vocational tasks?

College staff also felt there were dangers that possession of knowledge might be undervalued. For example, a knowledge component may require direct assessment (given the unlikelihood of it being demonstrated through application, but it nevertheless being important to respond appropriately if it does occur: e.g., identification of certain animal illnesses, etc.). They felt some consolation in that observation of performance constitutes the main, but not the sole, method of assessment in the new system. Again, they would reserve judgement until they saw whether the system accommodated this in practice as well as theory.

In summary it should be noted that while the specification of performance criteria represents a significant move towards criteria based assessment, normative assessments still take place. That is, the new criteria have to be interpreted and judgements based on them. However, who makes these judgements and upon what bases is critical to the overall success of the new system. Thus, the size of the task involved in securing regular and consistent workplace assessment should not be underestimated.

Indeed a number of colleges involved in work on work-based assessment drew attention to the tendency of work placements to seek administrative convenience in accreditation arrangements. For example, countersigning/verifying, etc. on a single day, or making generalised judgements about a person's overall competence, rather than recording achievement as it occurred. This whole area requires further study and without effective moderation some college staff felt they and others would have little confidence in the system.

3 Brief summaries of the sector-specific findings

This section gives brief sector-specific commentaries, in four vocational areas: agriculture, clerical, hairdressing and caring. Appendix 2 carries a further commentary upon the sector-specific findings, with more specific work being carried forward to Phase 2 of the Project.

3.1 Agriculture

Of the four vocational areas researched, agriculture was by far the most adequately prepared for the introduction of NVQs. The reason for this comes from the existence of an integrated infrastructure that has for many years linked workplace assessment to competent performance through the network of National Proficiency Testing Councils. Furthermore, the typical involvement of college staff and colleges in the administration and standard maintenance within local NPTCs means that there already exists the mechanisms for implementing NVQs in this area. Nevertheless, the effect that NVQs will have on this existing structure and on the provision of courses will need careful monitoring, as many college staff did not expect to change their current course content so much as re-juggle it into the new NVQ levels. One of the greatest concerns here, as elsewhere, was the need to reduce the paperwork, particularly for workplace providers. A further issue relates to NCVQ's specification of no minimum or maximum period of time in training and/or on work experience. This raises questions about how to build a variety of conditions into the assessment and the value of a residential component. Passage of time and experience of different place-ments, conditions (including weather), etc., were felt necessary to give students 'exposure' to at least some of the variety of circumstances which could be met in many branches of agriculture. Would possession of technical skills (especially in favourable conditions!) alone be sufficient?

3.2 Clerical

In the clerical sector the introduction of a competence based curriculum has taken place largely along two fronts. Firstly, the RSA, prior to the NCVQ's formal statement of levels, introduced its own definition of levels (although it was always intended that these should accommodate NCVQ decisions rather than being seen as a pre-emptive strike). Thus a model existed in the clerical and administrative sector, early in the day, with continuing piloting of the first two levels. However, it should be noted that in colleges, staff awareness of levels of any sort and competence based initiatives was found to be patchy at the time of the research. Those involved in YTS often appeared best informed.

The second front of developments related to the Administrative, Business and Commercial Training Group document (ABC document). This took some cognisance of the RSA work and set out the standards of performance that were to be incorporated into the first and second level qualifications in the new NVQ framework. The ABC document came in for some criticism for its limited approach to competence, but at the time of the research the effect of this document at the grass roots was found to be low.

3.3 Hairdressing

In hairdressing a number of sector-specific issues were highlighted. Firstly, the need to enable better and more trusting relationships between employers, who view each other as competitors, was identified. Moreover, the poor intra-sector communications between employers was further reinforced by the use of conflicting standards and procedures. A further concern was raised over the traditional view of employers that the college staff are the 'experts' in the field and that more workplace assessment and training would be viewed negatively. Further, in a competitive market little scope exists for trial and error and the expectation that colleges teach the students to a given standard (above that applied in many workplaces) will be difficult to bridge.

On the issue of standardisation of the workplace provision, many colleges favoured the introduction of registration of hairdressers as in France, the USA and Canada. This was seen by some as an important step to be taken if the full intentions of the Nationally Preferred Scheme were to be realised. However, the NPS itself came under fire from many college staff — including supporters of it. The main problem raised was the reduction of the science components in the lower levels and a view that the NPS represented very much the 'bare bones'. An alternative scheme (UBS) was often preferred by those with experience of both as giving 'better integration' of the work as a whole.

3.4 Caring

While there are undoubtedly major implications associated with the implementation of competence based curricula, in many ways, as argued throughout this report, the extent to which it requires a change in *orientation* among college staff in some vocational areas should not be overestimated. Thus, for example, staff associated with caring courses such as the NNEB have traditionally always viewed their task as being to develop students' *competence in a role*. To this end, great emphasis is given to performance in work placements and the development of attitudes and behaviours appropriate to carers. This consideration of role even influences the initial selection process: students are viewed not so much in terms of how well they could cope with the course academically but in terms of their motivation and likely commitment to their future role; for example, how far they have already demonstrated a commitment to caring through previous activities (paid, voluntary or domestic).

To some extent, caring may be a special case, insofar as a strong vocational attachment is often required of those wishing to enter the area and not just a willingness to undertake a particular course. What is of interest though is that the orientation of staff has never been that vocational education and training in caring is about passing courses — the aim has always been personal development of (mainly young) people such that they would make 'good carers' — where competence in a role is and remains central to that process. The recent introduction of BTEC courses in caring, with students now sometimes seeking entry to undergraduate courses through this route, may however affect staff orientations in the future, as not all future entrants may be seeking a career in caring. Some of these new students may alternatively see their current course in terms of individual progression: a stage in their journey, not their ultimate destination. Either way, for the time being even with demographic decline in the population of young people caring courses, particularly nursery nursing, still receive abnormally high rates of application.

One final comment about caring concerns the quality of *relationships* which lie at the heart of caring. Scrutinising these and making judgements on approaches taken by carers can be very difficult, especially as different workers can have very different styles and patterns of relationship with their clients, without one approach being seen as clearly superior. The difficulties that various working groups have had and are having in producing competence objectives with clearly specified criteria of performance is perhaps testament to the difficulties in applying the new framework in this area.

4 Major issues

In this section we draw together not only some of the major threads from the responses of college staff, but also incorporate material from other publications and debates in producing a commentary upon major issues involved in the implementation of competence based curricula. Once again, we will organise the commentary under the headings: curriculum development; staff development; institutional development.

One issue perhaps, however, lies at the heart of any debate about the practical implementation of competence based curricula. That is the issue of work based learning and assessment, including tutors' relationships with the workplace. As this issue both straddles and has major implications for our three major categories, it has been given a sub-section to itself.

4.1 Curriculum development

Much of the curriculum development which will be required will of necessity relate to progress towards development and implementation made in the various occupational sectors. A number of more general issues remain.

The first may seem somewhat academic and rather remote from colleges, but it concerns the various definitions and understandings of competence. However, it has led to a degree of confusion in the field, and if staff in colleges are to have a clear understanding of (and commitment to) the underlying aims and objectives, then they have to be given a lead. In particular, issues associated with the *breadth* of competence have to be addressed. Presumably the underpinning idea (the purpose of education) must relate to personal competence. Learners have to be capable of fulfilling a variety of roles as well as successfully completing vocational tasks. Even if attention is focused primarily upon vocational outcomes, then the arguments espoused in the New Training Initiative about the need for a versatile and adaptable workforce would suggest that a range of approaches to learning need to be 'owned' by the learner. Similarly the ability to perform in a variety of contexts and locations would seem necessary to give learners both some breadth of competence and to equip them with the potential for progression.

However, the argument needs to be taken further than this (and there was little evidence that this issue was being seriously addressed): transfer needs to accommodate both transfer *within* occupations and also *between* them. Back in 1985, MSC were arguing that occupational competence 'also embodies the ability to transfer skills and knowledge to new situations within the occupational area and beyond to related occupations'. This seems sensible in that many young people will not remain in the industry they initially enter, either for training or employment, in the medium-term let alone the long-term. Equipping people to facilitate transfer and progression then has implications for how levels of occupational competence are drawn in practice: assessment processes should be drawn so as to ensure these broader considerations are not neglected.

NCVQ has moved considerably in the past year in this direction and appears more aware of the need to incorporate a more substantive knowledge component and to address the issue of transferable skills. The increasing collaboration of FEU, NCVQ and the Training Agency also holds out the possibility that a clear and consistent line can be promulgated so as to facilitate the development of broadly based competence.

One key element of the quality control of the new competence led curricula will depend upon the quality of the moderation procedures. As in accord with 'good practice' elsewhere in the FE system, moderation should be used in a supportive role, not simply as a means to check standards. Where moderators are themselves 'learning on the job', care has to be taken to ensure consistency in the approach to moderation. Staff development can then be seen as important in this respect too (GCSE has shown the unease felt by practitioners when the moderators were given little time and few guidelines to formulate their approach). Time is required to enable moderators to explore ideas and attempt to reach consensus upon issues of interpretation and to share experiences once the moderation process gets fully underway. Thus, initially moderators (and any staff development) will have to communicate and interpret both the underpinning philosophy and specific advice (e.g., on assessment, technical details, etc.).

A second point is that regional models (more detail of these will be given in Section 4.2) have emphasised the importance of the relationship between moderators and individual centres: the number of visits and degree of support offered were both much higher than 'normal' where centres were grappling with new competence based curricula. However, this has direct cost implications. Moderation has traditionally been poorly paid, although there has been no shortage of volunteers because it was seen as valuable experience in terms of individual career development. However, if moderation is to become much more widespread, then some of its attraction (and exclusivity) may be lost. One result may be that the duties of a moderator are more tightly circumscribed. If they become verifiers and countersigning officers, who will give the support about learning and assessment which was traditionally part of the moderator's (avuncular) role?

The 'old' system of moderation seemed in tune with the system of assessment as a whole, being geared to high reliability and low cost (unfortunately validity was also low). Now a new system of assessment and moderation promises higher validity, but will it also require higher costs? Will people be willing to finance the type of moderation required? Or will moderation procedures be adapted to fit cost requirements?

4.2 Staff development

One striking feature about staff knowledge and understanding of the implications of the implementation of competence based curricula lay not in the variation, but rather the form of the variation. Rather than there being a continuum of people's knowledge and understanding, it was almost as if it could be represented by a bipolar distribution. That is, there seemed to be two opposing camps: on the one hand, there were those well-versed in what was happening or were au fait with the latest thinking of NCVQ, EAV bodies and the like, while on the other hand, there were those with only very hazy understandings of either the changes or their implications. Included in this latter group were some who had seen the initial outputs of industry lead bodies and were sceptical about both the value and the practicality of some of the proposals made. As a result they paid relatively little attention to subsequent developments.

Clearly as implementation of new curricula comes nearer in particular vocational areas, interest will presumably surge and mechanisms will be required to broaden the base of the number of people with a fairly full understanding. It would be unrealistic to expect change to come about simply by knowledge filtering down and through the system. In any case, such a trickle down approach to staff development, as well as being ineffective, could prove to be disastrous in another respect. If staff are not primed to prepare for change, they may carry on with existing practices and by so doing the momentum for change may be lost. If, after the heralding accompanying the much-vaunted reformation of vocational qualifications, staff continue much as before, then it will be much harder to institutionalise change at a later stage. Similarly, a 'catch as catch can' approach to staff development risks enshrining any parochial views, with the spread of 'poor practice' as likely as the spread of 'good practice'. Without a more comprehensive approach to staff development, it may be that not only are college staff not locating certain issues, but other people, especially those concerned with a national perspective, may be unaware of these shortcomings. A coherent strategy is required for staff development and one that firmly locates staff development within the development of the curriculum in its broader sense. Thus staff development must be placed alongside curriculum development and organisational development as part of an integrated approach to the challenge of the reformation of the system of vocational qualifications. Further, within this approach, there must be scope for formative evaluation to ascertain the effectiveness and direction of staff development. This will mean it is possible to refine the approach taken to staff development, in the light of overall goals. Only then will the process of a *competence led* curriculum start to take shape.

One possible way forward in promoting competence led staff development would be to utilise existing regional networks as foci for such a programme. The recent experience of two Regional Advisory Councils (YHAFHE and WMACFE) may be informative in this respect. Both developed curricula (Tradec and UBS respectively), which while open to all remained strongest in their own regions. They were also certificated by CGLI as alternative routes for the delivery of schemes, which were more genuinely national in practice. What is of interest here is not the precise fate of these particular qualifications, but rather that in order to maintain their existence they sought to make their provision align more closely to the requirements of NCVQ. (Now all EAV bodies involved with vocational education and training were at the very least re-examining their provision in the light of NCVQ and many were seeking to give it an explicit competence base). What makes the two RACs particularly noteworthy, however, is their *regional* dimension and how they were involved in trying to re-orient provision in colleges. That is, they have direct experience of a number of substantive issues involved in moving towards the implementation of competence based curricula and the process by which they sought to institutionalise change through their staff development programmes.

The first point to note is that they have involved a wide range of FE staff in the whole implementation process. Secondly, both regions were involved in a number of interlocking projects and developments concerning the implementation of competence based curricula. For example, the Tradec schemes have been re-oriented to introduce competence objectives and to pay greater attention to assessment. A development project on Work Based Assessment (WBA) has input findings into that re-orientation: especially as Tradec has always sought to emphasise importance of work experience. Another (NAFE Central Reserve) project has sought to help tutors utilise work experience. Similarly, UBS was developed in 1984 and has sought to fit the training specifications laid down by the dominant training organisation in different occupational sectors. This has already led to re-orientation and updating as major training organisations, including latterly the industry lead bodies, have developed their approaches. The skill and training specifications of these bodies are then seen as the training information base, around which units are constructed. However, UBS treats this information as a base, which requires embellishment through using a broader orientation of transferable core skills. The result is then seen as contextualised core skills, thereby addressing both occupational and broader concepts of competence.

We have repeatedly stressed how involvement in such development work can give people an edge in understanding the shape and direction of curricular change as a whole. The key is, however, the extent to which such potential advantages are realised for the benefit of staff other than those directly involved. The two RACs both sought to capitalise on such advantages but did so in different ways.

YHAFHE's approach seemed to rely upon its long-established tradition of curriculum working parties and moderation procedures associated with Tradec, to perform in addition a staff development function and coupled this with regional events, when the intelligence associated with involvement in development projects pointed to significant events looming on the horizon. This approach meant that intelligence about what was happening was spread quite widely among the colleges, although the information was still piecemeal and the base of those with some overall picture was still narrow. Existing intra-regional links, where these were good, could then perform a valuable role. That their effectiveness is limited by the lack of a more coherent and comprehensive approach to staff development can be illustrated in two ways. Firstly, the number of people reached by such haphazard means is likely to be fairly small and there are numerous opportunities for misunderstandings to arise as messages are transmitted around the system. Also it increases the likelihood that messages will be 'locked up' in separate departments/sections, and hence militates against the adoption of a college-wide response. Secondly there was no mechanism for translating what came out of the development projects into general practice through a complementary staff development programme. Thus the WBA project came up with an important finding: that tutors often viewed industry/workplaces in generalized terms, rather than looking at the particular workplaces associated with their students. Hence they were not always viewing the workplace as a learning opportunity. Now ideally this idea should be picked up in a regional staff development programme addressed to the implications of a competence led curriculum. Only at a regional level would it be likely to work through such a balance between policy and practice.

UBS is a much more recent development than Tradec and has sought from the outset to tackle major issues relating to competence and assessment. As a consequence, WMACFE have insisted that all staff involved with the scheme should take part in an initial two-day staff development programme. Moderation is seen as a key element of UBS, with college and workplace personnel cross-moderating each other's provision. Once again, moderation also performs a valuable staff development role as well as promoting integration. A commitment to continuing staff development was also seen as necessary in order to facilitate an effective interchange about practical problems 'on the ground' and a response to changes in policy at national level.

Irrespective of the future of these particular qualifications it is the involvement and commitment that was faciated and harnessed by regional organisations which is of relevance here. It makes good sense that FEU and NCVQ have recently agreed on the need to promote a Regional Staff Development and Support Service as part of a staff development programme to support the implementation of the NVQ framework. Involvement at this level can bring significant advantages in relation to cost, co-ordination and exchange of good practice. The service was to be available, via RACs, through the eleven Regional Curriculum Bases later in 1989. Problems with funding the programme mean the form and scope of the activities to be undertaken are uncertain. In any case, the RACs vary in the extent to which they are already seen as a focus of significant activity, including staff development, by individual colleges. Thus while the idea is sound, in practice greater efforts will be required in some regions than others to ensure the message gets through to staff at the requisite levels in colleges.

In conclusion, any programme of competence led staff development will need to take account of both the specific and more general issues highlighted in section 2.2. That is, it will need to remedy the patchy understanding of the nature of competence, but also be alive to the need to support the development of more flexible learning provision. Hence any staff development programme accompanying the implementation of competence led curricula should not be viewed in isolation, but needs to be placed in the broader context of staff development policy as a whole.

4.3 Institutional development

The scale and breadth of the changes required in order to produce successful implementation of new vocational qualifications has been reiterated throughout this report. It is apparent that it would be futile to attempt to meet this challenge with marginal changes to the existing curriculum, coupled with a small 'dose' of staff development. If colleges wish to remain major providers of vocational education and training, then they will have to reassess their organisational aims, structures, processes and resources to see if these align with what is required for an effective implementation of competence based curricula.

However, even where a process of self-scrutiny was underway, the impetus was likely to be only marginally related to the reformation of vocational qualifications. The impact of the Joint Efficiency Study, the Educational Reform Act, changing relationships with LEAs, proposed mergers and re-organisations, the prospect or actuality of falling rolls, even the introduction of GCSE could all seem more pressing concerns. Further, even if a review does touch upon course provision, it should be remembered that colleges may choose to boost GCSE, A-Level and HE access courses, arguing that demographic change will mean that young people will have good vocational prospects if they follow this route. Certainly they may regard it as prudent 'not to become prematurely wedded to a system within which they are unsure of their place'. Such considerations will mainly be one of balance, however, and sooner or later colleges will have to square up to the consequences of the reformation of vocational qualifications.

The evidence would seem to suggest that many of them were hoping it would be later rather than sooner, as most colleges were not framing a college-wide response to the implications of the implementation of competence based curricula. There would appear to be three principal reasons for this.

Firstly, so much effort from TA, NCVQ etc. has gone into stressing the *vocational* dimension, that less attention has been paid to the wider implications. The very different approaches and rates of change in the different vocational areas were seen as further evidence that a sectoral approach was sufficient. Secondly, the amount of change the system as a whole has been undergoing in the last decade was seen as exerting an inhibiting influence. This was succinctly expressed as: 'there has been so much change that many people are suffering from initiative fatigue'. There was an awareness that curricula in future would be competence led, but many staff were going to wait till the change actually arrived or at least appeared in a more tangible form (due to uncertainties about overall direction and the response of particular examining and validating bodies and ILBs and what this would mean for particular courses). On several occasions the researchers were advised 'to come back next year when we should have a clearer idea of what the changes mean'. This type of response was starting to give way, even over the short time-scale of our interviewing period, to a thirst for information from those most directly affected as the imminence of the changes in some sectors became apparent. The attention of those with institutional management responsibilities was still, for the reasons given above, mostly elsewhere. The third reason related to resources: getting course teams, departments or sections to consider the particular implications for them was seen as an ad hoc activity, which did not require commitment of official resources. By contrast, any college-wide response and commitment to action would have significant resource implications. The ethos of the 'responsive college' was seen as supporting the devolution of responsibility for change to course teams. Certainly, active consideration of implications of competence based curricula in their vocational areas by course teams is necessary, but is it sufficient? Does there not need to be a mechanism whereby emerging issues can be considered at different levels in the college structure? Work by the course teams will of necessity be largely *reactive*, operating within fairly narrow bands (even if the change within that particular band is marked). However, if provision is to be *competence led*, then a more thorough-going review is likely to be required, dealing as it must with major questions of college policy and management. The scale of the review required could be evidenced in the following exemplar.

In one college an ad hoc group of staff interested in NCVQ developments had a meeting and made recommendations to the Academic Board. Their recommendations are given in full in Appendix 2. The breadth of their proposals illustrates the chasm between what could be accomplished by course teams working alone and what could be achieved if a college-wide strategy were adopted. The latter case would require major changes in course delivery (modularisation), marketing strategy, industrial liaison, clients (more emphasis on training trainers and assessors), organisation of staff and patterns of responsibility, enrolment, credit accumulation and transfer, IT policy and staff development. Another interesting sidelight on this issue is that in the six months following the issue being raised with the Academic Board, no action had been taken or even proposed. Again this raises issues about the 'management of change': good ideas alone are insufficient. A commitment to action is also required. We shall return to this theme in Section 5.2.

Some college managements might defend their refusal to go far down this road on the grounds that it is necessary to understand the external context within which they have to operate. In particular, they may point to the inconsistency between attempts to improve the effectiveness of college provision and services on the lines suggested above and the way institutional performance is currently judged. (The FEU project 'Educating the Auditors' addresses such concerns). Notwithstanding such arguments, institutions still need to be considering what they can do within existing constraints to facilitate the implementation of competence led curricula. At the very least such active consideration of policy should ensure that staff are given a clear indication of the overall direction of change, that scarce resources are used to best effect (for example, that staff development policy is viewed as a whole and that activities undertaken interlock rather than compete) and that a case is assembled as to what is required to bring about the effective implementation of competence led curricula.

4.4 Work based learning and assessment

It is not appropriate to give in this sub-section a full exposition of all the issues that arose in relation to work based learning and assessment as many of these will be taken further in Phase 2. Indeed the uncertainty about how work based learning and assessment will operate *in practice* is one reason why there is so much project activity in this area. Whatever the detail of the systems which eventually do emerge, it has become clear that college staff may often find that they have a critical role in the implementation process, particularly in relation to how they interact with work placements. The precise portfolio of work they undertake may vary according to the vocational area and the particularities of both college and workplace environments, but given below are a range of possible areas in which they may become involved. Thus some possible roles for college tutors in relation to work placements could be:

— In planning/structuring of opportunities for learners to acquire necessary skills and knowledge and apply them at work placements (e.g., may need to move between placements to get experience of different contexts, especially where placements can be very diverse as in agriculture).

— To facilitate demonstration and accreditation of any competence acquired at the workplace (may not only require assessment at the workplace, but also support of off-job learning and assessment). In particular, tutors could help learners build up a body of evidence (including use of an agreed framework for recording performance) which could be used in the accreditation process.

— To make connections between work experience and related knowledge. That is, practical experience should demonstrate a need for related knowledge: in hairdressing, the use of chemicals; in caring, cognitive development, etc. Skills and knowledge can then be developed in a continuing and dynamic way.

   In practice, such integration can be difficult to achieve, e.g., in agriculture, while allowance can be made for the season, unforeseen contingencies can mean the matching between the two components falls short of the ideal. Integration can still be a valuable tool. (Needless to say, simplistic equations such as off-job = knowledge, on-job = practical skills, should not be drawn).

— Evaluation: reviewing the operation as a whole, including estimation of the real costs of the assessment system in practice.

— To help placements make an analysis of their training needs (in order that they are able to support the learners in performance of activities at the workplace in relation to learning and/or assessment).

— To help learners identify their particular learning needs (in relation to prior experience, current performance, placement opportunities and their chosen combination of units).

— To consider appropriate approaches to facilitate learning and assessment at the workplace (for example, different types of emphasis, location, sequencing, degree of supervision, specialisation, etc.). Note it is often necessary to build in opportunities for reflection, such that learners can be aware of what they have achieved and make connections between different components of their programme.

— To draw out the extent to which experience at work means more than just acquisition of competence in work tasks. That is, also consider the need for task management and the importance of learning to perform roles. This then links with issues about transferable skills, learning to adapt to changed contexts/circumstances and learning to perform a variety of roles. Work experience can then be used as a means to exemplify the need for a more catholic approach to learning, rather than reinforcing ideas that all that is required is the development of 'narrow' vocational skills.

— To monitor learners' overall performance in different contexts and locations. This should enable overall progress to be monitored, with any consequent changes of programme (for example, if any particular learning difficulties are revealed) and help to ensure that particular performances are recorded, especially if they can contribute to a unit of competence (or other form of qualification).

— Using feedback from learners to find out about particular work placements rather than relying solely on a generalized view of activities at work. This can then be used as a valuable means of updating college staff.

5 Possible ways forward for the project

5.1 Phase 2 and relationship to other work

Work has been continuing apace on curriculum development, narrowly defined — competence objectives, criteria of performance etc. — but little attention has been focused upon staff development and institutional development as part of a coordinated approach to the management of change. To forge ahead in developing one leg and neglecting the others may throw the system as a whole out of balance and may indeed undermine progress even on the leg upon which so much effort has been concentrated.

Thus Phase 1 of our work has identified that the activity designed to facilitate the implementation of competence based curricula in colleges varies widely according to geographical location and vocational area. However, even in situations where activity has been frenetic, it has invariably taken a very limited and narrow view of curriculum development. The absence of any strategic consideration is striking! To this end, if Phase 2 were to operate as originally intended it would risk exacerbating the situation: that is, to look at particular responses of colleges to specific issues identified as problematic in Phase 1 would contribute to 'being unable to see the wood for the trees'. The adoption of a broader perspective is required.

The new approach for Phase 2 is to apply our methodological frame for extracting key issues and putting them in wider context to the Mutual Development Fund R & D Projects. The intention is to ensure that a coherent and comprehensive approach is adopted to the implementation of NVQs in FE. Implementation should then be in line with a strategic rather than an ad hoc (or reactive) approach. The issues framework itself is predicated upon the assumption that effective change within the system needs to be evaluated in the context of:

— the development of the curriculum
— the continuing professional development of staff
— the institutional and organisational arrangements of colleges.

Phase 2 then will look at MDF projects, and the identification of any 'gaps' in coverage with a view to commissioning further work. The review also looks at what is happening in these projects in the light of developments elsewhere (e.g., NCVQ, Training Agency Occupational Standards Branch, etc.).

The overall intention then is to provide information and intelligence to assist in the development of a coherent strategy towards the implementation of NVQs within the FE system as a whole, ensuring that that process is competence led and enshrines a broad approach to curriculum development.

5.2 Management of change

Throughout this report, we have emphasised the extent and magnitude of the changes required within colleges in order to implement competence based curricula. The need for these changes were readily identified by many of our respondents. However, by the very nature of the research, our interviewees were among the most aware of the full implications of the introduction of NVQs. In any case, as we mentioned previously, there is a world of difference between informed staff in a reflective mode being able to identify the changes required and the realisation of those changes in practice. In order to promote effective change, the change process itself has to be *managed*.

If curricula are to be genuinely *competence led*, then a *process* of curricular change has to be actively promoted and supported. How is this to be achieved?

To effect translation of a major programme from theory to practice requires more than just dissemination of the underlying ideas. It also requires organisation change and system change. At least in this respect many of the organisational and systemic changes required for the implementation of competence led curricula complement or reinforce those required to support contemporaneous developments, such as the development of more flexible learning provision and the search for new clientele. However, although this may result in synergy, this may not necessarily be so. Developments may be viewed in isolation, effort and resources may be fragmented in wasteful duplication and/or competition.

There is a clear need for a strategic approach to the implementation of competence led curricula, whereby a clear picture of the type of provision to which people should be working is presented, together with practical advice as to how to move in that direction. Apocalyptic visions of the future rarely generate commitment nor do they offer much help or guidance in the short term. Similarly, resource constraints and practical difficulties with implementation are inadequate excuses for not seeking at least to move in the required direction. In this respect, the nature and quality of staff development becomes critical in generating a commitment to change.

Phase 2 of this project will then not only seek to identify the extent to which a coordinated strategy of curriculum development, staff development and institutional development is instrumental in the implementation of competence led curricula, but will also actively support attempts at its practical realisation.

APPENDIX 1: One proposal for a college-wide response to NCVQ developments

At one college an ad hoc group of staff interested in NCVQ developments argued for the adoption of a college strategy and 'action plan' to meet the challenge of NCVQ. They recommended that the strategy should be based on the following:

1   Establish a liaison group to ensure that the LEA officers are fully briefed on NCVQ matters and take an active part in the development of the co-ordination of these matters across the Authority.

2   Establish an adequate and accessible data base capable of providing the sophisticated records of student achievement and credit accumulation envisaged in the NCVQ documents. (This item is particularly relevant since it will be a vital element in the process of producing the information required in the Joint Efficiency Study).

3   Initiate an enrolment procedure which adequately reflects the need for the recognition of prior learning, credit transfer and credit accumulation and which recognises, in a structured way, the implication of student

counselling, achievement testing, student profiles and the full range of modes of delivery and costing implied in the documentation.

4   Initiate a marketing strategy to establish the College as the focus of NCVQ in the eyes of local industry.

5   Initiate a college-wide review of IT provision and a process of ongoing appraisal of the provision in the light of the competencies in this field likely to be highlighted by the various industry lead groups.

6   Establish 2 — 5 above as the main areas of staff development for the college, recognising the resource implications that this implies. Prioritise those areas requiring most staff development and having done so be more directive in implementing this staff development policy.

7   Generate the ideas required to develop the procedures outlined in 1 — 6 above by reinforcing the work of some existing individuals or groups, or by establishing new groups and by allocating time and responsibility to these individuals or groups to perform the following tasks:

a   To establish a pool of expertise in competency based learning and its implications for the curriculum.

b   To establish a marketing strategy to ensure that the College is in the forefront in the development of NVQ in local industry and commerce. This strategy may have to encompass the needs of industry and commerce with regard to:
   i   training programmes for work based assessors
   ii offering a consultancy service on assessment in the work place
   iii the provision of simulated work experience in the College
   iv the integration of 'college' based and 'work' based experience.
   (This task could be divided between two groups).

c   To recommend the procedures to be adopted for enrolment, recognition of prior learning, credit transfer and credit accumulation.

d   To recommend the procedures to be adopted with regard to student counselling, achievement testing, student profiles and course tutoring.

e   To recommend a suitable data base system capable of dealing with the sophisticated demands described above and the procedures required to ensure that the flow of information both into and out of the system will be sufficiently detailed.

f   To prioritise the staff development implications relating to NCVQ and recommend the direction of staff development funding towards prescribed areas.

g   To assess the resource implications of these recommendations.

8   Appoint a NVQ Manager and Deputy who will be responsible for implementing the Action Plan. A suitable amount of time should be allocated for the execution of this task.

9   Appoint an Assessment Coordinator and an assistant coordinator who will
     be responsible for implementing procedures for student counselling, achieve-
     ment testing, student profiles, recognition of prior learning, credit transfer
     and credit accumulation. A suitable amount of time should be allocated for
     the execution of this task.

APPENDIX 2: Fuller commentary on sector-specific findings

1. Agriculture

As reported in the text, in many ways the agriculture sector was the most advanced in
its preparation for the introduction of NVQs. Yet, in having well established industry
– college infrastructure, some resistance to change may result. This was particularly
indicated in college staff responses to what was meant by, for example, competence.
The replies here were often of the form 'competence is related to the NPTC standards
and tests'. Nevertheless, a range of definitions of competence were given covering all
the active categories referred to in 2.1. It should be remembered that the idea of
competence has been around for some time in this sector. Moreover, links with
industry are well established with the industry involved in course reviews and teaching
on a part-time and exemplary practice basis. In addition, college staff are involved in
the training of the NPTC assessors and the administration and operation of local
NPTCs. Further, a body of competent workplace assessors already exists, although it
was felt these might not wish to see their role expanded, particularly if this necessitated
additional paperwork. Similarly, doubts were expressed about how many workplace
supervisors would be willing to play an active role in the assessment process.
     As regards the setting of standards it was felt by some that the industry would
have benefitted from a more independent industry lead body than the ATB. However,
the roles of the NPTC and NEBAHAI were seen as important so far as moderation
was concerned. Although the standards had already been set for NVQ level one, it was
expected that at least a further year would be required to generate a complete and
acceptable set of standards to level two. Some concern was raised over whether these
developments would lead to minimum standards being enshrined as normal practice.
     Unlike the other vocational areas there was in general a higher level of manage-
ment awareness of the changes taking place. Furthermore, at the management level
the new initiatives were being viewed very positively as marketing opportunities.
There was an expected increase in the provision of assessed and accredited adult
education and retraining classes alongside new more practically oriented full-time
provision. The use of open learning was expected, particularly in the development of
introductory and bridging materials. Whilst there were calls for staff development in

new and appropriate teaching and learning strategies, the content of courses was not expected to change radically.

In this vocational area, as in others, there was some concern as to the effect roll-on roll-off courses would have on both the traditional three-term year and the students' personal and social development. It was considered important for students to have a peer group to whom they could relate — something with which more individualised programmes might dispense.

2. Clerical

The administrative and clerical sector have traditionally relied mainly on various forms of college based terminal assessments. Thus the more towards continuous and work based assessment will rely heavily, in this sector, on increased staff awareness, development and training.

Unsurprisingly, definitions of competence in this sector tended to revolve around performance in terms of speed and accuracy as well as skills training. College staff in this sector seemed to possess a limited conception of what was meant by both competence based and competence led curriculum. The former was related to skills in general and the latter to ideas of continual assessment.

Clerical staff in colleges recognised the need for staff development in course design and open learning development and facilitation. This was seen as related to the probable move to more roll-on roll-off courses which would provide for better access. Some saw a need for all courses to be modularised providing a basis for a menu of 'pick and mix'. However, as in other sectors, concern was raised over the likely fluctuation of numbers if a roll-on roll-off programme became the norm.

With regards to curriculum development, more forward colleges saw the need to develop specialised areas in which to deliver competences in a student centred approach incorporating greater use of independent learning. This route also implied the need for college staff to become greater generalists with skills in student guidance, counselling, resource management and assessment. Time would also be required to generate materials.

Particular areas of staff development that were raised related to the need to liaise more with, and learn from, the workplace. Along with this, staff argued there was also the need for more specific training in IT, student management and less static classes, the creation of assessment proformas, administration and record keeping.

In relation to assessment there was some concern over the impact of NVQ assessment recommendations. Traditionally, employers expected colleges to train and assess students and it was felt they would only respond if the paperwork was simple to use. This would result, it was suggested, in a lot more college staff time being spent in assessing in the workplace.

Overall, clerical staff thought that a lot of work would be entailed in setting up the new system of vocational qualifications in colleges. There was also a perceived need to sell themselves more effectively in the workplace and involve commerce and industry more in course developments. Nevertheless NVQs were in general considered a positive move, that would provide greater motivation to students in the form of a clearer picture of where they were and where they were going.

3. Hairdressing

College staff in hairdressing were generally well informed on the NVQ initiatives. In recent years with YTS, course improvements and changes made by the City and Guilds, the teaching of competence had already begun to take place. The major concerns raised in this sector related to increasing workplace involvement both in the provision of college courses and more specifically in work place assessment and programme delivery. Competition within the industry was seen as the major problem, along with a range of uncoordinated professional bodies.

However, some colleges were making a great effort to overcome these difficulties. In particular, some colleges were programming in time for staff to spend in placements, developing better relationships and links. These often stemmed from YTS arrangements but had been found to be invaluable both to monitor and counsel students in the workplace and to check on the type and nature of the experiences being received. They were also able to use this time to break down misconceptions about college staff and do some small scale staff development in terms of current commercial approaches and orientations. Hairdressing staff tended to define competence in terms of degrees of supervision.

The improved access that NVQ would create was viewed positively and a wide range of both intensive short courses, courses for adults and for (in some cases) holiday makers were being considered. Income generation was considered important for the future viability of hairdressing departments.

The use of staff from across a range of departments in the provision of hairdressing courses was seen to be important also. However, the reduced curriculum offered by the NPS was a concern for some colleges. In addition, some colleges saw a possible reduction in inter-departmental cooperation at a time when it was most needed.

Staff development requirements identified mainly in this sector were those relating to more frequent and detailed guidance and information on design and time-tabling of the new courses. Greater involvement with industry was called for by many in designing modularised courses. In relation to this, some colleges were not intending to introduce the NPS until it had had time to iron out its teething problems.

In summary, YTS has enabled a good relationship to develop between colleges and some employers. There still remained, however, role conflict with college staff being viewed as 'experts'. The need to resocialise the employers into recognising their own expertise and role in delivery and assessing competences was seen as necessary now, but would take time. Greater initial involvement of employers with college staff both in and out of the college was thus considered essential.

4. Caring

College staff discussions on the implications of NVQs tended to rotate around the BTEC/NNEB courses. In this context the potential of BTEC giving placement based assignments (though with college based assessment of them) was seen as a positive move, as it was felt that theory and practice were not linked in the NNEB courses. Further, the exam based (NNEB) versus work based divide was contrasted by some with the curriculum segmentation implied by the new NVQ framework against a need for more course integration.

Another issue highlighted by staff related to problems in distinguishing between roles of learner and worker, when students (from NNEB courses) were on work placement. That is, the learner was frequently seen, and sometimes viewed themselves, as a worker, not in any ephemeral, partial or training role but in its fullest sense. It was felt this could create major problems in getting assessment, accreditation, etc. carried out in the workplace. In theory, the relationship between college staff and the workplace could mean there is a substantial role for college staff in the accreditation process at the workplace. In practice, the conditions for observation may not allow that. That is, while the integration of activities in the two spheres may seem attractive, the practical difficulties may be considerable. This was certainly the experience of a recent project on work based learning in caring.

Moreover, whilst some college staff were involved in and aware of the wider issues of introducing competence based curricula, caring was found in general to be behind the other vocational areas in its developments. There appears to be only limited and selective involvement of the workplace in the design of courses but little involvement in the delivery of the college based programmes or assessment. With regards to the latter it was recognised that both awareness raising and substantial staff development were required. Indeed 'caring' college staff were particularly aware of staff development needs and they raised many of the staff development issues highlighted in the main body of the text.

Within the colleges, job fears and concerns were prevalent, with the need to 'shift staff attitudes' being recognised as a major block to the introduction of a more fully competence based curriculum into caring. It was suggested that the use of team meetings for staff development was one of the best ways of addressing the issue.

The nature and scale of the problems in trying to develop a competence led curriculum in caring has influenced the FEU into taking a different tack from that adopted in other vocational areas and it is currently supporting a separate development project in this area.

Acknowledgments

We would like to thank staff of the following for their cooperation in carrying out this project:

Colleges

Beverley	Hertfordshire
Bishop Burton (Beverley)	Isle of Wight
Blackpool	Kingston
Bolton	Merristwood
Brecon	Newham
Bristol	Norfolk
Brockenhurst	North West Kent
Cambridge	Otley
Chippenham	Park Lane (Leeds)
Dorset	Peterborough
East Birmingham	Southwark
Eastbourne	Tameside
Fareham	Telford
Guildford	Welsh Agricultural
Hampshire	Warwick
Hastings	Wirral
Hendon	Worcester
Henley (Coventry)	Writtle

Other organisations

Barbara Shelborn Associates	– NEBAHAI
BTEC	– NNEB
CGLI	– NPTC
CAST (Jordanhill)	– RSA
EARAC	– TA (formerly MSC)
FESC	– WMACFE
NCVQ	– YHAFHE

APPENDIX 3: Glossary of Abbreviations

ATB	Agriculture Training Board
BTEC	Business and Technical Education Council
CAST	Curriculum Advice and Support Team
CD	Curriculum Development
CGLI	City and Guilds of London Institute
CPVE	Certificate of Pre-Vocational Education
DES	Department of Education and Science
EARAC	East Anglian Regional Advisory Council
EAV	Examining and Validating
FE	Further Education
FESC	Further Education Staff College
FEU	Further Education Unit
GCSE	General Certificate of Secondary Education
HE	Higher Education
HTB	Hairdressing Training Board
ILB	Industry Lead Body
IT	Information Technology
LEA	Local Education Authority
MSC	Manpower Services Commission (now TA)
MDF	Mutual Development Fund (of FEU/TA)
NAFE	Non-Advanced Further Education
NCVQ	National Council for Vocational Qualifications
NEBAHAI	National Examination Board for Agriculture, Horticulture and Allied Industries
NNEB	Nursery Nurses Examination Board
NPS	National Preferred Scheme
NPTC	National Proficiency Test Council
NVQ	National Vocational Qualification
RAC	Regional Advisory Council
TA	Training Agency (formerly Training Commission; MSC)
UBS	Unit-Based Scheme
WBA	Work Based Assessment
WMACFE	West Midlands Advisory Council for Further Education
YHAFHE	Yorkshire & Humberside Association for Further & Higher Education

Chapter 12

Initial teacher training and the NVQ model

Michael Eraut

Introduction

This paper seeks to compare and contrast the assumptions about knowledge and its acquisition which underpin approaches to teacher training that are school based, and approaches to vocational training that are competency based. How significant are the differences, and to what extent do they stem from the distinctive nature of teaching as an occupation, from different views about the nature of expertise in general or simply from different historical traditions? More importantly, perhaps, what can each learn from the other that might modify its aims or improve its effectiveness?

For illustrative purposes, I shall confine my discussion to the 36-week Post Graduate Certificate in Education, which now accounts for over half the entrants to teaching. This course has a purely professional purpose and does not attempt to include any element of general higher education — though it can and, in my view, should be argued that it is highly educational and contains experiences of a kind that higher education as a whole would do well to develop further. I will also stick to the particular variant of the PGCE course that has been developed at the University of Sussex (Lacey and Lamont, 1974; Furlong *et al.*, 1988) though most but not all of my remarks would apply equally to variants funded in other institutions of higher education. No currently running PGCE course bears much resemblance to the strawman images criticised in a recent spate of articles, which appear to have been orchestrated to justify the licensed teacher scheme.

Key features of initial teacher training

Performance based

PGCE courses share important common features with the NVQ model of competence based vocational training.

> A large portion of the course (at Sussex about two thirds) is devoted to on-the-job training.
> Competence is assessed by direct observation of job performance.
> This assessment constitutes the largest and the most essential part of the teaching qualification.

Nobody is allowed to qualify who is not judged to be competent in the classroom, regardless of the brilliance of their intellect. At Sussex this assessment of classroom competence is made by designated schoolteacher tutors, then ratified by an examination board on which several practitioners sit. All borderline cases or likely failures are also seen by university tutors and the external examiner, and candidates may be asked to undertake a further period of teaching practice after the course has formally ended, in order to further develop and then demonstrate their competence.

Employer involvement

Another common feature is the heavy involvement of employers, though in teacher education this role is delegated mainly to individual schools. The day-to-day management of the course involves regular formal meetings (at least twice a term) between university tutors and schoolteacher tutors, in addition to the myriads of informal meetings when university tutors visit the schools. A significant amount of teaching at the unversity end is delivered by schoolteachers brought in for the purpose. Schoolteachers are full members of the course team, and several sit on the PGCE Programme Group, the formal University Committee for managing its initial training commitment. Course reviews and proposals for change are formulated by the course team or by individual tutors, then discussed in the Programme Group at considerable length. If approved, it is unlikely that significant changes will be made by either Education Committee or Senate. It should be noted that there is also strong employer representation on the University's Council in the form of Chief Education Officers and Committee Chairpersons.

Course approval and evaluation

The external approval and evaluation process is much tougher in teacher education than most vocational sectors. First, there is a national framework of criteria determined by the Secretary of State. Second, the course has to be approved by a local Professional Committee, shared with Brighton Polytechnic, which has a majority of schoolteacher members, senior LEA inspectors and industrial representatives. Third, the course is inspected by HMI whose report is published. Fourth, the course has to be formally approved by the Committee for the Accreditation of Teacher Education (CATE) which receives institutional submissions, and reports from both the Professional Committee and HMI. The intensity of the monitoring and evaluation process is indicated by the following list of events at Sussex between 1984 and 1989:

— Annual reports from teams of external examiners go to the Vice-Chancellor, who expects to see our response.
— Full inspection by HMI in Autumn 1984 (now published).
— Second inspection of Primary Course by HMI in Summer 1989 (to be published).
— Informal inspection of Secondary Course by mixed group of HMI and industrial trainers in Summer 1989.
— External review of whole department by six invited 'experts' in Autumn 1986 (published).
— Visit by CATE sub-group in Summer 1987.
— Departmental visit by UGC Education Sub-Committee in 1988.
— Visits from senior DES officials who have talked with students and schoolteacher tutors.

Requirement for trainer experience

Another tough regulation, seldom found in other occupations, is the CATE requirement that trainers have recent and relevant experience of teaching in schools. This regulation places a major burden on staff development programmes. While possessing an obvious commonsense validity, it is not based on any functional analysis of the teacher trainer's role. Indeed, this gap between the regulations entrusted to CATE and evidence of performance outcomes is responsible for teacher educators' growing interest in the NCVQ model as an alternative regulatory framework. Incidentally, CATE itself has only one member with recent and relevant experience of teacher education, surely a record minimum for any accreditation agency.

Assessment criteria

Arrangements for the assessment of teaching practice feature prominently in all the approval and evaluation procedures. These involve the use of checklists and performance criteria, but do not include ratings. There is a strong formative element with regular informal feedback on classroom performance being consolidated by formal reports towards the end of each term. We are now trying to develop a profiling system that will improve continuity of support and appraisal between training and the first year of teaching (hitherto called the probationary year). This will be helped by the general introduction of teacher appraisal in 1990. While these lists, criteria and profiles draw attention clearly and specifically to the various aspects of a teacher's performance, they do not constitute a set of competency statements in the NVQ sense. That is a further step which many teacher educators are now increasingly interested in exploring.

Components of teacher education other than teaching practice

It is the non-practice based components of teacher education which appear to be incompatible with the NVQ model. So I think they should be given some careful attention. Here I will simply describe their purpose and rationale. Later I will attempt to ask whether the divergence from the NVQ model is more apparent than real, whether it results from moving up to the professional level, and whether it indicates ways in which the NVQ model might be appropriately modified for lower levels as well. Perhaps all three of these statements are true? I shall focus on four main aims of teacher education, which the non-practice based course components address: developing a repertoire of practices, developing reflective practitioners, developing a wider professional role, and personal development.

Developing a repertoire of practices

While interactive skills are best developed experientially, planning and decision making can be usefully developed 'out of the firing line'. The aim here is both to provide beginning teachers with a good starting repertoire of methods, approaches and ideas; and to develop the skills of deciding which to use when, and how to translate intentions into practical action plans. This is the primary purpose of what we at Sussex call 'Curriculum Seminars and Workshops', though elsewhere the rather narrower term 'Subject Method' is used. Since the course is taught concurrently with teaching practice, it begins by helping students plan their early lessons, then provides a wider forum for pooling their observations and experience of practices in the schools where all the students work. The tutor is an experienced teacher of the subject, with close knowledge of those and other schools and familiarity with the literature about the teaching of that subject. He or she is thus in a good position to develop students' awareness of a wider repertoire of approaches than can be found in the particular school where they practice. Sometimes the students will be able to try out these approaches in practice, sometimes the opportunity will not arise. Hence part of the repertoire will be developed to a level of competent implementation, while part will remain at the awareness/comprehension level — albeit strengthened by the reading of the literature, by student colleagues' experiences and by seminar discussions. Often the detailed planning of some new approach will form the substance of a student's special study.

Simultaneously with this development of the repertoire, this component of the course tries to develop students' planning and decision making skills. How can a topic best be structured and made accessible to a particular class of pupils? What kinds of learning activities have to be planned and implemented? What activities will both motivate pupils and effectively promote the desired learning outcomes? These types of skill are developed by continuing discussion both in the practice school and in the university seminars.

Developing reflective practitioners

It is now generally acknowledged that the interactive skills of teaching are developed experientially and intuitively. Many aspects of classroom teaching cannot be worked out in advance. Indeed, it is difficult for teachers even to describe their practice with any degree of accuracy. Central to this problem is the need for teachers to develop routines in order to cope, which may then become barriers to further progress. The antidote is believed to lie in the process of reflection, in which teachers think about their experiences after the event in order to consider what had happened and why, and whether something different might have helped. The reflective process does not attempt to deroutinise, to make everything rational or to challenge every assumption; but it does enable a teacher to work at their practice, modify it and keep it under critical control. At a more sophisticated level it shades into some kind of action research. The concept of the reflective practitioner is thus increasingly perceived by teacher educators as central to the process of developing flexible teachers who will continue to learn after qualification and who will be able to respond to new challenges and opportunities in the future.

In Sussex this aim is the main reason why the course is designed with concurrent school and university components. Throughout the first six months after induction, students spend three days a week in schools and two days a week at the university. The encouragement of reflection on practice as it occurs is partly the responsibility of a schoolteacher tutor giving feedback on teaching performance and partly that of weekly personal tutor groups at the university. It is also promoted by the requirement that students keep a reflective diary in their course file, which forms part of their final assessment. The personal tutor group consists at secondary level of all those students working in a particular school, and the personal tutor is the main university liaison person with that school.

The other element feeding into the reflective process is educational theory, whose introduction is also the personal tutor's responsibility. I shall return to the role of theory in my concluding section. Here it is sufficient to state that theory is introduced to help students interpret and criticise their observations and experiences, not to present students with a corpus of validated knowledge. We recognise that students already have their own implicit theories which underpin the way they perceive situations and think about their work; and that the process of reflection involves elucidating and modifying personal theories in the light of evidence, experience and alternative viewpoints, while at the same time personalising some of the public theories by integrating them into their thought and action. Thus all reflection involves some degree of theorising, and one aim of the course is to develop the students' capability and disposition to theorise in order to lay the foundation for ongoing professional development (Eraut, 1985).

Developing a wider professional role

Hitherto we have focused our attention almost entirely on the teacher in the classroom. But the role of the schoolteacher is much wider than that including, for example, pastoral care, parent relations, curriculum development and general participation in the life of the school. At Sussex, induction into these wider aspects of school life is the responsibility of the general tutor for each school, usually a senior teacher or deputy head. Some of the education courses at the university also relate to this wider professional role. Thus policies for children with special needs, for equal opportunities, for school relations with business and industry and for TVEI are introduced in each school, then further discussed in a more critical comparative way at the university. Some induction into aspects of the educational system at local or national level is also needed in order to acquaint new teachers with the government and financing of education, with the new national framework for the curriculum and assessment, with agents such as advisers, HMI, school psychologists and educational welfare officers. Similarly, an introduction to the changing nature of schools as organisations and new developments such as school focused staff development, appraisal, and school self-review would seem important for new teachers embarking on forty-year careers.

In none of these areas is the course seeking to develop specific skills and competencies. The objective is a good comprehension of the issues and an awareness of the wider professional role of the teacher and the contexts in which it is performed.

Personal development

Personal development is a central goal of higher education, and it would be disastrous if it ceased to be taken seriously during preparation for an occupation which is acknowledged to be highly dependent on personal qualities. In one sense it is implicit in the aim of developing reflective practitioners, but it is also given more explicit form in option programmes and special projects. It is not the content of these activities which is critical, though it is usually highly relevant, but the skills and attitudes they engender. This part of the course is concerned with developing confidence and initiative, with assuring students that the academic skills developed in their first degrees can be harnessed to the development of educational knowledge and the solution of practical teaching problems. They are the knowledge creators of the future, and their motivation to improve practice, to strive for a better education for their pupils, and to develop themselves, their schools and their professions has to be mobilised and fostered, otherwise it will soon be dissipated.

Models of job performance

In order to derive a competency based model which is more than just a list of distinctive tasks, some kind of model of job performance is needed. While the models presented in other chapters contain some useful and interesting features, they are still a little restrictive in their approach; and this in turn constrains the potential of the NVQ approach from being fully realised. In this section I shall briefly summarise a two-dimensional model I prepared after a Training Agency conference in Leicester in 1989 which greatly informed and stimulated my thinking. This combines the notion of a performance domain which arose during discussions at that conference with a new idea, a model of a performance period. I have now added a third dimension, largely concerned with developing a knowledge base over time. Finally I discuss quite a different model, the Skill Acquisition Model of the Dreyfus brothers (Dreyfus and Dreyfus, 1984). In each case the presentation of the model is followed by some discussion of its application to teacher education.

The performance domain

My definition of a performance domain comprises three main types of variable:

1   the contexts in which the performer will have to operate, including likely locations and their salient features
2   the conditions under which the performer will have to work, e.g., degree of

      supervision, pressure of time, crowdedness, conflicting priorities, availability of resources

3   the situations which the performer may encounter, covering such factors as client types and demands, tasks to be tackled, interpersonal events, emergencies, etc.

These variables are not entirely independent of each other, but to properly characterise a performance domain the range of each of these variables has to be specified.

Applying the idea to teaching we immediately note that a teacher has to perform with a range of classes, to assess the needs of and respond to a range of children, and to work over a range of subject matter to promote a range of learning outcomes. Whenever we assess teaching practice we make inferences about a student teacher's capacity to extend their observed competence in a limited range of situations to encompass a much larger performance domain. Indeed one aspect of a university's negotiations with practice schools concerns the range of practice situations which each school can provide. We feel happier about these assumptions about transfer of competence, if we get additional evidence that the student understands the observed situations, made deliberate decisions about the appropriate form of practice, and has the knowledge, skills and attitudes to develop or adopt different forms of practice to suit other situations they may encounter in the future.

Another assumption which is only partially tested, is that the student can handle the pressures of a full teaching load over a prolonged period. While some students seem to become less pressurised as they gain in confidence, others seem to suffer more from the increase in their load. The short term nature of a teaching practice in a 'borrowed' class also makes it difficult to plan children's work over a long period with due attention to continuity and progression. Skills in record-keeping also may be insufficiently developed. Work outside the classroom such as pastoral care, talking to parents or working with teacher colleagues gets even less attention. Clearly it is urgent that we take a much closer look at the nature of the performance domain for a newly qualified teacher. Is it sufficiently covered by the assessment? How does it differ from the domain of an experienced teacher? How will the gap between the two be tackled by continuing professional development?

A model of activities during a performance period

The reason for focusing attention on a performance period is to distinguish between doing a job and doing a collection of separate tasks. This allows for the possibility of interference between tasks, and draws attention to problems of prioritisation and deciding which task to do when. The period itself will vary according to the occupation; in teaching for example one could consider the lesson, the period between two breaks or the day. A major aspect of school experience for both teachers and pupils is that many tasks do not get completed during a performance period, so there is a constant problem of 'picking up the threads' to add to the competition for attention which is the teacher's daily fate.

Two other considerations influenced the model: the need to incorporate the cognitive element in the right kind of way, and a desire to give equal attention to input and output. There tends to be a failure to recognise the extent to which even the most menial task carries a strong cognitive element, because people often equate cognition with explicit use of formally organised knowledge. The significance of implicit theory underpinning most kinds of performance was mentioned above; and those who have doubts on the point should try training animals to do the job instead. People are constantly thinking and making decisions as they go along, even though they could probably tell you very little about it afterwards. Similarly, a great deal of competent behaviour depends not just on being able to do certain things (output) but also in the correct reading of the situation (input) so that the appropriate action is taken. One advantage of using a performance period is that situations often develop over time. So, instead of a static model in which all decisions and plans are made at the beginning of a period, one has a dynamic model in which a constantly changing environment provides a changing input which leads to the constant modification of plans. Nor is it only the external environment which changes of its own accord. The performer is an actor who affects that environment, not always in totally predictable ways. So another role of input is to provide feedback on the effect of one's own performance. This applies whether one is making something and sensing it change, or talking to someone and listening to their reply and observing their reaction.

The 'period' base of the model can be seen in Figure 12.1 in the separate boxes for Initiation and Ending to indicate both the initial briefing and reading of the situation when the period starts and what has been made, assessed or learned by the time the period ends. The input side is shown by placing the activities within a context, which has changing conditions and a developing situation, with the opportunity for input by sensing and listening.

The interpretation of this input is just one aspect of the cognitive element, indicated by a central column marked 'Thinking'. Others include planning and monitoring one's activities, making decisions and solving problems. Hence 'Thinking' is shown in constant interaction with 'Doing' and 'Communicating'. These activities overlap a little in meaning; the distinction is primarily one between acting on inanimate objects and interacting with other human beings.

The developing knowledge base

This third dimension of my performance model is introduced to take account of the

Figure 12.1 Activities During a Performance Period

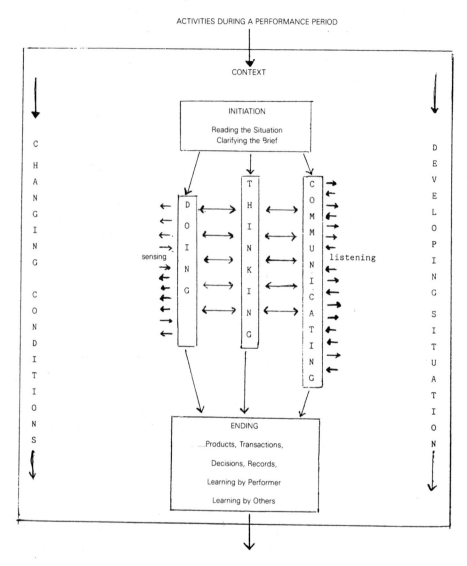

development of the knowledge base over time. It is what, apart from desirable outcomes, gets carried on from one performance period to the next. The most obvious examples are the accumulation of knowledge about the people with whom one is in regular contact and about contexts and situations with which one becomes increasingly familiar. Teachers get to know children, workers get to know colleagues, shopkeepers get to know their regular customers, doctors get to know their patients, managers get to know their subordinates. But do they do it well? Competence in learning about people and situations is a vital ingredient in many occupations, and especially important in both teaching and management (Eraut, 1988). More formal kinds of knowledge can be deduced by questioning and by direct observation over short periods. But this experiential wisdom and the ability to acquire it does not often feature in occupational analysis.

The learning of more formal knowledge can also be important in some occupations. The travel agent needs to learn about places, the financier about new laws and taxes, the doctor about new drugs. So the capacity for developing one's formal knowledge base may be needed in addition to the more experiential learning already discussed. People who have ceased to learn cease to be competent.

The Dreyfus Model of skill acquisition

The term 'competence' sometimes worries me. It is often used to set minimum targets which limit expectations. If this helps to reduce the load on initial training, I am all in favour. But if, once trained, people consider their competence as sufficient and ignore the need for further improvement, then mere competence is not enough. One should expect continuing improvement after qualification, and performance models need to take that into account as well. Only some activities are properly described by a binary model — either you can do it or you cannot. Others are characterised by gradations in performance. A competency model suggests that progression lies mainly in increasing the number of competencies rather than improving those you have already got. But to be a Jack of all trades is to be Master of none.

One great strength of the Dreyfus Model is its five stage description of skill acquisition: novice, advanced beginner, competent, proficient, then finally expert (Dreyfus and Dreyfus, 1984). Another is its attempt to consider the more experiential aspects of skill acquisition, the role of routinisation and the development of strategic approaches. One fascinating feature of the model is that it was originally developed from studies of chess players and airline pilots, then later applied to Information Technology. As a teacher educator, however, it is Benner's application of the model to nursing that I have found the most pertinent. Her analysis is briefly summarised in Figure 12.2 (Benner, 1982).

Figure 12.2 Summary of the Dreyfus Model of Skills Acquisition

---

Level 1

— *Novice*

Rigid adherence to taught rules or plans
Little situational perception
No discretionary judgement

Level 2

— *Advanced Beginner*

Guidelines for action based on attributes or aspects (aspects are global
characteristics of situations recognisable only after some prior experience)
Situational perception still limited
All attributes and aspects are treated separately and given equal
importance

Level 3

— *Competence*

Coping with crowdedness
Now sees actions at least partially in terms of longer-term goals
Conscious deliberate planning
Standardized and routinized procedures

Level 4

— *Proficient*

Sees situations holistically rather than in terms of aspects
Sees what is most important in a situation
Perceives deviations from the normal pattern
Decision-making less laboured
Uses maxims for guidance, whose meaning varies according to the
situation

Level 5

— *Expert*

No longer relies on rules, guidelines or maxims
Intuitive grasp of situations based on deep tacit understanding
Analytic approaches used only in novel situations or when problems
occur
Vision of what is possible

This model posits a significant qualitative gap between the competent and the proficient. Competency is the climax of rule guided learning and discovering how to cope in crowded, pressurised contexts, whereas proficiency marks the onset of quite a different approach to the job. Normal behaviour is not just routinised but semi-automatic. Situations are apprehended more deeply and the abnormal is quickly spotted and given attention. The sense of priority is clear and strategic approaches are used. However, more experience of successful problem solving and strategic planning is needed before expertise can be said to have been developed.

It would be fruitful to discuss how widely this model can be applied. For now, let us just consider what questions it raises. For example, if we consider a job to have a number of different aspects, i.e., a wide-ranging performance domain, then at what stage in the skill acquisition process for each aspect should the qualifying line be drawn? Could it be at the proficiency rather than the competency level for some aspects? Could it be below the competency level for others? Might the appropriate answer depend on the degree of supervision and subsequent training available? Wherever one stands on this issue, and whether or not one chooses to adopt the Dreyfus Model, one central point emerges from this discussion. In order to redesign a training system, one first needs a model of Knowledge Acquisition (using the term 'knowledge' in its widest sense, i.e., to include skills and practical know-how as well as cognitive achievement) which is graduated rather than binary in character. Only then can one decide where are the appropriate points to place the initial qualification and what are the briefs for continuing education and further qualifications.

This strategy might expose the arbitrary nature of the initial qualifying point in many occupations. It might also help to link occupational status more to the level of expertise reached and less to the level of the initial qualification. It is the latter which leads to unnecessary academicism and qualification inflation. Some third world countries have developed quite different approaches to levels of medical qualification, than those which we now take for granted, with lower levels dealing with common problems only and passing all the others to more qualified people with better care facilities.

My own view of the licensed teacher scheme is that it addresses the wrong problem by suggesting a different form of training to solve what is perceived as a problem of recruitment. We need a much more radical approach if we are to examine the teacher supply problem more seriously. We need to consider both how to help trainees become competent (in the sense of being capable of being left in charge of a class) and how to help them become proficient (the level of performance reached by good teachers after 3–5 years). Then we can consider different training models for achieving these goals. Only then do we raise the question of the point at which the initial qualification is awarded; and how we can link different levels of remuneration to the appropriate levels of skill acquisition. Cannot the length of each training stage also be varied to suit the learning rates of individual student teachers?

The role of theory in practical affairs

The NCVQ and the Training Agency recognise that job performance is under-pinned by knowledge, but argue that this knowledge need not be directly assessed because it can be observed in use. In practice, the time available for such assessment is often so limited that the sampling of the performance domain is inadequate. Hence the question of assessing knowledge arises in the context of inferring that performers can transfer their competence to unobserved situations. This can only be achieved by developing some model of the nature of the knowledge that underpins performance. However, adequate models are not readily available in the training literature, nor in the practice of examination boards. The problem arises, I believe, from a failure to appreciate the role of theory in practical affairs.

There are several reasons why people tend to regard theory negatively. First, it is easy to make it irrelevant by definition: when people start using a theory they stop calling it theory. This 'irrelevance' is then reinforced by the tendency of formal education to concentrate on people's comprehension of theory rather than their use of it. Also people become alienated by theory through being constantly subjected to other people's theories rather than encouraged to develop their own. Or if, in contrast, they go looking for theories to tell them what to do, they find that theory does not prescribe practice and become disillusioned with the whole idea.

Yet people use theory all the time; and it is their personal theories which determine how they interpret the world and their encounters with people and situations within it. In my earlier discussion of the concept of the reflective practitioner, I argued that in teaching and most other professions, performers should attempt to bring the largely intuitive aspects of their practice under some kind of critical control. Both transfer to a wider range of situations and further improvement of performance in familiar situations are difficult to achieve without this critical consciousness of what one is doing and why. Once one becomes more aware of the nature and effect of one's own theories, then it is possible to also consider those of others, whether they be immediate colleagues or authors of books. Similarly, by recognising the contexts in which one has developed one's theories, one is better able to judge when new theories are needed to cope with new kinds of contexts.

My challenge to those concerned with vocational training is to ask them how far this concept of the reflective practitioner is relevant to those personal qualities sometimes described as flexibility, adaptability, situational understanding and ability to learn from experience? There is a considerable body of psychological evidence to show that personal theories have a significant effect on how people think, act and perform (Nisbett and Ross, 1980). Perhaps trainers should give it more attention.

Another role for theory in practical affairs lies in strategic thinking. To be successful, this needs considerable understanding of the context, a sense of priorities, awareness of alternatives, and an ability to predict the consequences of various courses of action over the longer term. This kind of thinking is important in many occupations yet difficult to observe in practice. It is unlikely to show up in short observations of performance and may not develop very far prior to qualification. But does this mean that pre-qualification training should not devote any time to it? Given the lack of post-qualification training in so many occupations, one hesitates to cut those aspects of initial training which prepare people for the longer term. There is much to be learned from the way teacher education is gradually working out a role for theory that is appropriate for its own special mission.

References

BENNER, P. (1982) 'From novice to expert', *American Journal of Nursing*, 82, 3, pp. 402–7.

DREYFUS, H. L. and DREYFUS, S. E. (1984) 'Putting computers in their proper place; Analysis versus intuition in the classroom', in Sloan, D. (Ed.) *The Computer in Education: A Critical Perspective*, Columbia, NY, Teachers' College Press.

ERAUT, M. (1985) *The Acquisition and Use of Educational Theory by Beginning Teachers*. UCET Conference Paper.

ERAUT, M. (1988) 'Learning about management: The role of the management course', in Day, C. and Poster, C. (Eds) *Partnership in Education Management*, London, Routledge.

FURLONG, V. J., HIRST, P. H., POCKLINGTON, K. and MILES, S. (1988) *Initial Teaching Training and the Role of the School*, Milton Keynes, Open University Press.

LACEY, C. and LAMONT, W. (1974) *Partnership with Schools: An Experiment in Teacher Education*, Occasional Paper 5, University of Sussex Education Area.

NISBETT, R. E. and ROSS, L. (1980) *Human Inference in Strategies and Shortcomings of Social Judgement*, New York, Prentice Hall.

Chapter 13

Emerging issues:
The response of higher education to competency based approaches

Tim Oates

Introduction

This commentary provides an overview of the issues raised in group and open discussion during the *Competency Based Learning Symposium.*

Following tradition, discussions varied in the degree to which they directly addressed the topics raised in the formal presentations and the tasks presented to the working groups. However, whether oblique or coincident, the tenor and content of contributions during discussion reflected a perception shared by symposium members: that current developments in competency based learning are not whim or fashion, and will have a direct or indirect impact on Higher Education *irrespective* of whether it develops a specific policy response to those developments.

Although wide-ranging and animated, discussions centred on three main topics. Symposium members probed the origins and nature of the developments in competency based learning; examined how the techniques being developed might enhance curriculum development in HE; and explored the extent to which the developments are effecting structural change in the relations between agencies and institutions in the UK education and training system. Accordingly, this commentary is arranged into three main sections which reflect these themes:

— the rationale and development history of competency based learning
— technical characteristics of current developments in competency based learning
— future strategy in HE in response to developments in competency based learning.

The author has added selected text from relevant sources and illuminative comments where these help to elucidate and/or tease out the implications of issues raised.

The rationale and development history of competency based learning

The current development work by the National Council for Vocational Qualifications (NCVQ) on implementing a new framework of National Vocational Qualifications in England and Wales is assuming a high profile. For many, competency based learning is associated strongly — or even exclusively — with the work of NCVQ. NCVQ developers themselves stressed that this misrepresents the true picture. Both the history and the diversity of competency based learning need to be emphasised.

Firstly, the NCVQ development work is proceeding *in partnership with* the Training Agency (TA), industry and prominent bodies within UK VET (Vocational Education and Training). The importance of the partnership with industry is emphasised by both NCVQ and the TA.

The NCVQ partnership with the Training Agency (TA) is particularly important. NCVQ's implementation effort makes substantial use of networks and structures established by the TA, particularly the system of Industry Lead Bodies (ILBs). It is the ILBs which are responsible for identifying the 'employment led standards' which make up the new National Vocational Qualifications (NVQs). This is explored in more detail in the final section of this commentary.

Secondly, some HE institutions have made headway in developing competency based programmes — witness the practice based teacher education courses at Ulster and Sussex Universities, and the continuing use of periods of time in workplaces within sandwich courses, medical training, etc. Dissemination of the insights emerging from this work would help curriculum developers across the HE sector, but much still remains to be done. In particular, symposium members stated that further curriculum development work is required for ensuring that the workplace component is used for 'structured learning' and for ensuring effective linking, or integration, between the institution based and practice based elements of programmes.

Thirdly, the TA has commissioned the Enterprise Initiative in HE and investigative work on access to HE. The former is designed to promote entrepreneurial activity and greater engagement in the world of work by learners in HE. The eleven institutions which were successful in their bids for awards of £1 million (over five years) are implementing this across all disciplines, not just in areas which traditionally have included practice components or have maintained strong links with industry.

Finally, the developments currently labelled as 'competency based learning' have been growing in momentum over the last thirty years. They have their origins in profound concerns that traditional education programmes were failing to address the needs of both learners and industry. Current developments are therefore best characterised not as part of a one-off, 'inspirational' policy drive but as continuing appraisal and revision of the function and content of educational provision. 1957 saw the launch of Sputnik and a resulting wave of anxiety in the Western world regarding the orientation and function of education, particularly in science. Following the emergence of the so-called 'Black Papers' in 1969, concern over poor economic performance and rising unemployment during the 1970s led to Prime Minister Callaghan's speech at Ruskin College in October 1976. Here he emphasised that:

> . . . I am concerned on my journeys to find complaints from industry that new recruits from the schools sometimes do not have the basic tools to do the job that is required.

> I have been concerned to find that many of our best trained students who have completed the higher levels of education at university or polytechnic have no desire or intention of joining industry . . .

The seminal think-tank paper *Education, Training and Industrial Performance*, by the CPRS (Central Policy Review Staff) highlighted that learners emerging from education programmes generally lacked the capacity to *apply* skills and knowledge in the context of work. This was accompanied by a growing recognition that many manual and traditional skills were in decline. It was predicted that new skills and knowledge would increasingly be required, associated with understanding production systems, possessing strategies for coping with contingencies, etc. Commentators emphasised that transition to a 'post industrial society' was occurring, with an 'information based society' emerging from changing technology and work systems.

The New Training Initiative (MSC, 1981) formed the blueprint for strategies designed to increase participation in VET and for ensuring that the function and content of provision meets training needs in a rapidly changing and increasingly competitive economic environment. The formation of NCVQ in 1986 was presaged by the statement in NTI that ' . . . at the heart of the initiative lies standards of a new kind . . . ' (p. 6).

The implementation of NTI has proceeded through wide-ranging processes of consultation, partnership and intervention. How should HE perceive the current developments? Is it presented with a scenario where partnership is being proposed? Will this deteriorate into intervention? Is intervention simply being cloaked in the mantle of consultation? If the TA Enterprise Initiative in HE is characterised as 'partnership', how should the NCVQ developments be perceived? There are two important strategic issues. Firstly, initial NCVQ development work has focused on implementing a four-level framework which spans qualifications from the 'most basic' level to those approximating to higher national. The impact on awards above this is now prescribed by the invitation to NCVQ in early 1989 by the Secretary of State for

Employment to extend the framework to include qualifications at 'professional' level, including degree awards. This begs the question as to when a particular degree award is considered to be a 'vocational qualification', but there is immediate relevance to awards linked to professional bodies, and particularly to awards associated with the idea of 'licence to practice'.

Secondly, one of the most important aspects of NCVQ strategy is that the policy statements emphasise ' . . . the new forms of competence based qualifications . . . *lead rather than follow* education and training . . . ' (Gilbert Jessup, chapter 6, this volume). The dominant strategy is therefore one of effecting change in curriculum content through the qualifications themselves. Therefore, the process of who decides what will go into a particular award is critical. Within the system implemented by TA and NCVQ, the 'who' are industry interests. The 'what' is determined by the industry as a result of analysis of the functions which employees carry out, paying particular attention to purpose and outcome.

This represents a fundamental re-orientation in the pressures acting on curriculum development in HE. This will be explored in more detail in the final section of this commentary. The next section examines the technical characteristics of the current development activity and catalogues problems raised by symposium members relating to method.

Technical characteristics of current developments in competency based learning

Just what is the definition of 'competence' which lies behind 'competency based learning'? Symposium members immediately homed in on this issue; exploration of the definition was used as a means for establishing just how the aims and objectives behind competence based learning articulate with the aims and objectives under-pinning HE provision.

Discussion of conflicting views often begins with each antagonist painting a rough caricature of the opposition's position. The symposium was no exception. If the TA and NCVQ policy position was portrayed as promoting a narrow definition of skill which neglected development of the 'whole person' and precluded curiosity-motivated study, then HE developers were portrayed as advocates of learning provision which lacked precision in statements of aims and outcomes, and being committed to delivering knowledge and theory without support to learners on how to apply that knowledge and theory within the world of work. As the protagonists circled each other and explored the advantages and disadvantages of their respective positions, the caricatures began to decay and a consensus began to emerge.

The breadth of the definition of competence promoted by the TA provided reassurance to many. Though ' . . . unashamedly about the ability to perform effectively . . . ', the TA states that:

> . . . occupational competence is defined as 'the ability to perform the activities within an occupation or function to the standards expected in employment'. This is a wide concept which embodies the ability to transfer skills and knowledge to new situations within the occupational area. It encompasses organisation and planning of work, innovation and coping with non-routine activities and includes those qualities of personal effectiveness required in the workplace to deal with co-workers, managers and customers. It stems from an understanding to perform effectively in a work role an individual has to be able to combine
> — performance of various technical and task components
> — overarching management of the various technical and task components to achieve the overall work function
> — management of the variance and unpredictability in the work role and wider environment
> — integration of the work role within the context of the wider organisational, economic, market and social environment (TA, 1988).

Symposium members supported the breadth of this definition, and were further reassured by the technical effort currently devoted to including relevant knowledge in the standards which make up the new NVQs. It was recognized, however, that whilst the relation between the development work on competency based learning and HE provision was clear in some subject/discipline areas — engineering, medicine, teacher education, etc. — its relationship to other areas was by no means obvious. Indeed, reification of competency based learning might lead to anything other than highly instrumental provision being severely devalued. However, TA and NCVQ policy makers are sanguine about this area. They see room for the co-existence of curiosity-motivated and mission-oriented provision within HE, but emphasise that the rationales for these different areas need to be explicitly recognized and not confused/conflated. Additionally, they anticipate that any impact and takeup of approaches to competency based learning in HE will occur unevenly across different discipline areas, just as the work with professional bodies on establishing the NVQ framework at higher levels is expected to be ' . . . slow and uneven . . . '.

Within this debate, a key point surfaced briefly. Just where does learners' motivation to learn come from? Linking learning to the work role can be a key motivator for learners. Problems and issues emerging from an individual's work role can be used as a stepping-off point into much wider learning activities. Not least, this reflects the latest development work on the use of theory in practice. This emphasises that delivering theory in a way which is closely linked to practice can have a profound effect on a learner's ability to apply that theory in new, unfamiliar contexts.

The consensus emerging from the discussion of the definition of competence cut two ways. For the TA and NCVQ, there was confirmation that they should continue to ensure that the new qualifications protect the longer-term aims of learners and guarantee their occupational mobility. For HE curriculum developers, there was confirmation that HE curricula could be informed by analysis of its aims, objectives and outcomes, and perhaps enhanced by closer linkage with the demands of work role. Within this, there was recognition that in sandwich and other courses with a practice component, strategies were required for structuring learning in the workplace and for more effective assessment.

But two further, related issues are buried in the concerns regarding 'narrowness'. The first of these is that the new qualifications will be tied too closely to the requirements of a particular job in a particular occupational sector. Thus, ensuring that a learner obtains such a qualification does not mean that the *occupational mobility* of the learner is being secured. The second of these relates to the problem of updating the content of the qualifications. The new qualifications specify the elements and performance criteria which make up competent performance in considerable detail. This detailed prescription is seen by NCVQ and the TA as one of the keys to quality in VET. The qualification is a specification of content — '. . . leading rather than following education and training . . . '. If the content of the qualifications is tied so closely to working practices and work systems, how long is it before a particular qualification becomes a straightjacket, institutionalising out-moded practice rather than continuing to reflect existing best practice? At this point in time, the answer is uncertain. Qualifications in different sectors will become outmoded at different rates. Updating qualifications requires continuous evaluation and analysis of the link between each qualification and the work roles to which they relate. The prevailing view of policy makers is that the advantages of specifying the content of qualifications in detail outweighs any potential or emerging disadvantages. Again, a watching brief appears necessary here.

With discussion centering on the definition of competence, a small number of symposium members widened debate by emphasising that no matter how broad, well-grounded and egalitarian your definition of competence, it will count for little if the strategy for implementation distorts your intentions. Attention must focus on the analysis techniques which are used to identify what makes up competence in a specific work role.

The limitations of existing techniques such as task analysis, the imported DACUM approach (Developing A CurriculUM) etc., mean that they are not appropriate as analysis techniques for determining the content of the new qualifications. This is unsurprising, since they were designed for a different purpose, but developers in FHE have often appropriated analysis techniques and used them in ways which were never intended. The recognition of the limitations of existing techniques has led to the development of 'functional analysis'. A great deal hangs on the capacity of functional analysis to deliver its promise of comprehensive analysis of the requirements of occupational competence. The timescale for implementation, the effects of 'handing over' the responsibility for undertaking analysis to the Industry Lead Bodies may compromise the level of rigour which is expected, and thus compromise the new qualifications. The need for evaluation of the impact and takeup of functional analysis was highlighted by symposium members.

Incorporating specification of relevant knowledge within the standards has proved particularly problematic. The conception of knowledge as a 'bolt-on' to performance — dominant in the early work on assessment in TA programmes — was responsible for many of these problems. However, following consultation and intensive development effort, relevant knowledge is now being incorporated into standards; an approach which symposium members saw as essential.

One of the more significant aspects of the new qualifications is that they are to be 'more informative'; following the recommendations of the Review of Vocational Qualifications (MSC and DES, 1986). That is, they should offer more information about an individual's achievements to selectors in industry, and in education and training. The intention is that the new awards should offer 'a statement of competence'. For HE this introduces the question of how degree and other awards *communicate* an individual's achievements. What does it *mean* to 'possess a degree in physical chemistry' or 'possess a PGCE'? Selectors within the HE sector frequently discriminate between degrees in the same discipline awarded by different institutions. A 'league table' clearly exists; it is partly explicit, partly tacit. But the key question is this: those within the HE sector and a limited number outside it may well discriminate between awards in an informed way, but what of the majority of hapless employers? How can they find out just what curriculum content has been covered in a course leading to a particular award from a specific HE institution? They are, after all, 'end-users' of HE certification; should they be provided with 'more informative' records of learners' achievements? Symposium members were attracted to the idea of stating the outcomes of courses with more precision. Not least, *learners* would accrue benefits from this; they would have more explicit targets and greater awareness of their own abilities. But the consensus erred on the side of 'useful but difficult'. Making the outcomes explicit would involve some hard-hitting questions about why courses look the way that they do and the degree to which the different components of courses link together.

Another key question emerged: 'who is the client?'. With the ILBs determining the content of awards within the NVQ framework, who would be securing learners' rights and interests? Whilst the TA programme guidance emphasises the 'learner centred' character of both learning and assessment processes, input to the symposium from the TA emphasised that ' . . . the state is the primary client . . . '. This reflects the Government's concern to ensure a 'supply' of competent, qualified workers into the labour market. However, this notion of the state as the primary client, coupled with the role of the ILBs, caused anxiety amongst symposium members. Fundamental changes in the locus of control appear to be underway, and symposium members flagged the importance of retaining the notion of 'the learner as client' at the centre of curriculum design processes.

Future strategy in HE as a response to current developments in competency based learning

Whilst symposium members concentrated on the technical characteristics of functional analysis, issues relating to the shifts in existing power relations emerged throughout discussion. Just what does the emerging system look like?

The National Council is not a traditional examining or validating body. It develops policy for the vocational qualifications system as a whole, negotiates to achieve the objectives for the system which were enshrined in the White Paper *Working Together — Education and Training* (DOE and DES, 1986), and accredits (i.e, kite-marks) the qualifications of bodies offering awards within the national framework. But on its inception in late 1986, with whom was it to negotiate? Obviously, it had to deal with the examining, validating and certificating bodies whose awards were to fit into the framework. But the Government also gave it the role of working closely with the TA (then the Manpower Services Commission) and industry interests for specifying standards of competence across all occupations. In the same White Paper that established NCVQ (DOE and DES, 1988), the Government asked the MSC to take the lead in stimulating industry training organisations in this matter. This the commission did through nominating Industry Lead Bodies to represent occupational groupings. In effect, therefore, the Government, through the Training Agency, retained de facto control of standards setting. Thus, the NCVQ is left with the role of broker — between, on the one hand, the Training Agency and the ILBs who are setting standards and, on the other, the bodies which were to incorporate those standards in their awards.

As a broker, NCVQ operates through consent and consensus but with the possibility of legislation if insufficient movement in the system is perceived by senior civil servants and the politicians. This possibility was plainly stated as a threat in the White Paper: ' . . . the Government will not hesitate to act should it appear that legislation is necessary to make the new NVQ framework effective . . . ' (DOE and DES, 1986, p.23).

Within the new arrangements, endorsed by the recent White Paper *Employment for the 1990s* (DOE, 1988), it is the Industry Lead Bodies (ILBs) who generate 'employment-led' standards which make up NVQs at each level. They vary in composition, but can include different combinations of Industry Training Boards, non-statutory training organisations, employer organisations, unions and education interests. They are formally independent of both the Training Agency and NCVQ but the Training Agency offers a strong lead in setting up and defining the scope of each ILB. The intention is that the ILBs, in partnership with NCVQ, will fit revised and new qualifications into the levels framework, thus ensuring the coherence of the overall system. Centralised control will thus be maintained by NCVQ operating in partnership with the ILBs whilst the levels framework will be the main prop of the system. However, a substantial re-alignment of the balance of power may have been effected by the introduction of the National Record of Achievement (NROVA), which allows learners to accumulate over time the units which make up an NVQ. Both employers and learners may therefore demand collections of units which match their needs in a particular work role but don't 'add up' to a full NVQ. This 'bottom up' pressure may undermine specific full NVQs in an unpredictable way.

Nevertheless, whatever the effects of NROVA, the ILBs are therefore key agencies in ensuring that the standards which make up the new qualifications relate to effective performance in work activities. However, they are a mixed group, both in terms of the histories of the various bodies and agencies which come together to form an ILB for a particular sector and in terms of the way in which the respective ILBs' scope varies. The new ILB for trainers, for example, has scope which overlaps all the other ILBs' spheres of influence. Some of the reasons for this variation derive from the way that the ILB system has, over time, assumed an increasing number of functions. The origins of the system lie in MSC-initiated development work on qualifications for the two-year Youth Training Scheme, overseen by the now-defunct Youth Certification Board. The ILBs' initial focus on YTS was quickly expanded to include provision of standards based qualifications of the Government's adult-oriented New Job Training Scheme (NJTS) and the subsequent Employment Training programme (ET). Further expansion has occurred as ILBs have been called to provide qualifications at all levels of the NVQ framework. New ILBs have been added to the system, existing ILBs have increased their scope and, unsurprisingly, boundary disputes have emerged.

The potential impact of these developments on HE provision is focused through the NCVQ's remit to incorporate professional bodies' awards within the NVQ framework. The Government:

> ... has invited the Council to consult with appropriate professions and other bodies on how higher levels of professional qualifications can be best articulated within the proposed National Vocational Qualification framework ....

The original NCVQ's objectives — which emerged from the *Review of Vocational Qualifications* (April, 1986) — included:

> ... providing opportunities for progression, including progression to higher education and professional qualifications ...

The Government accepted the recommendation that the new national framework should be called the NVQ framework and that it should be designed to incorporate and embrace existing vocational qualifications up to and including higher levels of professional qualifications. The Government also said it believed that the NCVQ should be entitled to expect the full cooperation and commitment of professional bodies in fitting all appropriate qualifications below degree level into levels I—IV of the NVQ framework by 1991. It then invited the new national council to consult the appropriate professional and other bodies on how higher levels of professional qualifications, above Level IV, could best be articulated with the proposed new framework. Given that, in the Government's own estimation, there were some 250 professional bodies which examined and awarded qualifications at varying levels, this was always going to be a difficult task.

Therefore, key relationships will be those that exist between HE institutions and the professional bodies. Where an individual HE institution is an awarding body, it can only fully participate in the NVQ system if it satisfies the criteria associated with NVQ awarding bodies. Not least amongst these are the requirements for employment interests to establish the standards which comprise the award and for assessment of performance in the workplace to be the dominant mode of assessment.

Arising from this, a question asked but unanswered in the symposium remains critical: 'What will provide an incentive for HE institutions to participate in the NVQ system?'. Possible answers can perhaps be anticipated. Not least, external pressures may play their part:

— where institutions link to professional bodies which are recognised as NVQ awarding bodies, they will be drawn into the system
— with the capacity for credit accumulation, learners may approach institutions for 'topping up' collections of units so that they can attain a full NVQ
— learners holding NVQs will approach HE institutions for entry to courses. The issue of access to HE is being explored in TA-funded development work
— demographic changes, though uneven across different socio-economic groups, may mean that a growing number of 'adult returners' may approach HE for full awards and for professional updating. NVQs may be the 'currency' in individual learners' occupational areas; pressure will therefore be placed on the institution to deliver content appropriate to a particular NVQ.

Many symposium members emphasised that the techniques being developed within competency based learning — such as functional analysis, assessment of performance, etc. — could be mobilised within existing HE programmes. Not least, these could contribute to a clarification of the aims and outcomes of provision and to a refinement of learning and assessment processes. However, an undercurrent beneath comments and questions was that HE was interested in the techniques but was holding back from participating in the overall structural realignment of vocational qualifications. It was as if symposium members felt that they could lift parts of the functional analysis methodology and leave the structural revision of the UK VET system on one side. This may be possible, but is it a wise strategic move?

The implication of the animated and wide-ranging discussion at the symposium was that HE should take an active role in the development of competence based learning. It should take responsibility for declaring its interests and imperatives, for there are no signs that the emerging system of UK VET provision will simply wait on an input from HE interests.

Finally, the impact of competency based learning is not limited to a problem of staff development. In responding to the challenge of individualised learning, linking learning to the work role, new modes of assessment, new content, new patterns of attendance and new client groups, FHE institutions will need to adopt responses within curriculum development, staff development and institutional development. The current diversity of curriculum development processes in HE may well continue, but the developments in competence based learning may mean that greater pressure is placed on institutions to establish the *function* of their provision with a level of specificity which HE has never contemplated previously.

References

DOE (1988) *Employment for the 1990s*, London, HMSO.
DOE and DES (1986) *Working Together — Education and Training*, London, HMSO.
MSC (1981) *NTI — A Consultative Document*, Sheffield, MSC.
MSC and DES (1986) *Review of Vocational Qualifications in England and Wales*, London, HMSO.
TA (1988) *The Concept of Occupational Competence*, Sheffield, Training Agency.

Notes on Contributors

Alan Brown has been a Research Fellow in the Division of Youth and Further Education within the Department of Educational Studies at the University of Surrey since 1981. He has worked on a number of major action research projects concerning innovatory practice in youth and further education and is currently involved in an Anglo-German study of vocational preparation in declining and expanding labour markets, and an evaluation of the teacher training development programme to promote information technology in technical and vocational education.

In addition, Alan has extensive teaching experience in further and higher education in social science, technology and education. He recently acted as the UK consultant for the European Institute of Education and Social Policy in producing evidence for the European Commission on the skill requirements of modern industry. Other consultancy work has been undertaken for the Department of Education and Science, the Engineering Industry Training Board, the Further Education Unit and the Open University.

John Burke is a Senior Research Fellow in the Institute of Continuing and Professional Education, University of Sussex. He has a wide experience of teaching, spanning primary/middle/secondary and sixth form college, university undergraduate and postgraduate courses, as well as FE and adult education. For a number of years he was a training manager in industry and he has worked on a number of research projects for the MSC and NCVQ; these have included a study of the reshaped framework and Record of Achievement in YTS, the development of NVQs, and the implementation of NVQs in FE. His current research centres on the identification of school management competences and the development of generic competences.

Graham Debling is head of the Employment Department, Training Agency's Standards Methodology Unit. The Unit has been established primarily to support the

Training Agency's Standards Programme but it also provides professional support and advice to other initiatives and programmes. Previously Mr Debling was a member of the Her Majesty's Inspectorate for Further and Higher Education in Scotland. He played a central role in the implementation of the Scottish Action Plan — the conversion of the traditional syllabus defined further education curriculum to a modular, criterion referenced, output defined format.

Michael Eraut is Director of the Institute of Continuing and Professional Education, University of Sussex. He came to the University in 1967 from the University of Illinois, and became a Reader in 1976 and a Professor of Education in 1986. During this period his research has covered management education, business education, YTS and prevocational education and a variety of new approaches to evaluation. Current projects include the mapping of curriculum options in business education, whole school policies for information technology and groupwork with computers. He has also written a number of papers on the nature of professional knowledge, especially those aspects which are acquired experientially, and on how professionals learn different types of knowledge.

Ian Haffenden is Staff Tutor in the Division of Youth and Further Education within the Department of Educational Studies at the University of Surrey. He has previously taught mathematics and physics in secondary education; in further and adult education in the Engineering and General Education departments of a college of further education and in secondary/youth education in the Seychelles. He is currently co-directing a Training Agency/FEU funded national study of the impact and implications of the new vocational qualifications in Further Education. Ian has published in journals and books, and is currently co-editing a book entitled *Educating Young Adults: International Perspectives*.

Gilbert Jessup is Director of Research, Development and Information, National Council for Vocational Qualifications. He set up and became the first Director of the Work Research Unit (1974–78) in the Department of Employment, with the remit to improve the quality of working life in British industry. While at the MSC (1982–87), he played a central role in formulating the MSC strategy in developing employment-led standards and assessment methods leading to new forms of modular qualifications. He initiated many of the early development projects in this field and helped to establish competence-based training. He was influential in reshaping the framework of YTS and introducing the Record of Achievement. At the NCVQ (since 1987) Gilbert has devised an R&D programme, introduced the National Record of Vocational Achievement (NROVA) and has been influential in developing the NVQ model of qualifications. Gilbert Jessup was made honorary Professor of Occupational Psychology at Nottingham University in 1976.

Bob Mansfield was co-founder of Barbara Shelborn Training and Development in 1982. Barbara Shelborn Developments (BSD) Limited is the research and development division of Barbara Shelborn Training and Development, a private sector training, research and development organisation based in Wakefield, West Yorkshire. He joined an Industry Training Board in 1977 as a Senior Training Adviser specialising in group working systems, industrial relations, training design and management development. Bob is a consultant to a wide range of public and private sector bodies, and specialises in the development of standards, occupational analysis and accreditation systems. He is a member of the TA Technical Advisory Group which develops guidance on the design of competency based standards and qualifications.

Lindsay Mitchell is Director of Research and Development at Barbara Shelborn Developments (BSD) Limited. Following extensive research experience in educational processes and assessment, she became project officer of '16 + in YTS', a project designed to develop the work based accreditation of Scottish modules; she became research officer of the 'Accreditation of Work Based Learning Project' in 1986. Later that year, she was appointed Director of the Competency Testing Project (SCOTVEC/MSC). Two years later, she joined Barbara Shelborn as Director of Research and Development. Lindsay Mitchell has a national reputation in the design and implementation of accreditation systems, and works with a number of research groups, public agencies and Lead Bodies as a consultant and adviser. She has published widely in the field of assessment methods, models of competence, and work based accreditation, and is a member of the TA Technical Advisory Group.

Tim Oates has participated in a number of national evaluation projects in the education and VET field, and was a member of the evaluation team for the joint MSC/ESF-funded Core Skills Project and its associated satellite projects. As research officer on the TA-funded FESC Work Based Learning Project, which took the work of the Core Skills Project forward into new arenas, he contributed to development of instruments and approaches for implementing work based learning across UK VET. With renewed funding until August 1990, the author now occupies the post of Deputy Director for the Work Based Learning Project and its associated satellite projects. The project offers a policy studies capability to the Training Agency. Personal interests centre on the management of change and strategic research management.

Jenny Shackleton is Principal of the Wirral Metropolitan College, a large (Group 10) locally maintained college largely offering non-advanced further education to the Wirral and North Cheshire. Before joining the College, Jenny was the Senior Assistant Education Officer (MSC Co-ordinator) for Bedfordshire between 1983 and 1987. Jenny has worked closely with the Training Agency/MSC and other national and government organizations (such as FEU and FESC) since the mid-1970s, particularly in the role of advisor, consultant, and manager of numerous projects. She is currently a member of the Lead Industry Body for Administrative, Business and Commercial Occupations, and of the Post 16 Network.

Geoff Stanton is Chief Officer at the Further Education Unit (FEU). He joined the FEU in 1977 as a Staff Development Officer where he wrote *Experience Reflection Learning* and *Developing Social and Life Skills*; he was secretary to the working group which produced *A Basis for Choice* which is now viewed as a seminal document in VET. In 1983 he became Vice-Principal (Curriculum Evaluation) at Richmond-upon-Thames College, where he was actively involved in planning the College provision for YTS, CPVE and TVEI. He was the LEA TRIST Coordinator, and also chaired an LEA Working Group planning the introduction of a system of profiling and recording of achievement for school and college users. Since 1974 he has participated in various working groups and projects which have reviewed and recommended curriculum developments in FHE and he has also been the author of reports and papers in this field.

Eric Tuxworth is now a consultant in vocational education and training. He was formerly Reader in the Faculty of Education at Huddersfield Polytechnic. During graduate studies and some teaching duties at the University of New Hampshire in 1977 he concentrated on competency based education and training. His interests in this area are extensive — he has undertaken projects for FEU, City & Guilds, NCVQ, the Training Agency and the Health Service. He was involved in the national working groups for the development of vocational preparation courses such as CPVE and has worked with the Industry Lead Body for Administrative, Business and Commercial Occupations. Current activities centre on the relationship of knowledge to competence, the assessment of competence and continuing professional development through field based learning.

Alison Wolf is a Senior Research Officer in the Department of Mathematics and Statistics at the University of London Institute of Education. At present she is directing a number of research projects as well as running INSET courses for teachers. She is a member of the Training Agency's Technical Advisory Group. She is currently examining the specification of knowledge required for National Vocational Qualifications using the very different vocational contexts of catering, pharmacies and (technical level) accountancy to illuminate common issues. Curriculum Development is her other main concern, mostly for the post 16 vocational and pre-vocational curriculum.

Index

academic disciplines, standards in 89
Accreditation of Prior Learning (APL) 7, 109,
    113
  a checklist 114–5
  co-ordinators 115–17, 128
  interest in 128
achievement
  -led colleges 103–4
  personal 104–5
Administration, Business and Commercial
    Training Group (ABCTG) 30, 32, 151
agriculture
  and NVQs 150, 165–6
assessment 6, 88–90, 94, 184–5
  alternative models of 70–1
  continuous 141
  criteria based 149
  of learning processes 96, 99, 101
  NVQs and 148–50
  of potential 90
  systems 136–7
  of teacher training 172
  VET methods of 33

caring
  and NVQs 151–2, 168–9
Committee for the Accreditation of Teacher
    Education (CATE) 173
Caterbase 30
clerical work
  and NVQs 150–1, 166–7
cognitive theory 42

competence 10, 92, 100
  analysis of 17–18
  assessment of 51, 60–1, 135
  based
    learning 187–8
    qualifications 65, 98
  curriculum and 133, 138–40, 144–5, 148–57,
    162–4, 168
  employers and 66
  further education and 127, 158–60
  higher education and 193–6
  and knowledge 41–4, 46–7
  learning and 189–90
  models of 27–9
  NTI and 55–6
  occupational 43
  and performance criteria 135
  personal 138–40
  re-contextualizing 47, 50
  standards of 30–41, 80
  statements of 70–1, 75
  teaching 177, 181
  testing 47–8
  units of 71–3
Competency Based Education and Training
    (CBET) 4–6, 10–11, 15–17
  in USA 10–16
Competency Based Learning (CBL) 3–4
Continuing Professional Development (CPD)
    22
credit accumulation 72–3, 136
criteria referenced tests 47